Peter Weir

A Creative Journey from Australia to Hollywood

Peter Weir
A Creative Journey from Australia to Hollywood

by Serena Formica

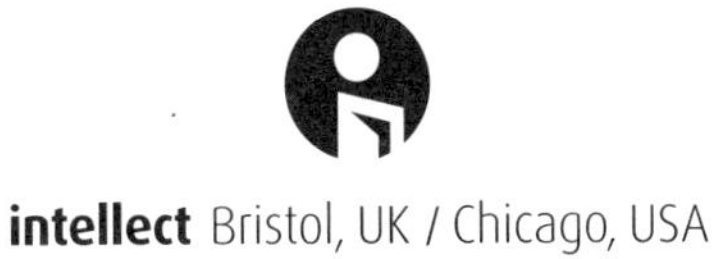

intellect Bristol, UK / Chicago, USA

First published in the UK in 2012 by
Intellect, The Mill, Parnall Road, Fishponds, Bristol, BS16 3JG, UK

First published in the USA in 2012 by
Intellect, The University of Chicago Press, 1427 E. 60th Street,
Chicago, IL 60637, USA

A catalogue record for this book is available from the British Library.

Cover designer: Holly Rose
Copy-editor: Macmillan
Typesetting: John Teehan

ISBN 978-1-84150-477-3

Printed and bound by Hobbs, UK.

Contents

Acknowledgements

I would like to thank Gianluca Sergi, Associate Professor at the University of Nottingham, for his suggestions during the research stages of this book and for making me believe that it was possible to interview Hollywood filmmakers.

I would like to thank all the academic staff of the Institute of Film and Television Studies of the University of Nottingham; in particular, Roberta Pearson, Sharon Monteith and Mark Gallagher for the guidance they have provided during the writing up of this book.

I am very grateful to the filmmakers who have agreed to being interviewed despite their busy schedule. I especially thank Peter Weir for his kindness, time and interest towards my topic; Russell Boyd for his time during several e-mail exchanges; and Philip Steuer for his availability during the Christmas holidays. I am also grateful to James and Hal McElroy for allowing me to use *Picnic at Hanging Rock*'s stills.

I wish also to mention my colleagues at the University of Derby; in particular, I wish to thank Teresa Forde and Felix Thompson, for their enthusiasm and constant support. Importantly, my gratitude goes to my editors, Melanie Marshall and Jelena Stanovnik. I would not have been able to finish this project without their continuous support.

A big thank you to all my friends in Rome and Nottingham – who are too many to mention by name for listening to my ideas and for their suggestions, feedback and enthusiasm. A particular mention must go to my friend Laura, for her passion of all things cinematic.

A very special mention goes to my family, for the support received during the writing up of this book. In particular, I wish to thank my mother for sharing with me her love for Hollywood classics and my father for encouraging me to watch film noirs and spy movies very early on. Last, but absolutely not least, special thanks go to Iestyn, for bearing with me during the most challenging times of this project.

Introduction

After all, this was *Hollywood*. This was a town that the whole world talked about.
They *thought* about Hollywood. Their dreams were painted here.

Paul Zollo[1]

Welcome to Hollywood. What's your dream? Everybody comes here.
This is Hollywood, the land of dreams.
Some dreams come true, some don't. But keep on dreamin'.
This is Hollywood. Always time to dream, so keep on dreamin'.

Pretty Woman (1990). Dialogue transcript[2]

Go thou to Rome, – at once the Paradise
The grave, the city, and the wilderness…

Percy Bysshe Shelley[3]

For [Rome] was the theatre of the world in its spring glory.
It was the school of man where he passed from infancy to maturity.

Charlotte Eaton[4]

A young upper class intellectual living in Europe between the eighteenth and nineteenth centuries would complete his classical education by taking the Grand Tour.[5] Compulsory destinations were the countries of Mediterranean Europe, because there Western civilization was born. The homeland of arts and humanities, these countries offered to the young intellectual of the period the contemplation of Roman and Greek heritage, and the beauty of Italian Renaissance masterpieces. As Shelley and Eaton recite in their poems, Mediterranean Europe was the natural destination of the first 'culture travellers' of the modern era; it was *the* place to complete one's education, because it was considered the site where the very idea of education was born.

The 'fatal attraction' of Southern Europe on the young intellectuals of the eighteenth and nineteenth centuries bears some similarities with the 'fatal attraction' for Hollywood on the filmmakers of the twentieth and twenty-first centuries. If Southern Europe was the compulsory destination for the first, Hollywood is the place of reference of the latter. Since the early decades of the studio system, Hollywood has attracted and hosted numerous filmmakers who have moved from their native cinematic contexts to America.

In this book, I am focusing on the migration of a contemporary filmmaker to Hollywood, Australian director Peter Weir, who moved professionally to America in 1985. Which are the factors that account for the differences and similarities in Weir's filmmaking in Hollywood and Australia? I am aware that Peter Weir does not stand out because he made this career choice, but the case is interesting *precisely* because he is part of a larger phenomenon involving Australian filmmakers in recent decades. Weir's career, in fact, mirrors that of a group of young Australian filmmakers who moved to Hollywood during the 1980s, such as directors Fred Schepisi, Bruce Beresford, Gillian Armstrong and, in the late part of the decade, Philip Noyce, and cinematographers Russell Boyd and Don McAlpine. These filmmakers had emerged in the 1970s, when Australian cinema was experiencing a revival after a prolonged period of crisis that had deep roots.

If is true that Weir's migration has to be studied within the larger phenomenon of Australian filmmakers' migrations, it is also true that the latter ought to be considered as part of a trend that has characterized cinema because it is very dawn. Every decade since the beginning of cinema, in fact, has witnessed migrations to Hollywood. In the 1920s, German filmmakers such as Friedrich Wilhelm Murnau and Ernst Lubitsch migrated to Hollywood attracted by the economic and technological possibilities offered by a rising studio system.

In the 1930s and 1940s, the systematic persecution of Jews during the Nazi regime resulted in the migration of filmmakers, such as Fritz Lang, Otto Preminger, Billy Wilder and Fred Zinnemann. In the early 1940s, the economic possibilities offered by the studio system – and the problematic situation of the British film industry during the Second World War – urged Alfred Hitchcock to move to America. Twenty years later, the Soviet invasion of Eastern Europe provoked the passage to Hollywood of, among others, Czech director Milos Forman. The reasons that led to these migrations of the past and their repercussions over both the cinematic contexts of origin and Hollywood have been investigated by scholars.[6]

Importantly, filmmakers' (and actors') moves to Hollywood are not a phenomenon confined to the past: on the contrary, they are an ongoing and increasing phenomenon. Filmmakers' migrations to Hollywood continued into the 1990s and 2000s, and involved filmmakers of different continents. In 1997, the handover of Hong Kong to China provoked the passage to Hollywood of several filmmakers, such as Ang Lee (who was already a Taiwanese émigré) and John Woo. More recently, the Italian director Gabriele Muccino made his first Hollywood film, *The Pursuit of Happyness* (sic) (2006), starring Will Smith. In Mexico, 'an inhospitable climate at home gives… top movie talents little choice but to cross the border to chase their dreams',[7] as Alfonso Cuarón, Guillermo del Toro and Alejandro González Iñárritu have done.[8] Migrations to Hollywood have indeed become a global phenomenon. In other words, we are witnessing an unprecedented circulation of labour (and technology) 'across and between film industries'.[9]

Filmmakers' migrations reflect an increasing global flow of people that concerns all levels of society and depends on factors that are historical (the end of colonialism), political (the end of the Cold War and more recently the enlargement of the European Union), economic (the growth of China and India) and technological (the burgeoning growth of mass communication). In the last fifteen years, theories on transnational migrations have been applied to the discipline of film studies.[10]

Despite increasing academic interest, I have identified an anomaly, because on one hand, these theories are not applied to actual case studies of contemporary migrant filmmakers who have made their move to Hollywood, and, on the other hand, contemporary migrant filmmakers are often only considered within the context of their original national cinema. An example is Peter Weir, who has been studied within the context of Australian national cinema, but scholars have overlooked the fact that Weir is also part of the Hollywood film industry, and have not investigated his status of transnational director.

The focus on filmmakers' moves to Hollywood is more prominent in film journals that occasionally feature interviews with such filmmakers. However, they have neither the scope nor the aim to frame the discussion within the broader context of transnational cinema. This book addresses this anomaly, and begins to fill this research gap by applying theories on transnational cinema to the case study of Peter Weir.

Although migrations to Hollywood have been a steady trend, its nature has changed. In the past, for a filmmaker, 'going to Hollywood' meant going to Los Angeles. It meant becoming part of an industry that was based in 'Hollywood, LA'. Now, 'going to Hollywood' does not necessarily mean going to Los Angeles: it has become necessary to make a distinction between Hollywood as a 'physical place' and Hollywood as a 'mode of production'. The first is an area of the city of Los Angeles, which is celebrated in the opening quotations by *Pretty Woman*'s anonymous passer-by and nostalgia by Paul Zollo. All the major studio headquarters, once situated in this Hollywood, have now moved geographical location, with the exception of Paramount.

The second Hollywood, as I analyse in this book, is a Hollywood that has expanded its geographical boundaries to different parts of the world. It has ceased to be a physical space, becoming a concept, 'Global Hollywood', which as Toby Miller and co-authors put it, is 'everywhere'.[11] In this book, I will take into consideration the existence of both the 'physical Hollywood' and of Hollywood as a 'mode of production' (if not specified otherwise, it will be the latter to which I will refer). The case of Peter Weir is particularly interesting in this respect, because, although he moved to Hollywood as a 'mode of production', he has never moved to Hollywood as a 'physical space', continuing to live in Australia.

To contextualize the case study of Peter Weir within transnational cinema, the first chapter of this book is dedicated to an analysis of transnational cinema theories and aims to identify the scholars' main hypotheses in the field, to apply them, in the fifth chapter, to the analysis of Weir's filmmaking. In line with my methodology which integrates the analysis of interviews with traditional research and textual analysis, the first chapter will also take into consideration the point of view of some contemporary filmmakers who have migrated from their own original context to Hollywood.

The second chapter is dedicated to a closer examination of existing studies on Peter Weir that sees scholars divided into two positions: a majority, who consider Weir to be an auteur, and a small minority, who do not. The chapter then considers and analyses interviews with Peter Weir in which the director, directly or indirectly, refers to his passage to Hollywood, and concludes with a look at two articles authored by Peter Weir.

Whereas the first two chapters of this book aim to provide a theoretical framework for the analysis of Weir's case study, the third chapter aims to investigate the production frameworks, as it were, within which Weir has been working as a filmmaker. In the third chapter, I analyse the production context of Australia in the 1970s and early 1980s, where Weir grew up professionally and then began to establish his international reputation. The chapter begins by investigating how the concept of national cinema applies to Australian cinema and concludes with a look at Australian filmmakers migrations to Hollywood in the 1980s.

The final chapter of this book ties in all the different threads that have emerged at theoretical and production level, and relate the findings of the previous chapters to a textual analysis of four films that I consider key Weir productions: *Picnic at Hanging Rock* (1975) and *The Year of Living Dangerously* (1982), made in Australia; *Witness* (1985) and *The Truman Show*, (1998) made in Hollywood.

Moreover, I aim to find out to what extent Weir and his collaborators' choices were informed by the production contexts in which they were made. In analysing the films, I will take into consideration the experiences and point of view of those directly involved in making them. In fact, this book aims to be not only a study of Weir's films but also a study of the people behind the films. In order to give voice to the filmmakers behind the camera, I have conducted interviews with Peter Weir and two of his collaborators: director of photography Russell Boyd, who has worked with Weir both in Australia and Hollywood, and Philip Steuer, executive producer of *The Truman Show*.

I have contacted several filmmakers, and among those contacted, Peter Weir, cinematographer Russell Boyd and producer Philip Steuer were willing to be interviewed. I interviewed Weir's collaborators because I acknowledge the 'collective nature of filmmaking',[12] and I believe that the final look of a film is determined not by the director alone, but by the director in collaboration with other filmmakers belonging to the different creative departments (chiefly cinematography, editing and sound). As aforementioned, the majority of scholars consider Peter Weir to be an *auteur*, with the result of overlooking the fact that a film is the product of collaboration among different filmmakers, a view that, with this book, I begin to challenge.

In my opinion, interviews with filmmakers can offer an insight into production practices, revealing in detail the processes that transfer a filmmaker's ideas from script to screen. They are a valuable tool to understand filmmaking as a collaborative practice rather than as the product of one person's (the director's) vision.

Notes

1. Paul Zollo, *Hollywood Remembered. An Oral History of its Golden Age*. New York: Cooper Square Press, 2002, xii (emphasis in the original).
2. *Pretty Woman* (Garry Marshall, 1990), Dialogue Transcript, http://www.script-o-rama.com/movie_scripts/p/pretty-woman-script-transcript-julia.html (accessed 11 April, 2007). These lines do not feature in the script by Jonathan Lawton and Stephen Metcalfe. See http://www.imsdb.com/scripts/Pretty-Woman.html (accessed 11 April, 2007).
3. Percy Bysshe Shelley, *Adonais*, Stanza xlix, in Roderick Cavaliero, *Italia Romantica: English Romantics and Italian Freedom*, London: Tauris & Company, 2005, 11, http://site.ebrary.com/lib/uon/Doc?id=10132932&ppg=22 (accessed 11 April, 2007).
4. Charlotte Eaton, *Rome in the Nineteenth Century* (1820), in Roderick Cavaliero, *Italia Romantica*, 186, http://site.ebrary.com/lib/uon/Doc?id=10132932&ppg=22 (accessed 11 April, 2007).
5. This practice actually began in the late sixteenth century, but became more popular from the seventeenth century onwards, having its peak in the eighteenth and nineteenth centuries. It involved English, German and also Scandinavian intellectuals. The Grand Tour often had England (London) as departure point and Italy (Rome, but also Naples) as final destination. Famous personalities who made the Grand Tour include poets and novelists such as Goethe, Byron and Shelley and painters such as Jean-Honoré Fragonard.
6. See Kristin Thompson, *Herr Lubitsch Goes to Hollywood: German and American Film after World War I*, Amsterdam: Amsterdam University Press, 2005; and Gene D. Phillips, *Hollywood Exiles. Major European Film Directors in America*, Bethlehem PA: Lehigh University Press, and London: Associated University Press, 1998.
7. Lorenza Muñoz and Reed Johnson, 'Mexico's creative brain drain', *Los Angeles Times*, February 24, 2007, LATimes.com, http://www.latimes.com/entertainment/news/business/la-fi-mexfilm 24feb24,1,4528084.story (accessed 9 May, 2007).
8. See Muñoz and Reed Johnson, 'Mexico's creative Brain Drain'; see also Paul Grainge, Mark Jancovich and Sharon Monteith, *Film Histories. An Introduction and Reader*, Edinburgh: Edinburgh University Press, 2007, 552–553.
9. Paul Grainge et al., *Film Histories*, 551.
10. See Elizabeth Ezra and Terry Rowden, *Transnational Cinema. The Film Reader*, London and New York: Routledge, 2006.
11. See Toby Miller, Nitin Govil, John McMurrin, Richard Maxwell and Ting Wang, *Global Hollywood 2*, London: British Film Institute, 2005.
12. Alan Lovell and Gianluca Sergi, *Making Films in Contemporary Hollywood*, 8.

Chapter 1

Migrations and Transnationalism in the Cinema

Introduction

Migrations are not a new phenomenon: people move for social, political and/or economical reasons, often in search of better living conditions. Since migrations tend to follow the flow of capital, the destinations of migrants have traditionally been the western and northern parts of the world. In recent decades, migration patterns have changed, capital has begun to flow more freely across the globe and so have people. Whereas the migrations of the past tended to involve less educated people, especially the lower classes, more recently they also involve upper classes and people who are more educated. In other words, every member of society is a potential migrant.

The modern social, political and economic configuration of the world and the increasing scale of these phenomena have prompted social scientists to rethink migration theories. The contemporary academic discourse has called the new form of migrations, 'transnationalism', a term born within Anthropology and later applied to Film and American Studies.[1] Indeed, as this chapter begins to show and as is analysed in the subsequent chapters of this book, filmmakers are not alien to the phenomena of transnationalism, and filmmakers' migrations, across different cinematic contexts and in particular to Hollywood, have been happening since the dawn of cinema. As people flow where the capital is, to the western and northern parts of the world, so do filmmakers going to Hollywood. However, in recent times, the flow of capital in the cinema has changed direction, or better, has enlarged its horizon, and, as the phenomenon of runaway productions show, it is becoming more common to shoot films in other English-speaking countries where economic conditions are more favourable. Through co-productions and runaway productions, transnational cinema has changed the very notion of Hollywood and the perception of it.

This chapter engages with the theories on transnational cinema, identifying their main hypothesis and considers if, and to what extent, these theories have been applied to the case studies of contemporary filmmakers who have moved to Hollywood. The chapter then takes into consideration the opinions of the direct protagonists of these migrations, the filmmakers, examining some interviews with filmmakers who have moved to Hollywood in recent decades. In the following chapters, I will attempt to apply the transnational cinema theories identified herein to the case study of Peter Weir, and I will examine o what extent he can be considered a transnational filmmaker.

Transnationalism in film studies and its implications for the notion of Hollywood

Elizabeth Ezra and Terry Rowden – in their introduction to *Transnational Cinema. The Film Reader*[2] – affirm that the concept of transnationalism is useful for a better understanding of the ways in which filmmakers imagine the contemporary world as a 'global system'. The authors consider transnationalism in relation to the concept of 'nation', reflect on the 'decline of sovereignty' and on the 'impossibility of assigning a fixed national identity to much cinema'. Factors that have problematized the category of 'national cinema', argue the authors, include the global flow of capital, the permeability of borders, an increased circulation of new technologies and the 'transformation of global cinematic landscape'.[3]

The domination of the American film industry over the other national cinemas is a phenomenon as old as the industry itself, and works not only at the financial and production levels, but also at the 'level of individual performers'.[4] Similarly, co-productions involving Hollywood and Europe go back 'at least as far as the Hollywood on the Tiber'.[5] Interestingly, Ezra and Rowden argue that Hollywood's dominance problematizes the concept of 'foreign film', traditionally associated with 'art-house' films representative of national cinemas. 'Foreign', 'art-house' and 'non-commercial', the authors point out, have been opposed to 'Hollywood' and 'commercial cinema' (as sites of this entertainment). Now, however, 'this traditional dichotomy has been complicated… by the fact that Hollywood has influenced cinematic traditions the world over, an influence reflected… in the terms "Bollywood" and "Nollywood"'.[6]

Nationalism, argue Ezra and Rowden, has played an important role in the legitimation of film studies; film is 'rapidly displacing literature' as the embodiment of a 'cosmopolitan identity',[7] and national cinemas are celebrated in proliferating film festivals. Cinema has become a 'visual currency',[8] and transnational cinema arises in the interstition between the local and the global. Because of the intimacy and communal dynamic in which films are usually experienced, cinema has a singular capacity to foster bonds of recognition between different groups.[9]

Transnational cinema, moreover, according to the authors, goes beyond the discourse of 'third worldism' and 'third cinema' (many third-world filmmakers were trained in the West), and 'binary opposition' have lost their value in light of the fact that many filmmakers now have 'hybridized and cosmopolitan identities'.[10]

Postcolonialism, according to the authors, is the closest attempt to recuperate a sense of national identity. 'The concept has not proved to be a flexible tool. Tied to imperial oppression, it is difficult to use the concept to define situations that have not been defined only by imperialism'.[11] However, the concept of postcolonialism, in turn, is rendered more problematic by the idea of transnationalism. The authors argue that transnationalism is determined by the permeability of national borders, and discuss the asymmetrical relation between the global diffusion of Hollywood products and the limited distribution of other national cinemas. Only the films that are better financed enjoy an international distribution, and they tend to be those that are more 'western friendly, adopting familiar genres, narratives, or themes in their hybrid productions'.[12]

Modern technology such as digital filmmaking has accelerated the rise of transnational cinema, allowing everybody to make, produce and circulate their own films, and is also posing a threat to national forms of censorship. Such a crossing of national borders has weakened states' authority over national cinema, leading to an increased availability of works by previously inaccessible filmmakers: 'Cinema will become', according to Ezra and Rowden, 'increasingly prominent as means of global legitimation and cultural critique'.[13]

With transnationalism films 'migrate' more freely, and diasporic populations are at the same time audiences of transnational cinema and objects of their representation. The experience of migrations, say the authors, complicates the notion of 'home', and transnational cinema is often 'generated by a sense of loss'[14] that is counteracted by the 'emotional construction of the homeland', as represented in Wolfgang Becker's *Goodbye Lenin* (2003). An increasing number of films depict people who live with displacement as a sort of permanent condition (such as Makhmalbaf's *Blackboards*, 2000). Nostalgia for the mother country is expressed in films such as *East is East* (1999) and *Bend it Like Beckham* (2002), which represent the generational clash between first- and second-generation migrants (the first still attached to the home traditions, the second attracted by the customs of the host country). Ezra and Rowden continue their review of cinema representing diasporas with those films that depict the paradoxical situations of 'non-places', in which the displacement of the subject is embodied by the impossibility of being at home and by the simultaneous impossibility of settling in another country, such as *The Terminal*, or by films that represent the ultimate 'non place, cyberspace'.[15]

From this analysis of Ezra and Rowden's work, it emerges that on the one hand, transnational cinema is the cinema made by transnational filmmakers, and, on the other hand, is the cinema that has transnationalism as its object. Moreover, the concept of 'transnationalism' is used by these authors as a conceptual umbrella that encompasses all those phenomena (diasporas, migrations of goods and people). Ezra and Rowden point out that transnationalism refuses to privilege the top (like capitalism does) or the bottom (like Marxism). Transnationalism 'both reflects and mediates power relations in the post-industrial digital age'. 'Is the world really "borderless"?' Ezra and Rowden finally ask.[16] The presence of workforce flows across the world, from southern and eastern to northern and western parts of the world, suggests otherwise.

Although Ezra and Rowden identify the traits that define transnational cinema (it works across borders, it both pre-supposes national cinema and transcends it, and it lies at the intersection between the global and the local), they do not provide a definition of the term. This lack of a definition could be due to the very nature of the concept itself, which, as the suffix 'trans' suggests, is something in permanent evolution. Another interesting factor that emerges from this analysis is that the authors do not apply their theory to any particular case study of transnational films (they only briefly mention, as shown, some films that have transnationalism as their subject) or, to the case study of transnational filmmakers.

Some of the defining traits of transnationalism according to Ezra and Rowden are also pointed out by Andrew Higson. In his essay 'The Limiting Imagination of National Cinema', the author problematizes the concept of national and concludes that, taken on its own merits, it does not account for the role of globalization in the modern world.[17]

The collection of essays *Contracting out Hollywood: Runaway Productions and Foreign Location Shooting*, edited by Elmer and Gasher, considers issues of transnational cinema (albeit without using this term, and I will return to this issue below), through the perspective of 'runaway productions'. In the introduction, Elmer and Gasher argue that 'Hollywood' is an 'inappropriate label for a film and television production industry that comprises a global network of locations, technical services, acting pools, even remote affiliate studio facilities'.[18] The major Hollywood studios have scattered their production in locations worldwide, and the very notion of 'location shooting' has changed its meaning (no longer defining only a film shot on location). According to Elmer and Gasher, a number of factors have to be taken into account to understand this concept, such as economic and aesthetic factors, the fact that new methods of production affect not only film but also policy-makers, and ultimately that location shooting has to be considered from a variety of points of view.

The terminology used to indicate 'location shooting' depends on who uses it and the context in which it is used. This difference is reflective of a different attitude towards these types of production. Elmer and Gasher give the example of Canada, where these productions are called 'foreign service production'. The use of 'foreign' distinguishes 'these projects from indigenous film and television productions and "service" denot[es] the fact that the Canadian contribution is primarily execution, rather than creation, of the project'.[19] In Hollywood, 'location shooting' productions are called 'runaway productions', where the adjective 'runaway' designates both the anxiety of below-the-line workers whose job is at risk (an argument that echoes Miller's discourse) and the fact that these productions are seen as a kind of 'cultural affront' for those who employ 'nationalism… as a political and economic strategy'.[20]

Elmer and Gasher underline that American professionals oppose runaway productions (such as the protests against a production about Rudolph Giuliani and the series *The X-Files*, both shot in Canada) and at the same time indicate the benefits brought to host countries by these productions, not only in terms of injection of cash in the local film industry but also as means of promotion of the locations featuring in such productions (as in the case of New Zealand featuring in the *Lord of the Rings* trilogy). Elmer and Gasher recognize that 'location shooting' is not entirely new, having been used since the early days of cinema, and point out that 'by the 1980s, Hollywood had a "split locational pattern", with pre-production and post-production work concentrated in the greater Los Angeles area and production activity scattered all over the globe'.[21] The authors dwell on both the 'push' and the 'pull' factors that determined the scattering of production, identifying the breakdown of the studios in the first category:

> [T]here are both creative and economic pull factors. Creative reasons for taking a production on location include, scenery, topography, weather conditions.... For host sites, location production requires little investment and holds the promise of significant benefits from a nonpolluting [*sic*] industry.[22]

Taking the television series *The X-Files* as a case study of runaway production, Elmer and Gasher observe that the 'cultural anxieties over the dissemination of generic or pan-American landscapes on the screen have focused on the *erasure* of national signifiers'[23] and conclude their work with the (worried) reflection that 'runaway' or 'foreign service productions' 'could very well reinforce Hollywood's global dominance'.[24]

In their essay 'The Policy Environment of the Contemporary Film Studio',[25] Goldsmith and O'Regan analyse the relationship between national and international. The authors analyse what they call 'international productions'[26] from the point of view of the producers and, in particular, from the point of view of the host countries. They highlight that the countries that successfully bid to host an international production have suitable locations, good film service infrastructures, and, more importantly, the backing of the local government, who encourage such production to take place.

Goldsmith and O'Regan argue that the presence of

> 'studio complexes' in the host countries... strengthen the competitive advantages of places competing for international production and... provide an opportunity for a place to win as much of a production as possible by offering the full range of production and post-production services in one location.[27]

Studio complexes are the evidence that Hollywood has truly become global.

According to the authors, it is important to stress that international productions are not only a Hollywood invention, as they put it, but also an invention of those places that seek these types of productions. In their analysis, Goldsmith and O'Regan concentrate on the pull factors that encourage Hollywood to contract out its productions and believe in the need to rethink the relationship between the local and the international production, and stress the importance of what they call the 'ecology' of the cities, the regions and the countries where international production takes place.

What is important to highlight in the economy of this chapter is that, while the productions analysed by Elmer and Gasher, and Goldsmith and O'Regan share the traits of transnational productions as identified above (international productions take place across borders, pre-suppose the national element, lie at the intersection between the global and the local), they actually never use the term 'transnational', preferring the expression 'international'. This further problematizes the concept of 'transnational'. Is transnational synonymous with international? Why use two terms instead of one? This book does not aim at answering these questions (nor does it aim at providing a definition of transnational cinema), but is more interested in pointing out that transnationalism is all but a straightforward and easy concept to deal with.

From a film studies perspective, transnationalism is not only changing the cinematic representations of the world, but also, at a deeper level, it is modifying the traditional notion of Hollywood and our understanding of it. 'Where is Hollywood?' ask Toby Miller and co-authors in their work, *Global Hollywood 2*.[28] This question, together with 'what is Hollywood?', has become important to understand the changed dynamics of this film industry. It is important to examine briefly these issues and the answers that scholars have given to these questions.

Today, it has become necessary to make a distinction between 'Hollywood as a geographical place' and 'Hollywood as mode of production' (or creative industry). The first is easier to identify. It can be pointed out on a map and has precise geographical boundaries. Is the 'physical Hollywood', the history of which is recalled with nostalgia by Paul Zollo in his book *Hollywood Remembered*.[29] The physical Hollywood is the 'land of dreams' referred to by the anonymous passer-by at the end of *Pretty Woman* (1990). It is the Hollywood towered-over by the famous sign, where past and present are blended together. It is the Hollywood of the historical Grauman's Chinese and Egyptian Theatres and of the more recent Kodak Theatre, permanent home of the Academy Awards. It is the Hollywood of the recent 'walk of fame' and of the memorable restaurants, Ciro and Musso & Frank's.

The second Hollywood, 'Hollywood as mode of production', is more difficult to categorize. It bears the name of the physical place but does not coincide with it. This Hollywood does not have boundaries. Is this Hollywood, the Hollywood of the major studios that are not confined in the 'physical space', any wider, taller or longer? Indeed, the burgeoning enlargement of the studio facilities has prompted them to push, literally, the boundaries of their geographical location. Some have moved to other areas of Los Angeles, Universal has created its own city, Metro Goldwyn Mayer has moved to Culver City, and of the major studios, Paramount alone has actually maintained its studios in Hollywood.

Other companies are not based in Los Angeles, let alone in Hollywood, at all. Dolby Laboratories and Lucasfilm, as but two examples, have their headquarters in San Francisco. Increasing production costs have encouraged the studios to expand their facilities overseas, where the below-the-line labour is cheaper. In 1998, Fox opened a studio in Sydney.[30] Paul Grainge, Mark Jancovich and Sharon Monteith observe that

> English-speaking countries such as Canada, Australia [and] the United Kingdom [are] emerging centres for runaway productions, a combination of tax incentives, currency imbalances and labour bargains meaning that studios could get more for their money using overseas production facilities... As result, feature film production in Los Angeles almost halved between 1996 and 2000.[31]

Although Hollywood as mode of production has expanded well beyond its geographical location, scholars have only recently examined the 'position of Hollywood within globalisation', remarks Melis Belhil in her doctoral thesis.[32] Moreover, the very term 'Hollywood' still generates confusion over its actual meaning. Belhil points out that, for instance, 'Hollywood' is occasionally used interchangeably with 'America'[33] 'in an age when this is no longer the case'.[34]

In the aforementioned book with the significant title, *Global Hollywood 2*, Toby Miller and co-authors, using a multidisciplinary approach (they draw from cultural studies, political economy and cultural policy analysis), investigate Hollywood's success and its dominance in the global cinematic stage. The main claim of the authors is that 'Hollywood's "real" location lies in its division of labour'.[35] The authors analyse the history of the industry's globalization and its dilemmas, and use the concept of New International Division of Cultural Labour (NICL) as an explanation of the phenomenon of runaway productions, and, more importantly, ask three questions: (1) 'Is Hollywood global? And in what sense?'; (2) 'What are the implications of that dominance?'; (3) 'Where is Hollywood?' Although I do refer to the book for the authors' detailed economic analysis of Hollywood's dynamics, here I report their conclusions.

As an answer to their first question, Toby Miller and co-authors affirm: 'Yes, Hollywood *is* global. It sells to virtually every nation, through a system of copyright, promotion and distribution that uses the NICL to minimise cost and maximum revenue'.[36] Responding to the issue of Hollywood's location, they somehow enlarge the division between 'Hollywood as a physical place' and 'Hollywood as mode of production'. The authors make a distinction between a Hollywood in a military sense, which is 'located in Washwood, a transversal between LA and DC'; a Hollywood according to a technological perspective, 'located in Siliwood, a transversal between LA and Silicon Valley', and a Hollywood according to the struggle between 'productive and mercantile capital [that] is between theatres and televisions versus games and computers'. Ultimately, there is the Hollywood 'of an old man walking through Greenwich Village, Santa Monica, Vancouver'[37] (the Hollywood of the runaway productions).

Toby Miller and co-authors do not directly answer the question of Hollywood's location, but make the point quite clearly that Hollywood is everywhere, and changes meaning and shape depending on the point of view from which it is looked at. Agreeing with this perspective is Tom O'Regan, who quotes an article in *Newsweek International*, which declares that 'Hollywood is no longer a place. It is a state of mind'.[38] The issue of Hollywood's dominance is a more complex one and so is the answer in *Global Hollywood 2*. In brief, Hollywood's predominance has created hundreds of jobs worldwide, but has also brought uncertainty in the job prospects of below-the-line workers of national cinemas, whose jobs were previously almost secure and now must be constantly negotiated with a considerable financial loss.

Working overseas: exodus, exile or carrier's plan?

Although it is true that Hollywood (as mode of production), as these studies show, is a centrifugal force that is extending to all the parts of the globe, it is also true that it acts as a centripetal force, because it has been attracting filmmakers (and actors) since its beginnings in the 1900s. In this section, I look at academic and other written studies on the subject of filmmakers' migrations to Hollywood.

In 1996, Harry Waldman and Anthony Slide published *Hollywood and the Foreign Touch: A Dictionary of Foreign Filmmakers and Their Films from America, 1910–1995*,[39] a collection of entries about 'significant foreign filmmakers who worked in Hollywood'[40] that attempts to be as inclusive as possible, taking into consideration not only directors, but also actors and actresses. In the introduction, the authors mention concisely the various phases of foreign filmmakers in America and Hollywood (from the early days in which 'the studios opened their doors to competent film people who made films in [many foreign] languages' to the experiences in Hollywood in the 1990s of the Petersens, Branaghs and Hallströms). Waldman and Slide's book is a useful tool for quick reference but does not – and does not claim to – provide a theoretical frame of analysis of the phenomenon of foreign filmmakers overseas.

A more insightful study of non-American filmmakers in Hollywood is Gene D. Phillips' *Exiles in Hollywood: Major European Film Directors in America*, published in 1998.[41] The author examines the works of those European filmmakers who migrated to Hollywood as a consequence of the Nazi regime, 'when Hitler nationalised the German film industry'.[42] Each chapter of the book is dedicated to a different director – Fritz Lang, William Wyler, Otto Preminger, Fred Zinnemann, Billy Wilder – the majority of whom were 'Jewish refugees who were looking for jobs on the basis of their experience in the German industry'.[43] Phillips examines the challenges that these directors had to face in America and analyses the impact that they had on American cinema, both technically and aesthetically.

As Billy Wilder, quoted by Phillips, points out, these directors belonged to a second wave of German directors going to Hollywood. The first wave had happened in the 1920s, when directors such as Friedrich Murnau and Ernst Lubitsch were invited by American studios because of their abilities. *Exiles in Hollywood* focuses on those directors who 'remained a permanent part of the Hollywood film industry'[44] (for this reason, it does not consider Jean Renoir, who went back to France after the end of the war) and whose work 'still appeals to filmgoers today'.[45]

Another study that concentrates on European directors in Hollywood is James Morrison's *Passport to Hollywood*,[46] which considers the period from the 1920s to the 1980s. Morrison analyses the work of those 'émigrés who came to the institution of Hollywood with a body of work behind them in European cinemas'.[47] The author on the one hand considers the directors already possessing their own style and reputation by the time they arrived in Hollywood, and on the other hand, he sees Hollywood as a cultural institution with its own practices and codes. Morrison examines the kind of representation that results from the meeting of these two realities and sustains that 'the films of European filmmakers in Hollywood remain illuminating examples of a particular strain of cultural hybridity'.[48] The author's analysis of the films made by these directors (beginning with Murnau's *Sunrise* (1927) and concluding with Forman's *One Flew over the Cuckoo's Nest* [1975]), is functional to understand and delineate the relations between American and European cinemas (such as the influences of European cinema movements on American film genres).

Although Morrison's work concentrates on European filmmakers in Hollywood, a broader view is adopted by Hamid Nacify in his *An Accented Cinema: Exilic and Diasporic Filmmaking*, published in 2001,[49] which concerns diaspora filmmakers who have been working in the West since the 1960s (in particular in Europe, America and Canada). Nacify aims to 'identify and analyze the common features of the cinematic productions of a number of filmmakers from diverse originating and receiving countries'.[50] He highlights how immigrants fuelled the American cinema both as spectators and as producers, contributing to the transformation of American cinema from an 'artisanal enterprise to an industrial system'. Nacify points out that in the early period of their American careers, immigrant filmmakers aimed their movies at an audience who shared their conditions as émigrés, obtaining mixed results.[51]

After the first wave of film 'pioneers' from Russia and Eastern Europe, an integration began between the two world wars, when Jewish filmmakers escaped from the Nazi regime and became part of the American film industry. In the post-studios era, 'ethnic' filmmakers ('the children of Irish, Italian and Jewish immigrants') made their contribution to the 'emergence of the New Hollywood post-industrial cinema',[52] making American films with underlying issues of ethnicity. Nacify does not adopt a univocal approach to his research, varying from the analysis of case studies to the examination of the careers of single filmmakers, and from the analysis of 'collective filming formations', to an examination of the Asian-Pacific American cinema. Waldman and Slide's dictionary, and above all Phillip's and Nacify's works are among the (few) examples of books dedicated to migrant filmmakers in Hollywood.

Regarding smaller-scale researches, one example of a study dedicated to non-American filmmakers in Hollywood is Pei-Chi Chung's article, 'Asian Filmmakers Moving into Hollywood: Genre Regulation and Auteur Aesthetics'.[53] The author explains the success of Asian filmmakers in Hollywood by demonstrating how they fit into established Hollywood genres and sustains that Asian filmmakers have used two different approaches to their work in America:

> On the one hand, there are Asian filmmakers like Wayne Wang and Ang Lee who came to the US in the '70s and began by making films for Asian immigrants in the US.... On the other hand, Asian directors like John Woo and Jackie Chan adopted different strategies.[54]

Woo and Chan both made the transition from Hong Kong to Hollywood in the 1990s and they have 'internationalised their images as *auteurs* by incorporating Hollywood style… into their own so that entertainment and violence dominate their films'.[55] Chung attributes the success of the films of Ang Lee and Wayne Wang in America to their being 'merely [an] Asian version of the Hollywood action films'.[56] On the basis of Jane Feur's study on genre,[57] Chung believes that 'genre formulas provide Asian directors with a convenient entrance into Hollywood'.[58] The author analyses the work of four different filmmakers, namely, Ang Lee, Wayne Wang, John Woo and Jackie Chan, applying the three different approaches – not mutually exclusive – indicated by Feur for an understanding of genre: the Aesthetic approach, the Ritual approach and the Ideological approach.

In the context of the Aesthetic approach, 'genre represents a system of conventions'[59]. According to Chung, 'Asian filmmakers… try to create their auteur status in Hollywood through the aesthetic approach'.[60] Chung takes the example of violence 'as a style of spectacle' in John Woo's movies. The Ritual approach is considered more as an exchange between the industry and the audience, where filmmakers become sellers who try to meet the audience's desires. This approach sees film as a 'cultural form that involves the negotiation of shared beliefs and values'.[61] Chung takes the example of Ang Lee who, with *Sense and Sensibility* (1995), 'chooses the theme of family conflicts and [the] individual's struggles to establish his auteur position in Hollywood'.[62] In the ideological approach, 'genre is considered an instrument that mainly serves the dominant power'.[63] The author, to illustrate this point, refers to action movies in which masculinity is constantly confirmed by the display of the male body. The examples provided are the films of John Woo, *Face/Off* (1997) and *The Killer* (1989), in which 'masculinity emphasises the importance of peer friendship'.[64]

According to Chung, genre imposes formulas that render it difficult to resist Hollywood's dominant ideology. The author sustains that to pursue success, Asian filmmakers present Asian culture in a stereotypical way, rendering it difficult to produce films 'that are based upon their own culture'.[65] Considering the work of the four filmmakers, Chung draws attention to the employment of US stars (like Nicholas Cage and John Travolta in *Face/Off*) to enhance the appeal of these films for the American audience. In the conclusion to the article, Chung affirms that Hollywood genre filmmaking seemingly 'provides Asian filmmakers with a convenient means to conquer cultural barriers' but the 'regulation of genre' does not leave the necessary space for Asian filmmakers to 'to express their ethnic concerns as freely as they were able to in their pre-Hollywood productions'.[66]

Remaining in the area of Asian filmmakers working in Hollywood, it is worth mentioning Tony William's article, 'From Hong Kong to Hollywood: John Woo and his Discontents',[67] published on *Cine Action* in 1997.

The author underlines that Woo's passage to Hollywood was not the fruit of a free choice, but rather the inevitable consequence of the hand-over of Hong Kong to China. 'As a result', writes Williams, 'many of Hong Kong's creative talents have sought refuge in the United States and Canada hoping to continue the recent achievements of Hong Kong cinema in a more hospitable climate'.[68] The author briefly mentions the previous waves of filmmakers' migrations to America and then analyses Woo's first two Hollywood films, the American and Japanese versions of *Hard Target* (1993) and *Broken Arrow* (1996). Williams focuses on the compromises that Woo had to undergo to be accepted by the American audience, who were unaware of his achievements in Hong Kong cinema. William's affirms that the director, in his productions (in particular, the American version of *Hard Target* and *Hard Boiled* [1992]) 'had attempted a stylistic and thematic synthesis between American and Hong Kong cinema'[69] and concludes his analysis affirming that, in Hollywood, Woo started to follow a different artistic path, challenging the audiences with the characters' direct gaze to the camera.

The common element that emerges from the analysis of the works of Pei-Chi Chung, Gene D. Phillips and Hamid Nacify is that they focus on filmmakers who went to Hollywood as a consequence of a situation over which they did not have direct control. In other words, they were all *forced* to leave their home countries to have a chance to express their creative talents. The Jewish directors had to go to America because of the oppressive Nazi regime, the Slavonic filmmakers as a consequence of Soviet oppression and Communism, the Asians as a result of Hong Kong's handover to China. None of these three studies focus on filmmakers who chose to go to Hollywood to (try to) establish a new career, *freely* accepting challenges and compromises.[70]

The view of filmmakers

Academic studies of past migrations to Hollywood are not the only way of looking at this phenomenon: there are also interviews with the protagonists of these migrations in which they refer to their passage to America. In this section, I concentrate my attention on interviews with filmmakers who moved to Hollywood and are still active. In 1981, the journal *Cinematograph* dedicated a dossier in two parts to the relationship between Europe and Hollywood: 'L'Europe à Hollywood: L'Age d'Or' and 'Europe USA: II'.[71] The first part of the dossier is dedicated to the first wave of European directors in Hollywood, such as Renoir, Murnau and Lang. The aim of the dossier is to 'position a subject historically, to suggest that a relationship of cultural forces is still developing nowadays, and is deeply rooted in the history of film'.[72] The second part collects a series of interviews with European directors belonging to the following wave of migrants to Hollywood (such as Jean-Luc Godard, John Brahm, Sydney Pollack, William Wyler). It is interesting to notice that, among the filmmakers, Roman Polanski is the only contemporary director interviewed.[73] Asked what Hollywood represented for him before actually going to work in America, Polanski says: a 'Mecca… capital full of mystery'.[74] Once in Hollywood, the director found it more serious and scientific than he imagined. Polanski sustains that it was Hollywood that formed him as a filmmaker, as previous generations of directors were influenced by the Russian school and later by the Italian Neorealism.

Comparing the Polish production system with the American one, Polanski affirms that it is 'more or less the same thing [there are fewer differences] between the American and the Polish systems than the Polish and French systems'.[75] This is because the Polish is a copy of the Soviet system, which was in turn, according to Polanski, modelled on the American one. However, Polanski states that differences between the Polish and Hollywood production systems are found at the level of commerce, because in the United States the investment is private, whereas in Poland it is the government that finances the film industry.

Dominique Maillet, dwelling upon this matter, asks Polanski how it is possible to reconcile the 'personal desires of the filmmaker with the commercial demands of the Hollywood system'.[76] According to the director, a good film generally has a satisfactory 'commercial career'. Polanski also notes the changes that had occurred in Hollywood since he first moved there in the 1960s, like the fact that a filmmaker now 'has a greater participation in the profits of certain films'.[77]

The interviewer then touches on the issue of Polanski being a foreign director in Hollywood and asks him how he reconciles 'his culture with the American subjects as it were'.[78] 'Americans are much more open to eccentricities than the European producers, above all the Polish ones',[79] says Polanski. Regarding more specifically how he adapted to Hollywood's way of working, Polanski affirms that he found it easier than the majority of his colleagues, such as Milos Forman, who was among those who suffered most.

A 1986 interview with Wolfgang Petersen, after he directed *Enemy Mine* (1985), is another example of a discussion concerning a contemporary foreign director in Hollywood.[80] The director declared that he was enthusiastic about the possibility of working with the special effects team at Lucas-film. However, unlike Roman Polanski and Bruce Beresford, also interviewed by the author, whose experience of Hollywood matched or exceeded their expectation, Petersen's first experience of America was not completely positive:

> I used to dream of being able to work there but, the more time I've spent in the United States the more I've realized that this [Germany] is my place. For a European, the atmosphere in America is rather superficial, the lifestyle too ritualized.... And I found it rather unpleasant to have to look on a film as something purely industrial. In fact, right now, after *Enemy Mine*, I need a little time to recover from the whole business.[81]

In 1996, the aforementioned Czech director Milos Forman was interviewed by Sally Sampson and Judityh Vidal-Hall[82] on his 'reluctant exile'[83] in Hollywood. The director declares that he wanted to move to Hollywood only for a couple of films 'to prove I could make it out there'[84] and he mentions that his American films, including *Amadeus* (1984), were banned in Czechoslovakia. Asked if he wanted to go back to live in Prague, he said after he took US citizenship in 1975, he decided to stay in America.

Like Bruce Beresford, Forman compares the cinematic reality of his home country with Hollywood: 'While working in Hollywood is not without its perils, its heady anxieties are a million miles from the old certainties of Communism'.[85] In a poignant metaphor, Forman compares Communism to a cage and America to the jungle: while in the former, there was no freedom but the certainty of being fed, in the latter there is the freedom to 'go where you like, but everyone's out there trying to kill you'[86]. Forman believes that in Hollywood market-forces determine what people want to see and consequently what a director can make. The director mentions, indeed, the difficulties of making a film like *One Flew over the Cuckoo's Nest*, which was considered 'uncommercial'. According to Forman, 'there's not one, monolithic "Hollywood", more like one behind every door; find the right door'.[87]

Conclusion

From the studies that I have analysed in this chapter, it emerges that scholars agree on the principal characteristics of transnational cinema, or, to put it in other terms, they agree that cinema, in order to be identified as transnational, has to have certain characteristics. Transnational cinema must suppose the national dimension, but, at the same time, goes beyond it: it takes place across borders, and finally, its products are somehow hybrid forms of cinema. Interestingly, however, scholars neither provide a proper definition of transnational cinema, nor do they justify the lack of such definition. Moreover, some scholars do not enter the discussion on transnational cinema, using the expression transnational cinema to describe products with similar characteristics.

What the studies analysed in this chapter make clear is that transnational cinema has multiple connotations, being present at the level of production, with co-productions and runaway productions. Moreover, transnational cinema not only exists at the level of representation (films that depict the lives of transnational and diaspora people), but also, importantly, it concerns filmmakers and actors who move within different cinematic contexts.

The latter consideration brings to the fore an anomaly in film studies. Although theories on transnationalism are applied to transnationalism as representation, the actual cases of migrant filmmakers are not considered within a transnational framework. There is a significant lack of studies on transnational directors: studies on migration filmmakers, indeed, mainly concentrate their attention on either past migrations (Charlie Chaplin, Ernst Lubitsch, F.W. Murnau, were attracted by the 'burgeoning movie business')[88] or on the migration of those filmmakers who were forced to leave their country for political and social reasons.

In other words, there would appear to be a paucity of studies regarding contemporary transnational filmmakers who freely moved to Hollywood. It is true that the issue of migrations concerning more contemporary filmmakers is addressed in interviews published in film journals. The very nature of these publications, however, is such that they do not have the scope and/or they do not intend to frame the interviews within a theoretical framework. It is interesting to notice, incidentally, that the filmmakers interviewed, who have a first-hand experience of two different production contexts, seem to reflect in more depth on the differences and similarities between Hollywood other national production contexts (i.e. their contexts of origin) than transnational cinema theorists do. From the studies analysed in this chapter, it emerges that although there is a theory on transnational cinema (albeit not a definition), such a theory has not been applied to a transnational director. Scholars have not tried to define what makes a director 'transnational'. Is a transnational director a filmmaker who makes transnational films? Or is he a director who makes films outside his or her country of origin? Moreover, scholars have not addressed the issue of how the move from the country of origin to a new production context affects a director's production.

In this book, I intend to address these anomalies, applying notions of transnational cinema to the study of Peter Weir's production, analysing how the Australian and the Hollywood production contexts have affected Weir's work, and I will be asking to what extent Weir can be called a transnational director. I am aware that other scholars have already studied the Australian director, but they have not done so within a transnational context. The next chapter provides a framework to the study of Peter Weir, looking at the approaches used by other scholars to analyse his production.

Notes

1. For anthropological studies on transnationalism see, for example, Arjun Appadurai, 'Disjuncture and Difference in the Global Cultural Economy', in Xavier Jonathan Inda and Rosaldo Renato (eds), *The Anthropology of Globalization. A Reader*, Oxford: Blackwell, 2002, 591 (originally published in *Public Culture*, Vol. 2, n. 2, 1990, 1–24); Steven Vertovec, 'Conceiving and Researching Transnationalism', *Ethnic and Racial Studies*, Vol. 22, n. 2, 1999, 1–25 and Ulf Hannarez, 'Flows, Boundaries and Hybrids: Keywords in Transnational Anthropology', in Ali Rogers (ed.), *Transnational Communities Programme Working Paper Series*, published in Portuguese as 'Fluxos, fronteiras, híbridos: palavras-chave da antropologia transnacional', *Mana*, Rio de Janeiro, Vol. 3, n. 1, 1997, 7–39. A recent application of transnational film theories is the new *Journal of Transnational American Studies* (http://repositories.cdlib.org/acgcc/jtas/cfp.html. Accessed 2 July 2009).
2. Elizabeth Ezra and Terry Rowden (eds), *Transnational Cinema. The Film Reader*, London and New York: Routledge, 2006, 'Introduction'.
3. Ibid., 1.
4. Ibid., 2.
5. Ibid.
6. Ibid., 3.
7. Ibid. Here, the examples are the cinema of Pedro Almodóvar, Mira Nair and Krzysztof Kieslowski, which have taken the place of traditional novelists.
8. Ibid., 4.
9. Ibid.

10. Ibid.
11. Ibid.
12. Jigna Desay, *Beyond Bollywood: The Cultural Politics of South Asian Diasporic Film*, New York: Routledge, 2004, cited in Elizabeth Ezra and Terry Rowden, *Transnational Cinema*, 5.
13. Elizabeth Ezra and Terry Rowden, *Transnational Cinema*, 7.
14. Ibid.
15. Ibid., 7–8.
16. Elizabeth Ezra and Terry Rowden, *Transnational Cinema*, 9.
17. Andrew Higson, 'The Limiting Imagination of National Cinema', in Elizabeth Ezra and Terry Rowden, *Transnational Cinema*, 15–25.
18. Greg Elmer and Mike Gasher (eds), *Contracting out Hollywood.* 1.
19. Ibid., 2.
20. Ibid., 3.
21. Ibid., 7.
22. Ibid., 8.
23. Ibid., 9 (emphasis in the original).
24. Ibid., 15.
25. Goldsmith and O'Regan, 'The Policy Environment of the Contemporary Film Studio', in Greg Elmer and Mike Gasher (eds), *Contracting out Hollywood. Runaway Productions and Foreign Location Shooting*, Lanham, MD: Rowan & Littlefield, 2005, 41–65.
26. Ibid., 41.
27. Ibid., 42.
28. Toby Miller, Nitin Govil, John McMurrin, Richard Maxwell and Ting Wang, *Global Hollywood 2*, London: British Film Institute, 2005, 7.
29. Paul Zollo, *Hollywood Remembered*, 1.
30. Fox Australia was one of the locations of runaway productions like *The Matrix* series (1999–2003) and *Star Wars Episode III* (2005).
31. Paul Grainge, Mark Jancovich and Sharon Monteith, *Film Histories. An Introduction and Reader*, Edinburgh: Edinburgh University Press, 2007, 550–551.
32. Among others, Belhil refers to the works of Franco Moretti ('Planet Hollywood', *New Left Review*, n. 9, 2001), Aida Hozic (*Hollyworld. Space, Power and Fantasy in the American Economy.* Ithaca, NY: Cornell University Press, 2001) and Toby Miller et al., *Global Hollywood 2.*
33. This book will enlarge the number of those who used the two terms interchangeably.
34. Melis Belhil, 'Home Away from Home: Global Directors of New Hollywood', unpublished Ph.D. thesis, University of Amsterdam, 2007, 35.
35. Toby Miller et al., *Global Hollywood 2*, 7.
36. Ibid., 362 (emphasis in the original).
37. Ibid.
38. R. Foroohar, A. Seno and S. Theil, 'Hurray for Globowood', *Newsweek International*, 27 May 2002, cited in Ben Goldsmith and Tom O'Regan, 'The Policy Environment of the Contemporary Film Studio', in Greg Elmer and Mike Gasher (eds), *Contracting out Hollywood. Runaway Productions and Foreign Location Shooting*, Lanham, MD: Rowan & Littlefield, 2005, 67.
39. Harry Waldman and Anthony Slide, *Hollywood and the Foreign Touch: A Dictionary of Foreign Filmmakers and their Films from America, 1910–1995*, Metuchen, NJ, and London: Scarecrow Press, 1996.

40. Ibid., vii.
41. Gene D. Phillips, *Hollywood Exiles. Major European Film Directors in America*, Bethlehem, PA: Lehigh University Press; London: Associated University Press, 1998.
42. Ibid.
43. Billy Wilder quoted in Gene D. Phillips, *Hollywood Exiles*, 13.
44. Ibid., 14.
45. Ibid.
46. James Morrison, *Passport to Hollywood. Hollywood Films, European Directors*, New York: State of New York University Press, 1998.
47. Ibid., 5.
48. Ibid., 7.
49. Hamid Nacify, *An Accented Cinema. Exilic and Diasporic Filmmaking*, Princeton and Oxford: Princeton University Press, 2001.
50. Ibid., 3.
51. According to Nacify, the most successful attempt was that of Yiddish film for the Jewish diaspora. See ibid.
52. Ibid., 3.
53. Pei-Chi Chung, 'Asian Filmmakers moving into Hollywood: Genre Regulation and Auteur Aesthetics', *Asian Cinema*, Vol. II, n. 1, Spring/Summer 2000, 33–50.
54. Ibid., 34.
55. Ibid.
56. Ibid., 48.
57. Pei-Chi Chung refers to Jane Feur, 'Genre Study and Television', in R. Allen (ed.), *Channels of Discourse, Reassembled: Television and Contemporary Criticism*, Chapel Hill: University of North Carolina Press, 1993, 138–159, in ibid., 35.
58. Pei-Chi Chung, 'Asian Filmmakers moving into Hollywood', 48.
59. Ibid., 35.
60. Ibid., 36.
61. Ibid.
62. Ibid., 37.
63. Ibid.
64. Ibid.
65. Ibid., 38.
66. Ibid., 48.
67. Tony Williams, 'From Hong Kong to Hollywood: John Woo and his Discontents', *Cine Action*, n. 42, February 1, 1997, 40–46.
68. Ibid., 40.
69. Ibid., 41.
70. Obviously, the case of Hong Kong filmmakers differs from the cases of Jewish and Slavonic filmmakers, because while totalitarian regimes had total control over the film industry, the same cannot be affirmed in the case of Hong Kong. In fact, China does not have total oversight of the Hong Kong Film industry in the manner of other totalitarian regimes of the past. Ultimately, the case of Hong Kong differs from the others because migrations of Hong Kong filmmakers to Hollywood have long preceded Hong Kong's handover to China.
71. *Cinematograph*, n. 65, February 1981, and n. 66, March–April 1981.

72. Jaques Fieschi, 'Avant Propos', *Cinematograph*, n. 65, February 1981, 1 (translation mine).
73. Dominique Maillet, 'Roman Polanski', *Cinematograph*, n. 66, March–April 1981, 13–16.
74. Ibid. (translation mine).
75. Ibid. (translation mine).
76. Ibid. (translation mine).
77. Ibid., 14 (translation mine).
78. Ibid. (translation mine).
79. Ibid. (translation mine).
80. Dieter Osswald, 'Boat Person. Wolfgang Petersen, Director', *Cinema Papers*, n. 57, 10 May 1986, 25.
81. Ibid. Despite his initial experience, Wolfgang Petersen remained in the United States where he has directed successful movies such as *Air Force One* (1977) and *The Perfect Storm* (2000).
82. Sally Sampson and Judityh Vidal-Hall, 'Milos Forman. It's Good out in the Jungle', *Index on Censorship*, Vol. 24, n. 6, November 1995, 129–135.
83. Ibid., 132.
84. Ibid.
85. Ibid., 133.
86. Ibid.
87. Ibid.
88. Larry Langman, *Destination Hollywood. The Influence of Europeans on American Filmmaking*, Jefferson NC: McFarland & Company, 1999, 3.

Chapter 2

Different Perspectives on Peter Weir

Introduction

This chapter looks at existing studies on Peter Weir, identifying the theoretical frameworks and methods used by other scholars in studying the Australian director. Scholars of Peter Weir are divided into two main positions: those who consider him an *auteur* in the tradition of the *Cahiers du Cinema* and those who do not. This chapter does not aim to discuss the entirety of the literature ever published on Peter Weir, which would constitute a too wide, and arguably, sterile exercise that would fall out of the scope and purpose of this book. The aim of this chapter is rather to give an informed and critical account of the leading studies that adopt an original and identifiable approach to the work of Peter Weir. Many studies of the Australian director, indeed, can be easily classifiable under one or the other label. Some studies and film reviews have been consciously and deliberately omitted, because rather than introducing elements of novelty to the study of the director, they can easily be re-conducted to an already existing wider approach.

I am referring, to, for example, Ian Hunter's short article 'Corsetway to Heaven: Looking Back to Hanging Rock'.[1] The article can be read as a study of Weir's *Picnic at Hanging Rock* (1975) largely based on textual analysis, a study that can be easily positioned alongside the numerous other reviews dedicated to *Picnic*. Hunter's approach is thematic and verges on the metaphysical interpretation of the film, and cannot be considered in any way innovative or original. The author appears more driven by an inner desire to dismiss the work of the director than by a genuinely academic interest, and this prevents the author from adopting an objective and detached perspective on the film.

Hunter's review is ultimately flawed and contradictory. After claiming that the film has 'nothing to do with this country [Australia]' the author immediately contradict himself by admitting that the picture demonstrates that 'our [Australian] culture is still bound by the deforming ties of the Victorian era'.[2] Morover, Hunter seems to resent the fact that the school girls in *Picnic* are 'Pre-Raphaelites maidens' and does not acknowledge the conscious choice, by the cinematographer and the director, to chose Pre-Raphaelite paintings as models for the look of the girls.

Another criticism made to the film is its favouring myth over the embodiment of time and place. By this, the author overlooks the fact that the film was never intended as a historical reconstruction and does not even attempt to position the film within the Weir's body of work at the time of his writing, in which case, he might have realized that previous films by the director, such as *The Last Wave* (1977), already intertwined their narrative with representations of myths. Ultimately, Hunter's work does not represent an original contribution to the study of Weir, but is better mentioned as noticeable numeric addition to *Picnic*'s reviews.

In this chapter, I firstly look at monographs on Peter Weir and then I take into consideration the books that have one or more chapters dedicated to the Australian director. Subsequently, as in the previous chapter, I have taken into consideration interviews with migrant filmmakers in Hollywood, and I look at journal and newspaper interviews in which Peter Weir mentions his move to America. Ultimately, I believe that a review of the works concerning Peter Weir should include not only the literature written on Peter Weir, but also the work written by Peter Weir. Hence, I briefly analyse two articles written by the director in 2001 and 2002.

Peter Weir: an *auteur*?

This section is dedicated to the review of the studies that, as Frank Beaver puts it, 'elucidate the work of individual directors whose ideas and cinematic styles make them the authors of their films'[3] and to the analysis of the studies of those authors who do not adopt what I call the 'auteur-oriented' position.

Weir as 'romantic mainstream auteur'

In the introduction of his book *Peter Weir: When Cultures Collide*, Marek Haltof specifies: 'My approach to Weir's films draws mostly on the critical concept of *auterism*. The focus is on the themes, structures and cinematic devices Weir employs in his films as well as on the cultural and ideological context of his films'.[4] To frame his analysis of Peter Weir's work, Haltof gives a brief history of the auteur theory. From Andrew Sarris' appropriation of the expression to the 'post-structuralist' phase (which was nurtured by semiotics and psychoanalysis),[5] Haltof clarifies that he is not concerned with Weir's biography but with the figure 'emerging from films authored by him. I look for and try to define his individual style'.[6] Although Haltof 's approach to the director is author-oriented, his methodology combines the chronological approach, which looks at the films in chronological order, with the thematic one, which considers the themes present in the director's body of work.

Haltof's analysis of Peter Weir's films is centred on a series of contrasts. In *Picnic at Hanging Rock*, for instance, Haltof identifies the following 'vivid contrasts': culture (civilization) versus nature (earth spirit); familiar versus mysterious; British (old land) versus Australian (Terra incognita); Appleyard College versus Hanging Rock; upper class versus lower classes; and British (aristocratic) versus Australian (democratic). Haltof's analysis somehow frustrates the expectations of the reader: instead of analysing in more detail each of the contrasts identified, he proceeds to diverge from them, thus undermining the relevance of his precise classification.[7] Interestingly, Haltof occasionally makes parallels between two films and, in conclusion, he reduces the conflicts present in Peter Weir's films into 'one fundamental conflict: the clash of cultures'.[8]

Haltof's view of Weir's production can be summarized with this statement: 'In spite of his refined, lush visual style it is difficult to think of Weir as an innovative filmmaker. He is rather an imaginative, intuitive, hopelessly *romantic mainstream auteur* who, while cannibalizing popular culture, is not absorbed by it'.[9] Whereas is possible to have a sense of what Haltof means by 'imaginative' and 'intuitive', it remains unclear what he means by 'romantic mainstream auteur', because Haltof does not provide his definition or interpretation of the word 'romantic'. Moreover, since Haltof aims to demonstrate Peter Weir's status as an auteur, it is surprising that he defines Weir as a 'mainstream' auteur, for the connotations of the concept of 'auteur' (original, independent, maker of 'art' films) do not marry with the concept of 'mainstream' (which defines more commercial productions).

When art film meets genre

In the first edition of *The Films of Peter Weir*, published in 1998, Jonathan Rayner did not specify which approach he used to study the Australian director. However, in the second edition, published five years later,[10] he felt it is necessary to add a preface to the book, to 'vindicate its subject or justify its approach'.[11] Rayner acknowledges that 'the study of film texts grouped on the basis of their authorship remains as critically controversial now as then'[12] and he justifies his position as follows:

> Despite a controversial half-century of usage, the auteurist approach maintains its importance for filmgoers, academics and students as one of the few reliable and enlightening organizing principles for textual appreciation.... It is one of the most obvious and pervasive ways in which film study is undertaken and considered.[13]

In the introduction, Rayner discusses the debate concerning the more commercial American cinema and 'art' European cinema and the impact that it had on the development of the auteur theory. Whereas, within the output of the American film industry it is possible to identify well-defined, conventionalized genre, the European production, being auteur-driven, has as many genres as many as there are 'author-directors'.[14]

According to Rayner, Peter Weir's films demonstrate an awareness of genre conventions that the director 'revises or subverts in ways reminiscent of the art-genre films'.[15] Peter Weir, by establishing his own 'visual and thematic hallmarks' and introducing them in 'his contracted Hollywood commercial material', is capable of reuniting 'European auteur style with the American *auteur*'s genre revision'.[16] Although Rayner's analysis of the films is chronological, he groups them into chapters following a thematic approach (according to style, genre and themes), thus occasionally stretching his argument to fit his theories.

Rayner follows a precise pattern of analysis. First of all, he determines where the film(s) examined stand within Weir's production. Then he compares it (or them) with other film(s) of the director – contemporary, previous or successive, considering certain features as echoes of previous work.[17] Subsequently, he does a textual analysis of the opening sequences of the films, in order to give the reader a sense of the whole work. Finally, the author does an analysis of the films, looking at their themes and motives, pointing out their similarities rather than differences. Rayner's analysis of Weir's production bears similarities with Haltof's. Like Haltof, Rayner uses textual analysis to identify the main thematic of Weir's films and, like Haltof, he identifies a feature common to the whole production of Weir – the conflict between a single individual and society.

Interestingly, Rayner also examines the influence that other directors and film movements had in the formation of Peter's Weir cinematic identity (especially the films of Kurosawa and Kubrick), and compares the films with the novels they are adapted from.[18] He points out their differences and similarities, and analyses the impact of the director's additions and omissions on the story. In the conclusion, Rayner returns to his original argument and affirms that the reason of Weir's success (in particular of his American films) is in the fact that the director succeeded in combining the elements of the European art film tradition with the features of the American genres, 'connotation and narrative', creating what he calls the 'genre of Peter Weir's films'.[19]

Exploring the sources of Peter Weir's films: the thematic approach

Michael Bliss, in his *Dreams Within a Dream:The Films of Peter Weir*, does not enter directly into the debate about Peter Weir's auteur status; however, his analysis suggests that he considers Weir an auteur.[20] Distancing himself from Rayner's and Haltof's analyses, Bliss is chiefly concerned in the identification of the psychological, philosophical and literary theories, which he believes are at the heart of the themes represented in Weir's films. It is interesting to consider Bliss' view on the representation of the 'other' (the non-white characters) in Weir's movies.

According to Bliss, Weir's representation of the black characters derives from Toni Morrison's concept of 'figurative blackness'. Black and non-white people are considered as 'symbols for ideas about the unconscious'[21] rather than as individuals. In Weir's later productions, black people are substituted by non-white characters or characters with the same function of representing 'the other', such as Max in *The Plumber* (1979) and the Egyptians in *Gallipoli* (1981). According to Bliss, this portrayal of black people cannot be regarded as racist, but must be examined in the wider context of Australian society, which used to be dominated by a 'white policy'. Bliss suggests that Weir mitigates the seemingly racist representation of black characters with the presence of positive characters such as Mr. Hardy in *The Mosquito Coast* (1986).

Another aspect of Weir's films underlined by Bliss is the dualism between 'the rational and unconscious',[22] the origin that would lie in Weir's education as a teenager. Bliss quotes a video interview that Weir released in 1983 for the Australian Film Television and Radio School, in which he affirms that during his college years, he began to distinguish between 'thought' and 'emotion', as two 'exclusively independent' realms.[23] Bliss uses Weir's propensity for the realm of emotion to draw a line in the director's career: according to the author, Weir's American career begins with *The Year of Living Dangerously* because 'aside from the fact that *Year* was completely financed by MGM… the film evidenced a dramatic change in the director's work, away from heavily symbolic rendering of abstract concepts… in favor of emotions as the arbiter of knowledge'.[24]

The originality of Bliss' argument lies in the fact that he explains the director's work applying Jungian and Freudian theories. The author bases his assumptions on the presence of the 'uncanny' (a concept extensively investigated by Freud) in those films where the protagonist finds him/herself in opposition with 'the upsetting forces of the unknown'.[25] According to Bliss, Weir shares Freud's view of the uncanny as nothing but the already known, and this is 'the necessarily ambiguous answer to the riddle that he… poses: what do we really know and how do we know what we know?'[26] Bliss quotes an interview by Michael Dempsey, in which the director refers to his fascination for the work of the early psychologists (such as Carl Jung), although he later 'lost interest in certain themes'.[27] Bliss does not believe in the latter affirmation and affirms that Weir 'has not abandoned Jung's ideas so much as integrated them into his own thinking'[28] and singles out the 'conception of the implicit connection among the unconscious realm, dramas and religion' as the 'most significant link' between Jung and Weir.

Ultimately, Bliss refers to interviews in which Peter Weir underlines his view on the cinematic concepts of 'style' ('It's a case of using one's talents to serve the idea rather than imposing a style')[29] and the idea of film as 'art' or 'craft' ('Craft was the correct emphasis for me').[30] A final consideration about Michael Bliss' work on Weir is that, given Bliss's view of Weir as an auteur, it is surprising that he would underline those passages where the director stresses his discomfort about the idea of being seen as auteur.

Peter Weir as an 'artist with a vision'

In 1980s, *Cinema Papers* dedicated an entire monographic special to the films of Peter Weir, written by Brian McFarlane. McFarlane declares from the beginning that he considers the director as an *auteur*. He begins his review of Peter Weir's films with a comparison with English novelist Ivy Compton-Burnett, pointing out that even though they work in different media, they share the 'witty perception of the disparity between the way things seems and the way they are'.[31] Both 'artists' believe that 'strange things happen, though they do not always emerge'. McFarlane does immediately make clear his own position on the director, saying that Wer is an *auteur* whose 'personal stamp is on all he does' and 'an artist with a vision'. In order to support his claim, McFarlane refers Richard Brennan, a film critic who wrote about Weir's prodigious talents in relation to his first short film, *Michael*, part of the *Three to Go* (1971) trilogy.

McFarlane's work follows a precise structure that mirrors the later work of Jonathan Rainer, by the same title (*The Films of Peter Weir*). First, he identifies the main themes of Peter Weir's films; second, he positions the film within: (i) Weir's body of work and (ii) other Australian films of the same period (the latter comparison does not happen for all the films analysed). The film is then analysed in more detail, its strengths and weaknesses are pointed out, and the analysis usually concludes with a statement that reinforces the main argument: Weir is an auteur. Indeed, McFarlane is keen to point out that weaknesses too are a mark of auterism: 'Weir relies too much on mystic and cryptic *frissons* and on bold statements about believes and laws. As an *auteur*, he is recognizable by his faults as by his strengths'.[32]

McFarlane analysis, in other words, follows quite closely a structure that is typical of auteur criticism, as Dugald Williamson points out in his book *Authorship and Criticism*. The author, in fact does identify the key themes of Weir's work already in the director's earlier shorts, the aforementioned *Michael* and *Homesdale* (1971) that already point out to Weir being a good filmmaker. McFarlane criticizes Weir's lack of attention to narrative is his films and his difficulty in integrating ideas into the 'texture of the films'.[33] Initially, he also points out that Weir is not an actors' director, stressing as this is a characteristic that is common of other Australian directors. However, in his analysis of *The Plumber* McFarlane contradicts his early claim, by stating that the three main actors in the film, Judy Morris, Ivar Kants and Robert Coleby do have the best performances of their careers.

Another distinctive characteristic of authorship criticism is to attribute all of the creative decisions to the director, therefore not taking into consideration or undermining the creative contribution of other filmmakers to the final look (and sound) of a film. McFarlane mentions twice cinematographer Russell Boyd in his analysis of *Picnic at Hanging Rock*. In the first instance, he highlights the ability of Boyd's camerawork in 'captivating the threatening nature of the Rock and the oppressive Victorian façade of Appleyard College'.[34] This recognition of the work of a filmmaker *other* than the director is soon muted down, because McFarlane immediately states that this was 'no doubt Weir's intention'.[35] By giving the merit of another filmmaker to the director's, McFarlane reinforces that idea of Weir as an 'artist with a vision'. The second time Boyd's is mentioned, he is indicated as the cameraman rather than the director of photography. This mistake highlights the lack of attention to any creative contribution other than the director's which is a characteristic of critics who adopt the auterist approach.

In reviewing *Picnic*, McFarlane criticize the lack of solution to the mystery of the girls' disappearance, in way that recalls the American critics and audiences' reaction to the film. McFarlane then poses an interesting question asking whether to value more the artistic enterprise 'that knows exactly where it is headed and arrives there, or the more adventurous work that is inevitable flawed but also richer in texture'. [36] This is not really a question but a further statement aimed at further strengthening McFarlane's argument. Either answer, in fact, counts as a recognition of Weir's abilities, whether in the form of 'artistic enterprises' or as 'adventurous work'. The author continues to praise Weir's 'prodigious talents' by stressing his ability to work, in *Plumber* within the tighter frame of a budget for a television film, and praises his control over the mise-en-scène (once more not considering the creative contribution of other filmmakers). The author concludes his article with the claims that Weir's *oeuvre* will be 'the chief claim of (Australian cinema) of the 1970s to a place in film history'.[37]

Questioning Peter Weir as auteur 1: Don Shiach

Don Shiach begins his *The Films of Peter Weir: Visions of Alternative Realities*, with a significant quote of the director: 'I think the word "auteur" has become devalued and we probably have to put it aside'.[38] Shiach mentions the origins and development of the auteur theory, sustaining that 'in its most extreme form [it] has largely been discredited'.[39] According to Schiach, this is due to the evidence of 'the collaborative nature of film-making'[40] deriving from the Hollywood studio system, in which director had a 'compromised role'.[41] However, he also acknowledges the different degree of control that a director might have over a film, depending on the period and on the production context. Shiach's exposition continues with a brief consideration of the role of the post-structuralist theory in unseating 'authors in literature and other arts',[42] putting an emphasis more on the text and its message rather than on its generator. However, Shiach is prompt in dismissing post-structuralism: 'The effect of post-structuralist analysis is finally reductive and repetitive' and 'pretends to a scientific objectivity that it cannot obtain',[43] because, according to the author, 'individual critics are not unprejudiced scientists'.[44]

Claiming that every theory is highly influenced by the social and political context in which it has been generated, Shiach informs the reader that he is not immune to the influences of the period in which he lives and states that his own reading of Peter Weir's films will be affected by many factors including '[his] maleness, [his] nationality, [his] age and [his] ideological stance'.[45] In opposition to Haltof, Shiach aims to study Peter Weir not as a critical construct but as an individual: he does not consider Weir as a 'dehumanized figure' but as an 'individual who has been shaped by his own personal experiences and affected by the times he has lived through'.[46] Ultimately, Shiach points out that Weir could only be a 'craftsman with a certain degree of technological know-how',[47] but at the same time he emphasizes his status as 'writer-director', and – considering that Weir does not always get the credit as co-writer during his Hollywood career[48] – poses the fundamental question of 'what relationship he, as director, has to the final movie product'.[49]

Shiach studies Weir in his context, considering 'the specific circumstances of the film industries (Australian and American) he has worked in',[50] and that is the approach that I adopt in this book. Moreover, Shiach does not align his work with that of other Peter Weir's scholars, who seem take the auteur-oriented approach for granted. Shiach's analysis of Peter Weir's work, however, does not follow completely his premise. Since he acknowledges the collaborative nature of filmmaking, the reader would expect a more thorough analysis of the contribution of other filmmakers to the films directed by Weir, but Schiach only occasionally mentions them.[51] In this book, I aim to begin to fill these gaps, taking into consideration the work and opinions of some of Peter Weir's collaborators.

Questioning Peter Weir as auteur 2: Dugald Williamson

Dougald Williamson intervenes in the debate concerning authorship with the book *Authorship and Criticism*[52] and traces the development of the idea of authorship from Romanticism to the present. A first observation that can be made is that, although very interesting, this historical overview appears to be more useful to an undergraduate student than to a scholar, who, presumably, should be familiar with the history of authorial criticism. The author analyses the authorial literary criticism dedicating each chapter to a different discourse.

In the first chapter, the author discusses the Romantic notion of original work of art (work of the imagination) and of mechanical product (work of imitation). The author analyses Abrams, Dixon's and, in particular, Woodsworth examination of the romantic concept of art and invention, and with it, the conception of the idea of the 'author'.

The discussion of the romantic notion of auteur leads the author to examine its influence on the auteur theory, developed by the *Cahiers du Cinema* and reprised in England by Wood and in American by Sarris, and following similar overviews of the development of the auteur theory, Williamson mentions Sarris' pantheon of directors. Moreover, the author is concerned with authorial literary criticism and considers F.R. Leavis and Q.D. Leavis' work. In order to examine the idea of authorship, Williamson also looks at Foucault's study *What is an Author* (1977), and argues that the romantic notion that the author is 'endowed with special insight'[53] persist in that criticism which is seeminglessly anti-Romantic. Says Williamson: 'Romantically-influenced notions of authorship have thus continued to play a significant role in recent times within literary and film criticism, even in some aspects which appear to repudiate them'.[54]

In the second chapter, the author examines the development of the idea of authorship after Romanticism and looks at different critical contexts before considering in more depth the ideas of Barthes and Foucault on authorship. Williamson's analysis commences with a look at the Marxist and Feminist perspectives, before looking in more detail at the psychoanalytical approach to authorship, which questions the idea of the author as a unique source of thought. This leads to a discussion of the role that the reader has – in relation to the author and to the text – in the construction of meaning. The author remarks that at the core of romantic notion of authorship 'lies an idea of human capabilities which may be called "humanist". This is the notion that mental, psychological and emotional capacities are all ultimately expressions of an essence of the individual, commonly identified with an image of universal human nature'.[55] Williamson also sustains 'that representational techniques have a central role in producing meaning for a subject' and do not succeed some 'pre-linguistic' process of thought.

In his analysis of the challenges to the Romantic idea of authorship, Williamson considers the role of semiotic and dedicates a quite lengthy section a review and examination of the concepts of sign, signifier, signified and signification, and mentions briefly their application to cinema. In my view, the most significant contribution made by Williamson in this passage is the idea that semiotic approaches are linked 'to what could be called a discursive or neo-rhetorical method'. This method, continues Williamson 'differs from post-romantic assumptions about authorship, because it emphasises the productive role of compositional techniques, their relation to cultural practices, and their role in forming subjects' psychological and intellectual capabilities'.[56] This discussion leads the author to consider, as aforementioned, Roland Barthes' idea of the death of the author and of the birth of the reader that puts into question the significance of the author's identity and defines the idea of *ecriture* as the circulation of multiple writings. In his analysis, Williamson gives account of Barthes' admission that 'the author is maintained as a principle of understanding art-forms, by institutional practices of criticism, literary history, biography, review and so on'.[57]

Williamson's review of Barthes' ideas is followed by an examination of Foucault's work *What is an author?* That maintains that 'the author is not an origin but a function of discourse'."[58] It is at this stage of Williamson's review that a matter that has more direct consequences on the re-production of works of art is discussed that is copyright. This is the first, and more important, of Foucault four features of discourse.[59] Through Foucault, Williamson's analyses the complexities of copyright and copyright's laws, their establishment with the introduction of the printed text and their development with the 1709 Act. Williamson stresses that copyright is internationally regulated, and, importantly highlights that not all texts can be considered 'authored texts' (a poster, or an instruction manual, are not authored texts). Williamson concludes the chapter arguing that Foucault's third feature of authorial discourse, 'that the author-function marks a dense network of discursive procedure' is crucial for understanding procedures of authorial literary criticism, to which he dedicates the following chapter.

In this chapter, the author makes his position clearer; he wishes to move away from the Romantic idea of inspiration and affirms a 'neo-rhetorical sense of composition'[60]. According to Williamson 'the circulation of key concepts and the protocols of criticism produce the effect of authorial individuality', and the relation between the author and the text is not 'something that we individually happen to see, but is the result to other critical and theoretical apparatuses'.[61] Williamson describes some of this apparatuses of literary criticism in the chapter; the first is 'to use to author's name as a means of classifying texts'.[62] This practice enables to distinguish between later and earlier work of an author, for instance, and is not fixed but continually shifting. The second practice, or procedure, is 'to treat the author as the origin of a work's form and meaning'[63]; Williamson sustains, citing Foucault, that such meaning is not intrinsic to the work, but is established through interpretation. The third producer of authorial criticism is 'that the author constitutes a principle of unity in writing'[64], which is also constructed through critical interpretation. This unity is established by a series of activities, such as comparisons, inclusion and exclusions of certain images, with the effect that a meaning is finally constructed, which can be attributed to 'an individual origin'.[65]

These apparatuses, however, do not cater for a study of the relationship between the text and modes of writing and reading that are not connected to only one individual author. Therefore, argues Williamson, an examination of alternatives modes of authorial criticism is necessary; the first proposed alternative is genre theory, which provides a 'productive interplay between convention and innovation, without reducing innovation to an idea of authorial originality and hence opposing it to the presence of technique'.[66] The author continues that search for an alternative to the authorial model with a brief look at Vladimir Propp's model that identifies specific narrative patterns across novels from different authors, and, sustains Williamson, anti-authorial, because 'the form of the stories is not connected to individual inspiration or expression, but to a culturally maintained pattern of story-telling, a formulaic organization of materials that gives raise to many possible re-telling and variations'.[67] Characters of stories are the product of a complex set of signs and the multiple conventions used in narrative forms, including 'medium specific techniques'[68] that, in modern fiction 'tend to be integrated into the dominant form of psychological character drama'.[69] According to Williamson, the study of these conventions is a demonstration that an alternative exist to the authorial study of 'the way in which writers and readers negotiate meaning in various kind of texts'.[70]

In the last chapter, Williamson takes Peter Weir as a case study and argues against that literary criticism that has identified him as an author (not as an auteur in the stricter sense of the word). Williamson gives account of those critics who have hailed weir as an artist, in particular Brian McFarland, and does stress that negative judgements, as well as positive ones, can be the markers of authorship (in this respect, the author reference a negative review of *Gallipoli* which sustains that Weir has failed to realize his own vision). Williamson starts his discussion by making a distinction between documentaries (which 'allegedly just report facts or ideas' and fiction 'which supposedly allows an individual, imaginative transformation of reality'[71], and argues that Weir is definitely a maker of fiction. The author continues by stating the use of the authorial name 'allows the recourse to the notion that a central, expressive purpose underlies the collective and material nature of filmmaking'.[72] At this point, it would be legitimate to expect the recognition of such a nature to argue against the existence of *one* individual creative mind responsible for a work; however, this is not the path chosen by Williamson to make his point. In my view, here the author incurs in the same error made by Don Shiach, who, albeit recognizing the collective nature of filmmaking, fails to give account of other creative contribution to the films directed by Weir. Moreover, when Williamson does mention another contribution, he denies himself the chance of exploring such contribution. The author, in fact, does mention the work of David Williamson, *The Last Wave* scriptwriter, but argues that 'the construction of [Williamson] as an author would merit its own detailed analysis; however, and so I restrict my discussion to the latter [the construction of Weir as an author]'.[73]

Williamson then uses two literary techniques, interviews and anecdotes, to disprove the belief that they do constitute proof of authorship. Williamson argues that 'it is only under the conditions imposed by the author-function that these forms can create the idea that, behind the text, authorizing it, giving it authenticity, stands the individual personality. Statements of experience and intention from the "author in person" constitute a further set of signs whose operations and effect need to be analysed in their own right'.[74] Answering Williamson's argument it is important to stress that interviews and anecdotes (which are generally told as part of an interview) not always are used as a marker of authenticity of the text and as a proof of authorship. This book does use interviews to other creative contributors to the work of Peter Weir with the purpose of investigating all of the elements that constitute 'Weir creative journey from Australia to Hollywood'. Williamson does not take into consideration the scope and nature of interviews does, in fact varies depending on the context (an interview published on a newspaper is different from an interview published on a specialized film journal) and time (an interview published before a film's premiere does differ from an interview published in occasion of a review on a director's work) of publication, and also depending on the audience in question (an interview on a fanzine does differ from an interview part of a DVD extra).

Williamson proceed to a textual analysis of two films and argues that Weir cannot be considered an author because he does work within cinematic codes conventions that pre-date and pre-exist the director. Wanting to sustain the idea that Weir is an author (which this book does question), it would be possible to respond that it is the constant use of the same pre-existing patterns and conventions within Weir films that are the markers of authorship. Another 'problem' of Williamson's study that, however, cannot be considered a limit or a flaw, is that it was published in 1988, well before more recent studies on the issue of authorship (such as the aforementioned Sergi and Lovell's book), and, when considered in relation to Weir, only three years after the director's move to Hollywood. Presented with the possibility of considering the first two Hollywood films directed by Weir, *Witness* and *Mosquito*, the author chose to limit his analysis to two Australian productions, *Gallipoli* and *The Last Wave*, which effectively narrows down the range of possible approaches to Weir's body of work, eliminating any possible consideration of the effects of the director's move to Hollywood.

Although Williamson provides a study of (two) Peter Weir's works outside of the authorial framework, his work present shortcomings. In fact, Williamson argument (Weir is not an auteur) shares the same origin of its opposite (Weir is an auteur), which is the text (the films) itself. In earlier paragraph, Williamson does consider cinematic structures (such as mise-en-scène) are nothing more than 'technical constructions' that automatically eliminates the need for searching for the individual responsible for the creation and execution of such constructions. In so doing, Williamson eliminates the need for the figure of the director, and, to a certain extent, renders a mere speculative exercise the answer to the question 'is Weir an auteur?' I argue that Williamson's approach to the study of a text is legitimate but limited, because it excludes *a priori* the study and consideration of the context within which a text is produced.

Featuring Peter Weir

Thus far, I have been looking at works that are entirely dedicated to Peter Weir, analysing and presenting the different positions. In the following sections, I briefly introduce those books in which the analysis of Peter Weir's films constitutes only a chapter or sections of a broader work (books dedicated to the Australian New Wave and books reporting interviews with Australian directors).

Acknowledging the contribution of other collaborators

In his book *The Last New Wave*, David Stratton looks closely at the revival of Australian cinema in the 1970s, and dedicates each chapter to a different director. Stratton's approach is different from that of the other scholars examined in this chapter; he is not concerned with the thematic of Weirs films and rather than concentrating on textual analysis, he looks at the pre-production, production, release, distribution and reception cycle of each movie. Stratton's work, indeed, constitutes a useful tool for a further investigation of the production history of Peter Weir's films until *The Plumber*.

Regarding Stratton's position on the Australian director, initially he appears to anticipate Rayner's and Haltof's 'auteur-oriented' approach: 'Weir has a very singular vision, one that he successfully followed through in each feature film he made during the period'.[75] However, considering the limited length of his chapter, Stratton goes on to acknowledge the contribution of others (filmmakers and producers) to Peter Weir's films. Stratton points out that his work 'is based very largely on the comments of the filmmakers themselves',[76] and analysing *Picnic at Hanging Rock*, he significantly affirms:

> [I]t is worth noting that *Picnic*, like all films, was a team effort. It is true that Hal and Jim McElroy produced the film, but they could not have done so without Pat Lovell,

who had had the faith, courage and foresight to spend her own time and money in the early stages, who had seen in Weir the right director for the project, who had initiated government funding, and worked closely alongside the McElroys and Weir throughout production. On the other hand, without the McElroys, the film might never have been made. And in the end, the credit must go to Peter Weir for the success he made of an extremely difficult subject.[77]

In this passage, Stratton stresses the collaborative nature of filmmaking and acknowledges that *Picnic* would not have been made without the commitment of the people involved in the pre-production phase, particularly the three producers. Stratton also recognizes the role of other filmmakers in making *Picnic* a success (in Australia). He gives credit to the editor, Max Lemon, for the idea to end the film with a montage of the picnic's scenes, acknowledges the creative work of director of photography Russell Boyd, and the 'brilliant use of Georghe Zamphir's hunting pipe music'.[78]

The 'direct approach'

The interview with Peter Weir by Sue Mathews occupies a singular position in the panorama of the works dedicated to Peter Weir. Mathews, indeed, is neither a film scholar nor a film critic: she is an Australian sociologist and journalist who, in 1981, interviewed five Australian directors and collected the interviews in a book.[79] Sue Mathew's position on the work of Peter Weir is not straightforward to identify. Although her book features only interviews with directors, the introduction suggests that she does not believe that a director is the sole *auteur* of a film: 'A movie', says Mathews, 'is the outcome of countless decisions made by a wide range of people with a very diverse set of interests'.[80] Mathews, indeed, dwells on the relationships that the directors interviewed have with their closer collaborators, such as, in the case of Peter Weir, his wife Wendy Stites (in the art department) and cinematographer Russell Boyd.

The interviews are divided into two main sections, regarding the directors' beginnings as filmmakers and their films, looked at in chronological order. In the interviews, Mathews discusses the qualities that give Australian cinema its distinctive characters, and asks all the directors, with the exception of Peter Weir (without explaining this omission), if they intend to continue to develop a national cinema or move to an international arena.

Interviews with Peter Weir

Considering that this book takes Peter Weir as case study of a filmmaker's passage to America, I believe it is important to take into consideration the director's view on his move. In this section, I therefore consider the interviews that regard or mention Weir's move to Hollywood. Firstly, I look at the interviews released during his Australian career in which the director talks of the possibility of eventually going to make films in America; secondly, I examine those interviews that were released around the time of Weir's passage (1985); and thirdly, I also briefly take into consideration the views of those who first collaborated with Weir in America, producer Edward Feldman and actor Harrison Ford.

To have a sense of the reception of Weir's Australian work in the United States, is worth mentioning two interviews that appeared on the occasion of the New York release of *Picnic at Hanging Rock* in 1979 in connection with a review of *The Last Wave*, the first of Peter Weir's films to be released in the United States. In the introduction to the interview with Weir, Diane Jacobs emphasizes that Peter Weir is the 'first of the Australian "new wave" of directors to win commercial distribution in this country [the United States]'.[81] In his review of *The Last Wave*, Vincent Canby affirms that 'though the inspiration of Mr. Weir and his associates run out before the end, *The Last Wave* is an impressive work from a director new to American audiences'.[82]

Jacobs and Canby's observations put to the fore two important points regarding the relationship between Weir and Hollywood: firstly, the increasing interest that the Australian 'New Wave' cinema was assuming for the American critics and public;[83] and secondly, the fact that Peter Weir's success in America did not come out of nowhere, but was prepared over the years by the American release of his films, which opened the way to his future establishment among Hollywood's directors.

The American releases of *Picnic* and *The Last Wave* are also mentioned by Kevin Thomas in the introduction to an interview with Weir published in August 1979 in the *Los Angeles Times*. Thomas writes that both films '[enjoyed] long runs locally' and 'have played – or will play – in all the major American cities'.[84] In the interview, Peter Weir expresses his satisfaction that '*The Last Wave* has been welcomed here in America'[85] and compares the different critical approaches to his films in his native country and in the United States. Although in Australia critics 'seemed mainly to discuss technique', says Weir, 'I became conscious of an openness here [in America]. One is encouraged to present different views here, but that's not true in our country'.[86]

Thomas reveals that, in 1979, the director 'was in [Los Angeles] for talks with Warner, where he is three months into a 12-month development deal'; '[P]art of the deal', confirms Weir, 'is that I come here for story conferences and script discussions at least three times a year'.[87] Even though the interview does not reveal all the details of the agreement between Warner and Weir, Thomas does mention that it was 'the first ever accorded to an Australian director by a Hollywood company'.[88] Talking about the possibility of going to Hollywood, Weir mentions that he 'got a call in Australia by John Calley',[89] who was 'very kindly urged' by Stanley Kubrick to see *Picnic at Hanging Rock*. Weir declares himself to be 'indebted to Kubrick. He's an unmet friend', says Weir, 'we've exchanged just one letter. I'm sure he's helped others'.[90]

The interview by Kevin Thomas shows that, in 1979, Peter Weir was at a crossroads, whether to stay in Australia or move to Hollywood. On the one hand, he felt that in Australia there was not the possibility to 'present different views', but on the other hand admitted that it was still 'exciting to work in Australia'.[91] The reason for this enthusiasm was partly because of the new route that Australian cinema was beginning to explore, looking at the 'Southeast Asia and [the] Pacific'. Moreover, the Australian government was keen on offering financial support. 'There's no excuse for anybody with talent to say he's been suppressed', says Weir, 'there are grants of all kinds available'.[92] Weir points out the amazement of Americans regarding this matter: 'People here [in US] are wide-eyed when I say that in Australia you can put in for a $200,000 grant'.[93] The interview suggests, furthermore, that the intention to go to Hollywood had always been in Weir's mind. 'Australia is my home', says the director, 'but I'd be happy to commute – to live here [in US] or wherever for a year making a picture'.[94]

Kevin Thomas' interview is not the only instance in which the Weir/Warner agreement is discussed. In the introduction to *Natural Dangers: A conversation with Peter Weir*, published on *New West*,[95] Stephen Farber gives further details on the matter: 'Weir has reached an important turning point in his career' being the 'top contender to direct Warner Bros' big-budget production of Colleen McCullough's international best-seller, *The Thornbirds*'. Interestingly, Farber does not only give an account of the facts[96], but he also offers his interpretation of them. According to Farber, what drove Peter Weir to consider Warner's proposal is that he did not want to be limited to directing low budget films for a niche audience (here Farber gives the example of the art-house filmmaker Robert Bresson). In other words, Weir's quest for bigger audiences and bigger financing 'than Australian film industry can provide'[97] had its natural destination in Hollywood. Farber then makes an observation from the point of view of the American major: 'For all their limitations, the studio bosses can still recognize talent as striking as Weir's, and he has already been offered a number of projects'.[98]

Ultimately, Farber speculates on the fact that the Weir/Warner agreement could lead to two opposite outcomes, pointing out that the combination of 'a talented, idiosyncratic director and a piece of pulp material'[99] had, in other cases, resulted in both 'exciting' and 'less happy' movies.[100] Farber concludes that '*The Thornbirds* might be the movie that gives Peter Weir the freedom enjoyed by only a handful of directors around the world, or it might be a disaster that sends him back to Australian television'.[101]

The interview by Stephen Farber delineates the phases in which Weir was considering the direction of *The Thornbirds*: the initial rejection by Weir because he 'simply could not find a way to get involved in the material', his reconsideration of the project: 'I spent some time working with Ivan Moffat on the screenplay… and I became interested in the potential of the film', and, finally Farber's own prediction 'Weir will probably direct the movie'.[102] These passages show how leaving Australia for Hollywood was, for Peter Weir, not a straightforward or easy step to make. The director was not going to accept just any project that came into his hands at the time.

Farber believes that *The Thornbirds* would have suited 'Peter Weir's talents'[103] and analyses the different consequences that the making of the film by Weir could bring: 'although one can understand Weir's attraction to certain elements in the novel – particularly its detailed depiction of nature and the cataclysms wrought by fire, drought and flood – the romantic slop at the heart of the story threatens to defeat him'.[104] Even though Farber does not consider the different aspects of the challenges that a passage to Hollywood entails (the difficulties of dealing with a Hollywood major rather than with Australian independent producers, for instance), his analysis of Weir's possible passage to Hollywood remains interesting, because he does not simply give an account of the facts but he also puts them into context.

Marcia Magill, in her interview with Peter Weir, published in 1981 on *Film in Review*, gives an account of the conclusion of the Weir/Warner agreement regarding *The Thornbirds*. The interview, on the one hand, suggests the interest that the American critics were beginning to show for Australian filmmakers that 'are attracting a lot of attention these days for the intelligence and visual beauty of their movies'[105] and, on the other hand reveals the director's feelings towards America. Weir appears to be conscious of the importance of the critics' evaluation of his work: 'the... ordeal is the not knowing but waiting to know, particularly in New York, the final votes of the critics, then waiting for the public vote'.[106]

Magill dwells upon Weir's relationship with Hollywood and asks what 'went wrong' with *The Thornbirds*.[107] Weir reveals: 'I signed on to the project and found to my horror that I just could not get the script right working with the scriptwriter, Ivan Moffat',[108] and then reaffirms his love for America '[after *Gallipoli*] it would be quite a thrill to make a picture here. The United States, in a sense, invented the narrative form and is the greatest practitioner of that, in fact of almost all mass entertainment', 'I have half an idea', continues Weir, '[of] a theme for a film I would like to make here in the US. My agent mentioned this writer he thought I would get along well with, and we're going to talk for an hour and see if it gets us anywhere. It seems like an unnatural way to do it, but I'm going to try'.[109]

When the actual passage of Weir to Hollywood finally takes place in 1985, it attracts an ever wider interest by American press, who report not only Peter Weir's point of view, but also the view of the people who first worked with him in Hollywood. In an article published on the *New York Times*,[110] producer Edward Feldman gives an account of why he chose Peter Weir to direct *Witness*: 'because they're able to look at America in a different way'.[111] This passage is significant because it suggests that Weir had a chance to work in Hollywood not *despite* the fact that he was a foreigner but *precisely because* he was a foreigner.

In the interview by Maslin, Feldman reveals other details which suggest that Weir had to make some compromises in order to render *Witness* more attractive for the Hollywood audiences, like adding more action especially at the end of the film. At the same time, Maslin says that Weir obtained certain changes to the script, like the elimination of unnecessarily violent scenes. The picture that begins from the review of these interviews is that Weir's passage to Hollywood was to a certain extent based on negotiations.

The role of Feldman in the making of *Witness* is further analysed in the article/interview by Mike Bygrave, published in *Still* in May 1985. Bygrave also mentions the importance of Harrison Ford in improving the script that was, according to Weir, 'half-way decent'.[112] In the introduction, Bygrave poses a fundamental for the understanding of Weir's career plans, at a time when '*Mosquito Coast* [was] getting nowhere'.[113] Did Weir intend to 'extend his American career or, like his colleagues-in-exile, Gillian Armstrong and Bruce Beresford, return to help recharge the cinema at home?'[114] Bygrave sustains that Weir 'has always wanted to work in America', and affirms that 'the feeling is reciprocated'.[115] According to Bygrave, the reason for this mutual 'affection' ought to be sought in Weir's 'high-gloss craftsmanship on big projects like *Gallipoli* [which] proved Weir has the kind of skills Hollywood has always sought in its directors'.[116] However, this strong statement is not further analysed or motivated, and Bygrave continues exposing the circumstances that brought Weir to eventually work in Hollywood. Rather than being valuable as a critical assessment of the director's passage to Hollywood, the interview is important for what Peter Weir affirms. The director emphasizes the importance of Harrison Ford and Edward Feldman in the pre-production phase of *Witness*. Feldman, according to Weir, 'proved to be the perfect collaborator' and the first was a precious aid in the revision of the script: 'The concerns I had about the original script', Weir remarks, 'fortunately turned out to be the same concerns Harrison felt'.[117]

Roderick Mann's interview with Peter Weir, published in 1985 on the release of *Witness*, returns briefly to the role of Feldman in the making of the film. According to Mann, Feldman 'felt that Weir would have been the ideal director for his story'.[118] Peter Weir reveals to Mann why he accepted to direct the film: 'to be honest', says Weir, 'I took the assignment because I decided it was a good idea not just to make films which obsessed me. [I] wanted to be like those directors in the '40s who took assignments from their studios and got on with them'.[119] This affirmation suggests that Weir, in order to work in Hollywood, had to change the vision of himself as a director. In his Australian career, indeed, Weir had always chosen his projects, and it is possible to presume that he considered himself an independent filmmaker, free to choose his films, as opposite to being a filmmaker under contract who receives assignment from a studio.

According to Roderick Mann, it was fundamental that Weir started his American career with a project that would suit him and Mann is ready to recognize the key role of *Witness* in the director's career: '[It] is an important film for him, in part because it is his first American picture, but also because his last movie *The Year of Living Dangerously* wasn't a box office success'.[120] The author, however, does not comment further on this statement. To say that *Witness* is important because it was Weir's 'first American film' does not really explain *why Witness* is important. Mann puts in relation the importance of *Witness* with *The Year of Living Dangerously*'s gross so it is possible to assume that, in Mann's view, it was vital for Peter Weir to achieve a financial success with *Witness*.

In an interview with Harrison Ford, published in the *Los Angeles Herald Examiner*, Jeff Silverman discusses with the actor the reasons he accepted the role in *Witness*,[121] and gives an account of how Peter Weir became involved in the direction of the film. Once Ford 'attached himself to the Paramount project, the film was a go. The next step', writes Silverman, 'was to find a director', and 'the man [Ford] wanted [to direct *Witness*] was Weir'.[122] Ford was, as Silverman points out, a celebrity, famous for his roles in the *Star Wars* trilogy and in the first two *Indiana Jones* films,[123] and Silverman predicted that Ford's status would contribute to the film's success.

In the Silverman interview, it emerges that Ford was free to work on the characterization of his character, 'I felt more free to create [a] behaviour [for the character] because of the experience I had' and adds, 'I do whatever physical action I can because in the midst of all this physical action there is a lot of opportunity for characterization'.[124] The interview by Jeff Silverman ultimately highlights that Ford had a clear perception about the film from the very beginning. He says

> The material represented a unique opportunity. I had not seen this movie before. Eighty-five percent of the scripts I read I know where they came from. It's a second-generation effect. This was more or less a literate script for adults. I saw a movie when I read it. It felt like a movie to me, and many things do not. On paper, *Witness* looked real. More than that, it had something to say.[125]

Peter Weir on Peter Weir

Weir is not only the object of scholar's studies, but he is also the author of two articles namely, *The Director's Voice 2: Peter Weir* and 'Peter Weir:Gallipoli: Shooting History', published in 2002 and 2005, both interesting albeit for different reasons: although they are both significant for their contents, the second is more significant for the context of its publication.

The Director's Voice 2 is based on a paper that Weir gave at the Australian Screen Directors Association and is included in *Third Take*, the third volume of the *Australian Filmmaker Talks* series, edited by Raffaele Caputo and Geoff Burton. The aim was to give voice to Australian filmmakers, allowing them to discuss their own works and the works of their colleagues, and they also look at the contributions of Australian filmmakers in America, including an interview to cinematographers Don McApine and an article by John Seale.

Weir's article is, in fact, a long answer to a series of unwritten questions on 'filmmaking': the director briefly expresses his views on the different aspects of filmmaking (directing, acting/casting and writing) illustrating his points with some anecdotes. Says Weir: 'Writing, producing and directing are quite often treated as a separate strand of the film-making process; although for me they are completely interdependent and I think some of the most profound creative decisions are made by producers'.[126] Interestingly, in this passage, Weir refers to producers as part of the *creative* process, a function that is not often recognized or seen as part of the producers' role, which is mostly associated with the financial aspects of production.

About directing, Weir dwells on the issue of style: 'After *Picnic at Hanging Rock* (1975) and *The Last Wave* (1977), I felt uncomfortable with what was perceived as my style – mystical' and continues, saying that from then on he tried to avoid making films that could be associated with that kind of style. 'For me,' Weir adds,

> style is to be used where necessary to help express an idea, it's simply a tool, a terribly dangerous tool, of course, in that a filmmaker can become a 'prisoner of the style'. [I] think it's fortunate to be in a position where you can write as well as draw on the material of others… or if you are able to work with a partner.[127]

This statement is helpful in examining Weir's position on the issue of 'directors having a particular style', and, although not expressed in this terms, on the issue of auteurism. First of all, Weir believes that some directors do indeed have a particular style. However, he also believes that it is wrong to 'become prisoners' of this style, which is why after *The Last Wave*, he sought to direct films with different subjects. This suggests that he sees himself a director who goes beyond the issue of 'style associated with a director'. Moreover, Weir acknowledges the importance of having the possibility to 'write with a partner', which again suggests that the director is keen on sharing the views of other collaborators.

Towards the end of his article, however, Weir somehow contradicts himself by affirming that when he receives a script written by somebody else, he has 'to consume it in such a way that it becomes organically [his own]', and adds that 'this approach doesn't always sit well with scriptwriters but makes me invulnerable to the studio executives'.[128] These contradictions put to the fore that, if on the one hand Weir emerges as a director who appreciates collaboration, on the other hand he wants to come across as a director in control, who feels he has to protect his work from the pressures of the studios.

The other article written by Peter Weir, 'Peter Weir. Gallipoli: Shooting History' is published in, *Amongst Friends:Australian and New Zealand Voices from America*,[129] a collection of essays, speeches and lectures given by Australians and New Zealanders who were professionals, academics and military personnel at the Center for Australian and New Zealand Studies (CANZS) at Georgetown University (Washington). The book aims to simultaneously celebrate and raise awareness of the multiple connections existing among these three 'English speaking democracies'.[130] Although, according to Patty O'Brien and Bruce Vaughn, the friendship among these three nations has been reinforced by the common participation to World War I and the recent 'war on terror', the interests of Americans towards Australian and New Zealand issues, is, partly, due to a stable presence of Australasian filmmakers and actors in Hollywood.

Although, this is not the context to examine the other essays of the book, it is interesting to notice the variety of contributors chosen by the book's sponsors to be ambassadors of the Australian and New Zealand cultures in America, which, alongside military personnel and academics include Peter Weir, film director. This is telling on the one hand of the international status reached by Peter Weir, and on the other hand of the recognition of Australian cinema as promoter of the Australian culture abroad.

In the article, Weir writes about *Gallipoli* and affirms that he made the film for the Australian soldiers who died during the battle. He narrates his personal and emotional journey during the visit to the battelfield in Turkey, and says how the account of the events by historian C.E.W. Bean inspired him to focus the movie on the friendship of the soldiers rather than concentrating on the bigger picture of the war. The article opens with a reflection on the significance of ANZAC Day[131] for a young Australian, and *Gallipoli* comes across as a personal celebration of a national myth. This nationalistic emphasis does not, however, emerge so strongly in the director's other discussions of the film,[132] thus this article should be read in the broader context of a book that illustrates Australian and New Zealand myths for the benefits of a niche American audience.

Conclusion

The examination of the studies dedicated to Peter Weir puts to the fore two interesting factors. Firstly, the majority of studies dedicated to Weir adopt an 'auteur-oriented' approach and overlook the contribution of others to the films directed by Weir; secondly, despite the fact that Weir has been directed films in Hollywood for more than 20 years, scholars approach the study of Weir's work mainly within the context of Australian national cinema rather within the context of transnational cinema.

The auteur-oriented position regards the director as the main person responsible – if not the sole person responsible – for the final look of a film and this leads commentators to overlook the contribution of other filmmakers. Here, I assume a different position. I argue that it is not correct to overlook other people's contributions, because it is thanks to all the different contributions that a film assumes its final form. Gianluca Sergi and Alan Lovell, in the introduction to their book *Making Films in Contemporary Hollywood*, responding to a statement made by Bordwell and Thompson that 'the director has most control over how a move looks and sounds',[133] affirm: 'The identification of the director as the key figure does not automatically mean that the contributions of other filmmakers will be ignored but it certainly has encouraged neglect of them'.[134]

In the conclusion of their book, in which they analyse several case studies (such as *Chinatown*, *Jurassic Park*, *When Harry Met Sally* and *Bonfire of the Vanities*) and the different contribution of various filmmakers to each one of them, Sergi and Lovell argue:

> It is important to note exactly what is being claimed for the director. It is not that they have *total* control; the claim is a qualified one – the director has *most* control. However… it is important to be clear about what 'most' entails. It could entail that the director has *much* more control than anyone else, or that they have a *little* more control than anyone else. There is an important difference between the two situations. If the director has much more control that anybody else, then the claim they are the author of the film has more weight than if they only have a little more control. In practice, the amount of control varies enormously.[135]

Sergi and Lovell give the examples of the case studies used in their book, in which the control was, from time to time, in the hands of the director alone (*Titanic*, James Cameron), or was divided between director and the producer (*Great Expectations*) and 'in the hands of the producer, not the director (*Top Gun*)'. In other instances, 'the star… or the writer has to be taken into account'. In this book, I aim to fill the research gap identified in this chapter and take into consideration the contribution and point of view of some filmmakers who have collaborated with Weir.

The second main point that emerges from the examination of the literature on Weir is the use of the Australian framework to study the entirety of Weir's career, without taking into appropriate consideration the Hollywood production context and its effect on Weir's career. Given the academic awareness of the phenomenon of transnationalism and of its impact on cinema in general, the lack of this approach to the study of Peter Weir is striking, especially considering the attention that film scholars have always dedicated to past migrations to Hollywood. Herein, I do not claim that scholars ignore Weir's passage to Hollywood, but they tend not to investigate its dynamics and the impact that it had on Weir's career and way of working. Despite the fact that Weir has now being steadily directing film in Hollywood for the past 27 years, Weir is still considered within the context of Australian cinema rather than within the context of Hollywood cinema.

As it emerges from the review, chapters of books dedicated to the Australian director are within the context of Australian national cinema, and there are not accounts of Weir's work within a context of a study dedicated to Hollywood cinema, or, as would be more appropriate, within a study on foreign contemporary directors working in Hollywood. In this book, I do neither consider Weir solely as an Australian director, nor do I claim that he is solely a Hollywood director, but I will argue that Weir could be rather considered a transnational director.[136] In the next two chapters, I take into consideration the Australian production context where Weir emerged and established himself as filmmaker and the Hollywood production context where he has been working with several major studios and some of the most prominent actors and actresses.

Notes

1. Ian Hunter, 'Corsetway to Heaven: Looking Back to Hanging Rock', in Albert Moran and Tom O'Regan (eds), An Australian Film Reader, Sydney: Currency Press, 1985, 190–193.
2. Ibid., 191.
3. Frank Beaver, 'Foreword', in Marek Haltof (ed.), *Peter Weir. When Cultures Collide*, New York: Twayne Publishers, 1996, ix.
4. Marek Haltof, *Peter Weir. When Cultures Collide*, New York: Twayne Publishers, 1996, ix.
5. Ibid., xii.
6. Ibid.
7. Ibid., 25.
8. As is shown below, Haltof is not the only scholar who identifies the clash of cultures as the major conflict present in Peter Weir's films.
9. Marek Haltof, *Peter Weir.* (ed.), *Peter Weir. When Cultures Collide*, New York: Twayne Publishers, 1996, 129.
10. Jonathan Rayner, *The Films of Peter Weir*, 2nd Edition, New York: Continuum, 2003.
11. Ibid., 1.
12. Ibid.
13. Ibid.
14. Ibid., 4.
15. Ibid., 8.
16. Ibid.
17. *Fearless*, for example, echoes, in its thematic, *The Last Wave*, whereas *Michael* previews *The Truman Show*.
18. *Picnic at Hanging Rock*, and the eponymous novel by Joan Lindsay; *The Year of Living Dangerously* and Christopher J. Koch's novel; *The Mosquito Coast* and Paul Theroux's book and, finally, *Fearless* and Raphael Yglesias' novel.
19. Jonathan Rayner, *The Films of Peter Weir*, 261.
20. Michael Bliss, *Dreams Within a Dream. The Films of Peter Weir*, Carbondale and Edwardsville: Southern Illinois University Press, 2000, 4.
21. See ibid., 6–7.
22. Michael Bliss, *Dreams Within a Dream. The Films of Peter Weir*, Carbondale and Edwardsville: Southern Illinois University Press, 2000, 12.
23. According to Bliss, Weir prefers the emotional and mystical dimension to the intellectual – and academic – one, and this position is reflected in *Picnic at Hanging Rock* and *Dead Poets Society*. See Michael Bliss, *Dreams Within a Dream*, 12. Bliss' investigation of the origins of the major themes of Weir's film recalls Neil Hurley's study of the work and the persona of Alfred Hitchcock. As Bliss ascribes Weir's dualism to his education, Hurley refers Hitchcock's moral conflicts to his Jesuitical education. Hurley talks of the 'limited dualism' between good and evil present in Hitchcock's films such as *Vertigo* and *Psycho*, and he claims that it is derived from the study of the Jesuitical spiritual exercises. See Neil Hurley, *Soul in Suspense. Hitchcock's Fright and Delight*, Metuchen, NJ, London: Scarecrow Press, 1993.
24. I discuss the matter of whether *The Year of Living Dangerously* is an Australian or an American film in chapter 4.
25. Bliss, *Dreams Within a Dream*, 25.

26. Ibid. Bliss' considers Weir's films as though they were written texts rather than audiovisual media. Bliss does not indulge in discussion of cinematic devices as means of representation of what many critics call 'the director's view', but he discusses this view directly, as if it was conveyed by a written text. On a parallel level, Bliss seems to consider Weir more a philosopher than a filmmaker. For Weir's mention of his fascination for the work of psychologists, see Pat McGilligan, 'Under Weir and Theroux', *Film Comment*, n. 22, 27–28, 1986; M. Judith Kass, 'Peter Weir', www.peterweircave.com/articles/articlei.html (last accessed 18 September, 2006) and Michael Dempsey, 'Inexplicable Feeling: An Interview with Peter Weir', *Film Quarterly*, vol. 33, n. 4, 1980, 10.
27. See Michael Bliss, *Dreams Within a Dream*, 22, and Michael Dempsey 'Inexplicable Feelings: An Interview with Peter Weir', 10.
28. Ibid., 22.
29. Bliss quotes Weir commenting on *Witness* in 'Weir, Dialogue on film', *American Film*, vol. 11, n. 5, March 1986, 14.
30. Bliss quotes Pat McGilligan, 'Under Weir... and Theroux', *Film Comment*, n. 22, 29.
31. Brian McFarlane, 'The Films of Peter Weir', *Cinema Papers*, April–May 1980 special, 4.
32. Ibid., 18.
33. Ibid., 10.
34. Ibid., 12.
35. Ibid.
36. Ibid., 20.
37. Ibid., 22.
38. Brian McFarlane and Tom Ryan, 'Peter Weir, Towards the Centre', *Cinema Papers*, n. 34, September- October 1981, 322–329, quoted in Don Shiach, *The Films of Peter Weir. Visions of Alternative Realities*, London: Letts, 1993, 1.
39. Ibid., 2.
40. Ibid.
41. Ibid.
42. Ibid., 3.
43. Ibid.
44. Ibid.
45. Ibid., 4.
46. Ibid.
47. Ibid.
48. As in *Witness*, *The Mosquito Coast* and *Dead Poets Society*.
49. Don Shiach, *The Films of Peter Weir.*
50. Ibid.
51. Director of photography Russell Boyd, producer Ed Feldman and Patricia Lovell are mentioned once; more consideration is given to John Seale, who is mentioned three times, like Maurice Jarre.
52. Dugald Williamson, *Authorship and Criticism*, Sydney: University of Sydney Press, 1989.
53. Ibid., 16.
54. Ibid., 18.
55. Ibid., 27.
56. Ibid., 30

57. Ibid., 33.
58. Ibid., 34.
59. For a detailed examination of the other three features, see Williamson and see also Foucault's *What is an Author?* in D. Bouchard (ed.), *Language, Counter-Memory, Practice*, Ithaca, New York: Cornell University Press, 1977.
60. Dugald Williamson, *Authorship and Criticism*, Sydney: University of Sydney Press, 1989, 50.
61. Ibid., 50.
62. Ibid., 43.
63. Ibid., 44.
64. Ibid., 45.
65. Ibid., 46.
66. Ibid., 52.
67. Ibid., 56.
68. Ibid., 56.
69. Ibid., 58.
70. Ibid.
71. Ibid., 65.
72. Ibid., 67.
73. Ibid., 74.
74. Ibid., 73.
75. Ibid., 57.
76. David Stratton, *The Last New Wave: The Australian Film Revival*, London: Angus & Robertson, 1980, xvi.
77. Ibid., 71.
78. Ibid.
79. Sue Mathews, 35 mm, *Conversation with five directors about the Australian Film Revival*, Ringwood, Victoria: Penguin Books Australia, 1984. The book features interviews with Fred Schepisi, Peter Weir, Gillian Armstrong, John Duigan and George Miller.
80. Ibid., 1.
81. Diane Jacobs, 'His Subject – Mysteries of Different Cultures', *New York Times*, January 14, 1979, 17.
82. Vincent Canby, 'Film: "Last Wave," Storm of Occultism: Mysticism Down Under', December 19, 1978, http://movies2.nytimes.com/mem/movies/review.html?_r=1&title1=Last%20Wave%2c%20The%20%28Movie%29&title2=&reviewer=VINCENT%20CANBY&pdate=19781219&v_id=28407&oref=slogin (last accessed, 21 July. 2006).
83. The extent to which Weir was known to the American public depends upon the scale of the distribution of his films in American theatres. Since Weir was a promising director of the emerging Australian revival, distributors were keen to release his films in America, starting from a small range of theatres to test the reaction of the public before eventually opening them to the bigger market. *Picnic* and *The Last Wave* were distributed in the United States by United International Pictures and Atlantic Releasing Corporation, respectively. The distribution of Peter Weir's films also depended upon their success in international festivals (*Cars*, for instance, won the grand prix at the Teheran film festival and was critically acclaimed at Cannes. It was distributed in the United States, by New Line Cinema with a different editing and title, *The Cars that Ate People*).

84. Kevin Thomas, 'Peter Weir Climbs Hollywood Beanstalk', *Los Angeles Times*, August 30, 1979, 21.
85. Ibid.
86. Ibid.
87. Ibid.
88. Ibid.
89. John Calley at the time was the vice-chairman of the board of Warner Bros Inc.
90. Kevin Thomas, 'Peter Weir Climbs Hollywood Beanstalk' Los Angeles Times, August 30, 1979.
91. Ibid.
92. Ibid.
93. Ibid.
94. Ibid.
95. Stephen Farber, 'Natural Dangers. A Conversation with Peter Weir', *New West*, November 11, 1979, 99.
96. Farber reports that after Herbert Ross dropped out of the *Thornbirds* project, Warner sought for an Australian director and 'Weir has emerged as a first choice'. The reasons of this choice are explored by Marcia Magill in her interview with the director that I examine below. See Marcia Magill, 'Peter Weir', *Film in Review*, vol. 32, n. 8, October 1981, 478.
97. Stephen Farber, 'Natural Dangers', 100.
98. Farber does not specify to which other projects he is referring. See ibid.
99. Ibid.
100. Ibid. Among the successful cases, Faber mentions Francis Ford Coppola's 'transformation' of *The Godfather* and Roman Polanski's 'perverse sense of humour' which 'enriched *Rosemary's Baby*'; among the failures he refers to John Boorman's *Exorcist II* and Jan Troell's *Hurricane*.
101. Ibid.
102. Ibid. David Stratton also mentions the possibility of Weir directing *The Thornbirds*. According to Stratton, 'Weir was unenthusiastic about the book', and about his meeting with producer Edward Lewis. Stratton is of the opinion that Weir turned down the project 'reluctantly': 'The prospect of making a big budget American film', says Stratton, 'had excited him… It was a difficult decision to make, because he hadn't worked on a theatrical feature for three years (and making television commercials, while lucrative, can be debilitating)'. In his book, Stratton introduces the new information that Weir was working on Australian television, making commercials – a fact that few critics point out – and attributes Weir's desire to leave Australia to the desire to move away from television work. Stratton also suggests that Weir was keen on leaving Australia because in America Weir would have had the availability of bigger budgets. See David Stratton, *The Last New Wave*, 81–82.
103. Stephen Farber, 'Natural Dangers', 100.
104. Ibid.
105. Marcia Magill, 'Peter Weir', 474.
106. Ibid., 474–475.
107. According to Magill, 'with the relative success of his first films and by virtue of the Australian New Wave… [Weir] was a logical choice to direct the screen adaptation', especially considering that the film was set in Australia. Ibid., 478.
108. Ibid.

109. Ibid., 478–479. Weir is referring to *The Year of Living Dangerously*.
110. The interview by Janet Maslin opens with an account of how Feldman chose Harrison Ford for the leading role. See Janet Maslin, 'Cooper film an Inspiration for "Witness"', *New York Times*, February 8, 1985, 20. The interview accompanies the review of *Witness* by Vincent Canby, which drives the attention on to the star of the film rather than on the director. This suggests the different 'Hollywood status' of the two: Weir was unknown to the larger audiences in America, whereas Ford, having already played in five major box office successes (the original *Star Wars* trilogy and the first two *Indiana Jones* films), was a major Hollywood star. See Vincent Canby, '"Witness" with Harrison Ford', *New York Times*, February 8, 1985, 16.
111. Feldman adds: 'I thought of Gary Cooper wearing the Quaker outfit… and I asked myself, "Who today is a reactive kind of actor who would also look funny in an outfit like that?" Harrison Ford came to mind, and the movie was on its way'. Janet Maslin, 'Cooper film', 20.
112. Mike Bygrave, 'Down Under in LA', *Still*, no. 19, May 1985, 47.
113. Ibid.
114. Ibid. It is interesting to notice the use of the word 'exile', which suggests that the move of the Australian directors to Hollywood was not voluntary but due to the circumstances. Bygrave, indeed, sustains that Beresford and Armstrong 'have been careful to emphasize their allegiance to Australia and *their relative indifference to Hollywood*' (ibid., 48. Emphasis added). A different view, however, comes across examining what Beresford and Armstrong say about their respective moves to Hollywood. In the interview by Gary Crowdus and Udayan Gupta, Beresford says: 'If you want… to do *Tender Mercies*, I'll come over and to it straight away'. See Gary Crowdus and Udayan Gupta, 'An Aussie in Hollywood: An Interview with Bruce Beresford', *Cinéaste*, vol. 12, n. 4, April 1, 1983. Gillian Armstrong, talking about her first movie realised in America (*Fires Within*, 1991), mentions that she had 'a very unhappy experience', but she does not refer to any reason that might have forced her to go to America. Her experience was unfortunate because she did not encounter a 'sympathetic producer who shared her vision' (*Fires Within* was produced by MGM). Indeed, the film was completely re-edited and 'totally changed'. Nonetheless, Armstrong chose to go back to work in America to direct *Little Women*, persuaded by the producer Denis DiNovi (see Gillian Armstrong, '*Little Women*: little by little', in Raffaele Caputo and Geoff Burton (eds), *Second Take. Australian Film-makers Talk*, St Leonards, NSW: Allen & Unwin, 1999. In the light of these considerations, Bygrave's definition of Armstrong and Beresford's condition as an exile does not seem appropriate.
115. Bygrave, 'Down Under in LA', 48.
116. Ibid.
117. Ibid.
118. Roderick Mann, 'Peter Weir pays Witness to the Amish', *Los Angeles Times*, January 27, 1985, 17.
119. Ibid.
120. Ibid.
121. Jeff Silverman, 'Harrison Ford Takes off his Fedora and Turns Humble', *Los Angeles Herald Examiner*, July 2, 1985, B/1 column 1, B7.
122. Ibid.
123. *Indiana Jones and the Last Crusade*, the third film of the trilogy, was made in 1989, several years after Ford's involvement in *Witness* (1985).
124. Jeff Silverman, 'Harrison Ford Takes off his Fedora', B7.

125. Ibid.
126. Peter Weir, 'The Director's Voice 2', in Raffaele Caputo and Geoff Burton (eds), *Third Take. Australian Filmmakers Talk*, Australia: Allen & Unwin, 2002.
127. Peter Weir, 'The Director's Voice 2', 61.
128. Ibid., 64.
129. Patty O'Brien and Bruce Vaughn (eds), *Amongst Friends. Australian and New Zealand Voices from America*, Dunedin, NZ: University of Otago Press, 2005, 54.
130. Australia and New Zealand both took part in the First World War alongside the Allied countries. See Richard W. Teare, 'Preface', in ibid., 5.
131. The annual national holiday to commemorate the Australian and New Zealand soldiers killed and maimed in the two World Wars.
132. See, as one example, Katrine Tulich, 'Peter Weir', *Cinema Papers*, vol. 80, 1990, 9.
133. Lovell and Sergi, in the introduction to their book, quote the passage from Bordwell and Thompson at length: 'Most people who study cinema regard the director as the film's "author". [I]t is the director who makes crucial decisions about performance, staging, lighting, framing, cutting and sound… For the most part it is the director who shapes the film's unique form and style, and these two components are central to cinema as an art'. David Bordwell and Kristine Thompson, *Film Art. An Introduction*, New York: McGraw-Hill, 33, quoted in Alan Lovell and Gianluca Sergi, *Making Film in Contemporary Hollywood*, London: Hodder Arnold, 2005.
134. Ibid., 8–9.
135. Ibid., 114.
136. In Chapter 4, dedicated to a comparative analysis of a selection of Weir's Australian and Hollywood films, I will discuss to what extent Peter Weir can be considered a transnational filmmaker.

Chapter 3

Australian Production Context in the 1970s and Early 1980s

Introduction

In this chapter, I examine the Australian cinema production context in the 1970s and early 1980s, at the time of Peter Weir's emergence and professional growth as a filmmaker, a period that has been referred to by some scholars as the revival of the Australian film industry.[1] To set the context, I first investigate how the notion of national cinema applies to Australian national cinema. Then I analyse the policies of the governmental body that financed the films of the revival, the Australian Film Commission (AFC) and its activity through the lenses of two reports commissioned by the government. In the second part of this chapter, I examine the production context from the point of view of the producers, analysing interviews with the McElroy brothers and with Patricia Lovell. In the concluding section, I look at the production context of the 1980s, the decade in which Weir left Australia for Hollywood.

The developing notion of Australian national cinema

Although earlier scholars (Graham Shirley and Brian Adams,[2] and David Stratton[3]) do not clearly state what they mean by Australian national cinema, it is possible to infer that they consider it to be a cinema representing the specificity of Australian culture, the myths and narratives typical of the culture, and the Australian character. These scholars identify those characteristics in the cinema produced during the period of the revival (1970s to early 1980s).

In the 1990s, Tom O'Regan provided a different angle of analysis of the Australian national cinema, describing the characteristic of Australian cinema as follows:

> Like all national cinemas, the Australian cinema contends with Hollywood dominance, it is simultaneously a local and international form… is has a significant relation with the nation and the state, and it is constitutionally fuzzy. National cinemas are simultaneously an aesthetic and production movement, a critical technology,… an industrial strategy and an international project formed in response to dominant international cinemas.… Australian cinema is formed as a relation to Hollywood and other national cinemas.[4]

The multifaceted nature of Australian national cinema is not, however, a direct reflection of the nature of Australia itself, seen by O'Regan as a 'European derived society', a 'diasporic society', a 'new world society' and a 'multicultural society';[5] each of these elements does not produce a corresponding cinema, but they are combined in different forms and different ways of considering Australian cinema. Firstly, there is a cinema that, as it were, compares and contrasts itself with Hollywood productions. For example, *Mad Max* (1979) is one of the films 'that are if not imitative, then consonant or interchangeable with the international product', whereas other productions 'complement' Hollywood (seeking local specificity in domestic events or myths, as in *Sunday Too Far Away* [1975]) or seek an alternative to Hollywood (as in the case of art films such as *My Brilliant Career* [1979]).

Secondly, there is a cinema seen as a local and international forum, in the sense that 'national cinemas' are part of internationalization and not an alternative to it. 'Going local' opens the possibility of a 'commercial exploitative cinema' and 'the prospect of a quirky, eccentric cinema' in order to establish 'international attractiveness'.[6]

The third aspect of Australian cinema is the cinema of film festivals that 'circulates in the non-Hollywood ("festival") space of the "foreign film" in world cinema markets'.[7] Since the revival, a good number of Australian directors have been recognized internationally and their work regularly circulated in film festivals such as Cannes, Berlin and Toronto. Such presence allowed the international circulation of local contents and cultural values, and the film festival circuit provides an alternative to Hollywood cinema. The cinema of festivals has been influenced by European 'art cinema', and this has eased its integration within the 'local and international art film circuits'.[8]

After Andrew Higson's work on national cinema and Tom O'Regan's discussion on Australian national cinema, scholars have ceased to take for granted the idea of Australian national cinema as an expression of national specificity and of cinema funded by the government, and have developed a more flexible notion of Australian national cinema. Studying the analogies between the British and Australian cinemas, Brian McFarlane and Geoff Meyer argue that Australian cinema is indebted to the classical narrative cinema of the Hollywood melodrama,[9] and those Australian and British cinemas both responded to the dominance of Hollywood. In his study on contemporary Australian cinema, Jonathan Rayner[10] agrees with Andrew Higson that the notion of a national cinema is fluid and 'subject to ceaseless negotiations'[11] and echoes O'Regan's view that 'the standard to which all other national forms of film expression are compared is that of Hollywood'.[12]

More recently, the study of Australian cinema has been framed within the transnational discourse. Natalie Brillion, in her article, 'Mexicans with Parkas and Mobile Phones: Transnational Cinema at Hollywood's Edge', looks at the 'ways in which the national cultural polices supporting [the] industries intersect with the transnational at the economic and cultural level'.[13] Brillion concentrates attention on the panorama of Australian cinema in the last two decades, especially looking at Hollywood runaway productions and co-productions between Hollywood and Australia.

Brillion examines the 'intersections of the runaway transnational films and the national funding policies', in particular co-productions. According to her, there are different types of intersections: 'treaty co-productions', 'equity co-productions' and 'films with transnational elements'. The first are recognized by the government, and give the right to local funding and other benefits. The second are 'non treaty co-productions', where international partners are investing in a Hollywood product but they no longer only possess the territorial rights but also have some creative rights. [T]he contract is basically between international conglomerates which by-passes national co-productions treaties, therefore stepping aside any national cultural agenda. Finally, there are films that have transnational elements, balanced in such a way that they do not 'threaten the qualification of the film as national' but are not part of co-production agreements between states. Brillion describes the peculiar policy that the Australian government has for the recognition of a film as Australian, 'films may be described by the AFC as "Australian" even if they are 100% foreign (US) financed'.

Brillion also argues that the popularity of Australian films with domestic audiences is due to a strong sense of Australianess conveyed by the films.[14] Furthermore, the constant representation of national themes in the Australian cinema rendered it highly recognizable both at a national and at an international level. Interestingly, Brillion points out that at a national level there is the willingness to reclaim as Australian those stars who have had international success, such as Russell Crowe (although he is a New Zealander), Cate Blanchett and Nicole Kidman. Brillion argues that a shift has occurred in the discourse surrounding Australian national cinema; from the traditional 'art' versus 'commerce' contrast, the emphasis has shifted to 'local' versus 'international', an example of which is given by the debate over the Fox studios in Australia and the production of *Moulin Rouge* (2001).[15]

The recent production *Australia* shows a reversal in the trend and a renewed interest of Australian filmmakers and stars in their national cinema. The film, released in 2009, is an American/Australian co-production, being produced by Baz Lurhman's company Bazmark films and by Twentieth Century Fox, was filmed on location in Australia and partly in the Fox Moor Park Australian studio in Sydney, was directed by an Australian director return to make a film in Australia after shooting *Romeo + Juliet* (1996) and *Moulin Rouge* in the United States, and stars an all Australian main cast (Nicole Kidman – considered an Australian actress at the time Hugh Jackman, Bryan Brown, David Wenham, David Gulipilil, Brandon Walters), and importantly, in contrast with *Moulin Rouge*, was marketed worldwide as an *Australian* film, with a publicity campaign (that – belatedly – matches the marketing of Peter Jackson's *Lord of the Rings Trilogy*), which promotes the landmark film locations as tourist destinations.

What emerges from these studies is that the notion of Australian national cinema is an evolving one and that its analysis, as in the case of any other national cinema, cannot neglect consideration of the larger international context within which Australian cinema operates.

The wake-up call: the revival of the 1970s and the institution of the AFC

By the end of 1960s, Australian cinema was struggling amidst several difficulties; overseas production had overtaken local features and audiences had turned to television, which had more Australian content. This gloomy situation provoked serious concerns among film critics and filmmakers about the status of cinema and they began a debate, fuelled by film societies, about the necessity of 'national cinema' to express the national culture.[16] In their seminal book on the Australian film industry, Dermody and Jacka report the cultural rhetoric discourse surrounding the role that a national cinema ought to play in Australia:

> Film is a crucial part of indigenous culture deserving support because of its contribution to the richness and self-reflexiveness of Australian experience and because, equally it contributes a large, exportable body of imagery, truths about Australia. It is claimed to be "our best ambassador", always with the coda that "trade follows film". Australian narrative and imagery are seen as reflecting and developing a process of national identity which is a process that may be proudly and advantageously projected overseas. An Australian film industry, it is argued, enables Australia to talk to itself, recognise itself, and engage the attention of the world in doing so.[17]

In this passage, the authors identify the main issue that defined what came to be known as the decade of the revival: the necessity of state support, cinema as ambassador of a national culture, and the tension, that I examine below, between cinema as art and cinema as commerce.

At the end of the 1960s, Australia did neither yet have a national cinema, nor did it have a proper industry that could produce films aimed both at local and international audiences. Government intervention was seen as crucial for its development.[18] The financial help from the government was needed to increase the quantity of Australian features produced, but also to raise their quality. Lobbied by the Federal Government Film and Television Committee and by the Australian Film Institute, the government promoted an investigation of 'government-funded film and television industries abroad'[19] that resulted in a report with indications and recommendation for the re-launch of the film industry.

Following the indications of the report, the government, supported by the opposition, set up the Australian Film Development Corporation (AFDC) that had the function to 'assist the financing of feature films and television programmes' and the aim of establishing 'a commercially viable industry',[20] to implement investments in the film industry.[21] The government also set up the Experimental Film and Television Fund (EFTE) and a film and television school.[22] The AFDC began operating in March 1971 and its first significant investment was Bruce Beresford's *The Adventures of Barry McKenzie* (1972).

Even though after 1970 the number of film released had increased dramatically, the industry was failing to produce films that could perform on the overseas market.[23] To find a solution, in 1972 the government set up the Tariff Board of inquiry into the film and television industry, with public hearings of producers and other industry personnel. The inquiry wanted to examine 'all the aspects of the distribution and exhibition of overseas and Australian films',[24] the activities of the AFDC, and find ways to assist the film industry.

Shirley and Adams report the more significant responses that the directors gave, which highlight the several problems of the cinema industry, showing that an injection of financial aid into the industry was not sufficient to resolve the long-standing issues inherited by decades of uncertainties and lack of organizations[25] (issues that neither the Royal Commission of the 1927[26] nor the Vincent Report had resolved). The directors' opinions, interestingly, also put to the fore contrasts between the different agents of the film industry, whose priorities had not always coincided. According to Tim Burstall, Australian producers, exhibitors and distributors were unaware of the audience's expectations and their biggest mistake was to release Australian movies and import overseas productions – which overshadowed local products – at the same time. Phil Noyce lamented the costs 'hiring cinemas' that 'led the Coop to screen regularly at unlicensed premises'.[27] The AFDC came under attack from the Film Producers' Association of Australia (formed from a merger between the Australian Motion Picture Studio Association and the Australian Film Producers' Association) unsatisfied by its policies and with the film traders angry at its attitude towards the Australian production.

In their analysis of the tariff board's report, Shirley and Adams quote a declaration of Eric Davis, managing director of Twentieth-Century Fox Australia, that is telling about the difficult relationships between foreign production companies and the local industry: 'For an overseas company', says Davis, 'to invest in an entirely Australian film and have no script involvement would be "very difficult"'.[28] Despite all the difficulties highlighted, the tariff board had the merit to raise new awareness of the importance of a film culture in Australia and of 'what constituted an Australian film, and more broadly, a film culture'.[29] A debate arose over the characteristics that an Australian film should have in order to appeal to the international market, and professionals agreed that 'a film which exhibits both quality and craftsmanship and national characteristics is most likely to achieve international acceptance'.[30]

As the mid 1970s approached, the government organizations gradually stopped supporting only the commercially viable films. The Tariff Board Report recommended that the AFDC would in future 'assist projects of quality which would not necessarily have good commercial prospects, and also projects of developmental or innovative value'.[31] The first of these projects was going to be Peter Weir's *The Cars that Ate Paris* (1974), with a contribution of 250,000 Australian dollars (AUD) by the AFDC.

Dermody and Jacka argue that the main problem of the Australian film industry was the lack of precedents on multiple levels, such as finance, management, creative skills and even generic models of audience receptivity. According to Dermody and Jacka, the period from 1970 to 1975 – which they regard as the first period of the Australian film industry's development – is characterized by an amateurish film industry, due to a 'virtually complete vacuum' of expertize at all levels (financial, managerial and creative), and by an unclear relationship between production on the one hand, and distribution and exhibition on the other hand. In this first period, the AFDC did not have clear policies and 'funded individual films on the hit-and-miss basis; there was not clear relationship between production, on the one hand and distribution and exhibition on the other'.[32]

Interestingly, producer James McElroy's view on the AFDC contradicts Dermody and Jacka's observations. In a personal communication to the author, the producer describes the AFDC as the body who effectively presided over the 'halcyon days of the revival in the seventies' and adds that the AFDC was 'the least intrusive of the any of the government agencies'.[33]

By June 1974, the AFDC had provided less than 5 million AUD for cinema production and the government began to ponder the destiny of the organization. In 1972, a Labour government had taken power for the first time in 23 years, and, following the recommendation of the Tariff Board, established the AFC which replaced the AFDC. Following the recommendation of the Tariff Board, the government declared that the commission should have a closer relationship with the industry, and, most importantly, should, among its long-term aims, 'demonstrate that high artistic standards and box office are not mutually exclusive'.[34] In the following passage, Graham and Adams report the Board's recommendations:

> [The Commission should encourage] the making of those films of high artistic or conceptual value which may or may not be regarded at the same time as conforming to the current criteria of genre, style, taste but which have cultural, artistic or social relevance.... Thematic concerns, Australian content, artistic value... will make to the development of [an] Australian film industry of high international standard.[35]

To make sure that the AFC was close to the film industry, the board suggested that the AFC's members should have some knowledge or direct experience of filmmaking, an aspect that was lacking in the previous AFDC. However, the AFC's status was still an open issue: should it be controlled directly by the government or should it have a statutory status?

The definitive statute was passed in March 1975, establishing the mission and the areas of control of the Commission. The AFC had the power to deliver grants and could oblige exhibitors to show a quota of short films that were certified as Australian. Furthermore, the Commission 'could... help state government authorities to acquire educational Australian films'[35] and should promote film archival activity. The annual grants conceded for film funding were around $5 to $6 million in the period 1970–75, reaching $10 million in 1980–81.

Dermody and Jacka regard the period from 1975 to 1980 as the second period of the Australian film industry development, characterized by the control of the AFC over the film industry that 'became consolidated as a government-subsidized and guided industry'.[37] In this second period, the production level was still 'artisanal', with independent producers who managed the financial aspects (being a liaison between the AFC and the directors). The exhibition and distribution levels, however, already had an international character.

A third period of the development of the cinema industry commenced in 1981 with the introduction of tax concessions, and stretched until the end of the decade. This period could be defined as the 'coming of age' of Australian cinema and is characterized by an increasing professionalism, technological improvements (such as the introduction of the Dolby system and the steadicam) and the significant increase of film budgets after the introduction of the tax concessions for film investors.

It is significant, in the context of this book, to highlight that Dermody and Jacka identify Peter Weir's films as the marker of the passage from one period of the development of the film industry to the next. For the authors, *Picnic* (1975) signals the passage from the first stage to the second for three reasons. Firstly, because it was one of the first films to be financed by the Greater Union Organization that covered one-third of the entire budget; secondly, it 'brought considerable prestige to its producer, the South Australian Film Corporation';[38] and thirdly, it 'had a higher budget of any film to date'[39] and was able to recoup its costs within ten weeks.[40] *Gallipoli* (1981) marked the transition from the second to the third phase because its record-breaking budget 'was by far the highest budgeted Australian film made in the period from 1970'.[41] The criteria used by Dermody and Jacka to single out *Picnic* and *Gallipoli* are predominantly economic and this shows that Peter Weir's relevance for the renaissance of the Australian cinema goes beyond the aesthetic contribution to the films of the revival but extends to the financial impact of the director's production on the film industry.

In Australia, Weir was able to obtain a considerable amount of money for his films, pushing the limits of the average film's budget. *The Last Wave* cost almost twice as much as *Picnic* ($800,000). The AFC that had partially financed *Picnic* was willingly to put its money into *Gallipoli*, which, as aforementioned, cost nearly $3 million. Peter Weir not only grew as filmmaker within the industry, but he also contributed to the growth of the industry in economical terms.

'Art' versus 'Commerce' in the Australian cinema

Alongside the mainstream productions, Australia had a lively production of 'alternative movies' that were mainly funded by the Experimental Film and Television Fund (EFTE). To be financed by the EFTE, a film ought to be 'original in approach, technique or subject matter' or '[an] experimental [film] by inexperienced but promising filmmakers'.[42] These two criteria, however, did not help to identify which film to effectively support. In an article in the *Sydney Morning Herald*, Margaret Jones sustained that the films financed with the EFTE funds were those that were *too* experimental to be understood by a general audience[43] and the EFTE should privilege the promotion of young talents rather than the production of commercially viable films.

Herein resides the eternal dilemma of 'commerce' versus 'art' that had animated the debate among filmmakers, the industry and critics because the realization that cinema could be considered as a form of art alongside the more traditional arts and could be used as a flagship of the national culture. Dermody and Jacka maintain that 'art cinema' combines two aspects. The first regards the films' textual characteristics, their aesthetic and their thematic concerns;[44] the second regards 'their display of signs of national differences, country of origin, geographical and cultural "sights"'.[45] An art cinema with these characteristics had to fight for self-affirmation in opposition to Hollywood. A national film industry 'seeks to assert its right to exist and its cultural necessity'.[46]

Dermody and Jacka, in their analysis, indicate 'art' and 'commerce' as the two main areas of concern for the Australian film industry, and identify 'two almost physically distinct industries'[47] which they call 'industry 1' and 'industry 2'. The first is concerned with the search for an Australian identity, produces low-budget films for local audiences, has an 'interest for other arts' and is 'university educated', is in favour of a government-regulated industry and opposed to cultural imperialism. The second industry stands for the opposite values; it favours entertainment, considers Australia as part of the world, is against the idea of message-films, is anti-art and pro-Hollywood, is in favour of a free market and denies cultural imperialism.[48]

Dermody and Jacka underline that, in the 1970s, only 'industry 1' existed, the values of which were backed by the majority of the producers and by 'most of [the] directors, writers and actors'. The films produced by 'industry 1' had a 'modest artisanal and democratic' style of filmmaking and were 'socially concerned, gentle, humanistic [and] sometimes didactic'. The second form of industry surfaced after the introduction of tax concessions at the beginning of the 1980s, and was embraced by 'latter-day producers, film financiers, packagers and brokers', whose main preoccupation was 'the quality of the deal'. The films made by 'industry 2' followed an 'industrialised, professionalised, streamlined and undemocratic' style of filmmaking and were 'international blockbuster or the formula genre piece'.[49]

Signs of this division between the two industries were already clear in the early 1970s. Indeed, of the two main governmental film organizations existing in Australian in the early 1970s, the AFDC financed more commercially viable films (such as *The Adventure of Barry McKenzie*, although that was still a long way from the commercial blockbusters that appeared from the early 1980s onwards), whereas a movie funded by the EFTF was immediately labelled as 'art'. The Tariff Board Report gave great importance to the issue of experimental cinema that was seen as the training ground for talented directors.[50]

Overview of government inquiries into the AFC

In May 1985, the Policy Unity of the Executive branch of the AFC promoted an 'overview of all the major federal and government enquiries since the Tariff Board Review that began in 1971'.[51] The document had a double purpose; on the one hand, it served as an assessment of the past achievements of the film and television industry, whereas on the other hand, it represented a tool for the preparation of future inquiries. Although the overview covers inquiries into both the film and television industries, I focus my attention on the three inquiries more directly related to the AFC: *Towards a More Effective Commission: The AFC in the 1980s*, the *ABC/AFC Woking Party on ABC Purchasing Policy: 1984* and *The Cultural Activities Review. Australian Film Commission*, of August of 1984. A closer look at these inquiries provides an important insight into the activities of the AFC, facilitating the understanding of its policies during the period of the revival. Each overview presents the background of the inquiry, a summary of the recommendations and the actions taken as a result.

Towards a More Effective Commission: The AFC in the 1980s refers to the 'management consultancy review of the Commission activities'[52] that the AFC undertook in 1977, interviewing industry professionals, filmmakers and representatives of the state authorities, with the aim of assessing the AFC's policies and defining its future development within the new trends of the film industry. The recommendations encouraged the AFC to plan on the basis of a further five years of state commitment – subject to a further review in 1984–85 and to invest in those projects that offered more possibilities of a recoup of part of the investment. The inquiry points out that the AFC financial estimate is based on three years and 'operates on the basis of continued government commitment to the film industry'.[53] The recommendations also discussed that role the AFC should play in film production. The AFC was encouraged 'not [to] enter into feature film production on its even account nor act as commission agent in distribution'.[54] However, in contrast with this recommendation, the AFC is also advised to become a shareholder of companies 'which produces Australian films'. The last recommendation also encourages the AFC to 'continue to fund organisations associated with film culture'.[55] Examining the actions that followed the 1977 review and the actual policies undertaken by the Commission, it emerges that the AFC acted only partially upon the recommendations: it invested in those projects which gave more financial returns, but *did* enter into film production, and ultimately continued to fund film-related organisations.

The second inquiry, in 1984, regards the AFC and the purchasing policy of the Australian Broadcasting Corporation (ABC). A closer examination of the review is interesting because it shows that the AFC's role as Australian cultural watchdog, as it were, was not only limited to feature film but was also extended to television. The AFC was concerned about the lack of Australian content in the ABC, due on the one hand to 'the lack of support given by the ABC to independent productions', and on the other hand to the 'little independent material available'.[56] In view of a possible acquisition of the ABC, the AFC consulted all the interested parties (the Television Production Association of Australia, the Film Industry Standing committee and the Australian Film and Television School) and an ABC/AFC Working Party was established in 1983.

The recommendations to the ABC mostly echo the ones that the Tariff Board had given ten years previously to the AFC, but it is possible to notice some differences. The board of directors is encouraged to establish 'joint ventures with independent producers' and to 'use... supplementary private investments'.[57] Otherwise, the inquiry reflects a conservative policy on the nature of the programmes to purchase, recommending the acquisition of 'high quality, independently produced Australian drama and documentary programs'.[58] The ABC is also advised to 'acknowledge a special commitment to the acquisition and broadcasting of low budget, innovative and experimental Australian programs'.[59] Regarding the actions taken as a consequence, the AFC 'expressed disappointment... on the slow progress of ABC's proposed increased acquisition of independent programs'[60] but acknowledges the purchase of a number of independent documentaries and the broadcasting of a collection of independent films made by students of the Australian Film and Television School.

This closer examination of the review shows an insistence on the 'Australianess' of television programmes. This is hardly surprising, given the pre-occupation of the Australian cultural – and political – milieu regarding the affirmation of an Australian national culture, in relation to both feature films and television programmes. What is surprising is the total lack of criteria for the determination of what is intended by 'Australian programme' and 'Australian film'. In the 1980s, the Australian film industry was increasingly becoming the stage of foreign investments, namely by Hollywood majors.[61] Was a Hollywood-financed film still to be considered an Australian product? The issue remained pending. What is clear is the position of the AFC regarding the nationality of actors and actresses to employ in Australian films, stated by the Actors' Equity Policy.[62]

It interesting to mention briefly the last inquiry of the overview, a 'review of the AFC's responsibilities to cultural activities',[63] which followed the 1983 proposal of dividing the Creative and Development Branch (CDB) of the AFC into two separate branches; script and production funding, and organization funding and film culture.[64] Among its objectives, the review aimed to 'define and review the nature and extent of cultural activities in Australia',[65] and to establish to what extent those activities relied on the support of the AFC, as well as identifying underdeveloped areas and establish new activities. Several organizations took part and a draft policy was adopted.

The policy guidelines covered various aspects of the AFC's activities, such as distribution, organization, exhibition and travel grants, and recommended the implementation of each area with AFC support. The policy regarded a vast array of propositions; assistance for film-related publications, support for awards, festivals and conferences, assistance for travel grants and support of film-training programmes in response to local needs. The guidelines also demonstrated the AFC's intention to implement production facilities with investments for the acquisition of better equipment. Ultimately, the AFC aimed to define its funding criteria and, importantly, to 'facilitate the exchange of information' between personnel of the 'funded organisations and film workers'.[66] The actions taken regard the administration of funding to applicants, subject to scrutiny of their 'financial position... policies, and program'.[67] Echoing the review on the AFC policies in the 1980s, the 'Cultural Activities' review encourages 'greater state government involvement in film culture'[68] and a closer connection between the AFTS, the AFC and funded organizations.

Although the document states its objectives very clearly, it does not, however, go into details in its findings, nor it does illustrate specifically the actions undertaken (which are, for instance, the organizations funded?), as a consequence of the numerous recommendations. This examination of the three inquiries reviews leaves the impression of high expectations and noble intentions that were not completely fulfilled by the review's addressee, the AFC. In my opinion, the intrinsic problem of these inquiries is that the *commissioner* and the *receiver* of the inquiries are, although under different names that reflect different functions,[69] the *same* organization: the AFC. Therefore, any evaluation of the outcomes of these inquiries has to be done with the benefit of the doubt. The actions undertaken by the AFC following specific recommendations, like the introduction of the scheme 10BA, are certainly to be considered an achievement of the AFC, but an achievement of a self-imposed goal.

Herein, I am not disputing the effectiveness of certain measures (the 10BA scheme, for instance, *did* bring fresh money into the industry), but I am questioning the nature of these reviews, because on the one hand, any praise of the AFC's activities ultimately comes from the AFC itself, and, on the other hand, and there are no consequences or penalties for any unfulfilled recommendation. I believe that those reviews could have been more effective if carried out by an external body or authority that could have put more pressure on the AFC for the achievement of set objectives and could also have taken measures for its shortcomings.

The Interim Report on the Australian Film Industry (1969–1980)

The 1980s opened with the introduction of the 10BA tax incentives scheme, aimed at facilitating private investment in the film industry. Two years into the scheme, the AFC, together with other government film organizations and the Film and Television Production Association of Australia, promoted a survey of the areas affected by the legislation, and presented the *Interim Report on the Australian Film Industry: A Survey of Industry Activities from October 1980 to October 1981 Against the Background of Industry Development from 1969 to 1980*,[70] the results of which were presented to the 'government, the industry and other interested parties'.[71] It is worth examining the report more closely, because it represents another important tool of information and insight into the AFC at the beginning of the third phase of the Australian film industry's development. As noted above, in this period, the industry stopped producing only films aimed at local audiences and at art house international audiences, and began to produce more commercial products increasingly aimed at international mass audiences.

The 'objectives of the survey were to establish the levels of production and investment activity in the film industry during 1981, and the attitudes of producers and investors' representatives to the present functioning of the tax incentive schemes'.[72] The survey was designed having in mind 'both the production side of the industry and the sources of production investment',[73] and was divided as follows:

- production survey (members of producer associations and persons acting 'in the capacity of film producer')[74]
- finance survey (investors contemplating entry into film production, and professional advisers such as stockbrokers and lawyers, and financial intermediaries)
- casting agencies survey
- facilities survey ('companies involved in film processing, editing and mixing services as well as production equipment hire and sale')[75]

The survey was tailored to the different categories addressed and was conducted with a combination of questionnaires and interviews.[76] The broad spectrum of categories covered demonstrates that the Australian film industry had reached, during the period of the revival, a very complex structure with a variety of professional figures (such as stock brokers) becoming involved in the industry's activities. The report shows that the AFC, in addressing these other professional figures, was becoming aware of the changes that were occurring within the industry. Such awareness, however, as it emerges from the response to the survey and from the interviews with producers that I examine below, was not necessarily accompanied by an understanding of the actual needs of all the parties in the industry.

The interim report gives details of the production level during the 1969–1980 period, and points out that the investments in the film industry were of two different types: 'industry investment' and 'private investment' (directly related to government support made available through state film organizations).[77] In the first half of the 1970s, the industry was characterized by low-budget productions and private investment was more significant. The report shows that, after 1975 (when the industry received a dramatic government financial boost with the establishment of the AFC), private investments failed 'to keep pace with the growth of the industry' (150 features were produced) and, declined in the biennium 1979/80, causing a dramatic drop of production. In the period of the second half of the 1980s, there were 'unusually high levels of government and industry investments and an insignificant level of private investments'[78] but only three films commenced production. The announcement of the introduction of the tax incentives had the desired effect and more than twenty films began production before June 1981[79] (and about ten others afterwards).

The Interim Report summarizes the main points, comments and pre-occupations raised by the responses of the producers who answered the survey,[80] which regarded film development, finance, investment, deals with brokers, and, more specifically, the tax-incentive scheme. The questions can be grouped into the following areas:

- Production (number of features in development; stage of development – treatment, scripting and packaging)
- Finance (costs, how the finance were raised – government, producers, other; presence of a broker or intermediary and their role; investment)

- Investment (structure adopted – more than/less than 20 investors; typology of investors (individual tax payers, size of business run)
- Tax-incentive scheme (how the 27 May 1981 legislation affected feature film investment; factors that mitigated the benefits of the legislations – difficulties of completion on time, excess demand of post-production facilities during March/June 1980, seasonal setting implications)
- Further suggestions

According to the report, the main pre-occupation of the respondents to the production survey regarded the difficulty of complying with the required deadline for the completion of film production to be eligible for the tax deduction (30th of June – the so called '12 months rule'), because certain productions had specific needs (such as requiring specific seasonal settings). Furthermore, producers signalled that the scheme provoked a 'bunching of production schedules, leading to competition for and inflation in costs of production crews and casts'.[81] Producers also pointed out problems of interpretation of certain legal expressions in 'the absence of effective guidelines'.[82] The production schedule was also an issue, because it required 'investments to be raised during the least advantageous period of the financial year'.[83] Regarding the certification, the respondent pointed out 'definitional concerns in respects of the different types of films'.[84]

Lastly, the production survey highlighted that 'development activity for future films appears quite high… with producers clearly dependent on continued direct support from government film organisation'.[85] This statement suggests a certain uneasiness, on the part of the producers, to be dependent on government funding, and, by extension, to have to comply with the series of requirements (Australian content, Australian actors, film completion by certain date) in order to be eligible for funding.

Respondents to the 'finance survey' identified film financing as one of the possible investments legally regulated, alongside more traditional ones such as 'real estate' and 'primary production'.[86] Investors responding to the survey, furthermore, expressed concerns regarding the legal aspects involved and the required deadline for the completion of film production. On the strictly financial side, the investors rejected the idea of 'finance for the development and marketing of films as distinct from production'.[87]

The report does not have a conclusion and does not indicate the path to be followed for the rectification of the problems highlighted. In the covering letter accompanying the report, there is only the suggestion that 'the task of monitoring the financial aspects associated with the development of the film industry, commenced under the auspices of the survey, to be continued'.[88]

The government, however, did take into consideration some of the concerns raised in the survey, and, in January 1983, modified the tax scheme in relation to the 12-months rule, so that 'investors could again claim in the year of expenditure, with the restriction that the film had to be completed by the end of the financial year'.[89] With the introduction of the tax-incentive scheme, the industry saw a 'fundamental reorientation', changing 'from a public service organisation to a servicing agency for private investors'.[90] According to Dermody and Jacka, if the AFC's clients, before the introduction of the scheme, were 'individual independent producers, writers and directors, after 1981... the clients were effectively the investors'.[91] In the biennium 1982–83, however, the film-financing industry became depressed and government funding returned to being important.

Australian production context: the producers talk

Having examined the production context from the point of view of the AFC's policy, in this section I will look at the industry, taking into consideration the views of the industry professionals. I will examine interviews with Patricia Lovell and also with two of the most important producers of the period, Jim and Hal McElroy, whose discussions with Scott Murray, published in *Cinema Papers*, provide a valuable insiders' view into the condition and the development of the Australian film industry from the late 1970s to the early 1990s.

In the first interview by Scott Murray, in 1974,[92] Jim and Hal McElroy discuss a series of issues, from the limited number of good producers in Australia, to the fact that all the work available was taken by the handful of best filmmakers, leaving newcomers with scant possibilities of gaining experience. Through the narration of the McElroys' experience in producing *The Cars that Ate Paris*, the interview provides an interesting insight regarding the financial aspects of production in the mid 1970s.[93] Jim McElroy says that the best way to approach a possible investor is to have a clear picture of the costs involved in the making of the film; the producers consider the exhibition costs, the advertising costs and the producers' percentage (eventually split with the investor).

Producer Patricia Lovell (*Picnic at Hanging Rock*), interviewed by Scott Murray and Antony I. Ginnane for *Cinema Papers*,[94] also discusses the Australian policy about the amount of money returned to producers of a film's gross, which in 1976 was 75/25 (75 per cent for the investors and 25 per cent for the producers). According to Lovell, this type of deal does not take into account the risks taken by the producers and such a low percentage of the profits does not always guarantee enough money to invest in the following project. Australian producers, says Lovell, believe that a 60/40 deal would be more appropriate, also considering that overseas, especially in Europe, 'producers have a fairer go'. Lovell stresses that the Australian way of conducting this type of deal is 'highly unprofessional'.[95] In the interview, Lovell also points out that the role of a producer involves more than just finding investors: it also entails finding the director, and sometimes – as in the case of *Picnic at Hanging Rock* – taking part in the casting.[96]

In 1977, in a brief article in *Film and Filming*, Jim McElroy expresses his concerns regarding the state of film financing in Australia:

> [It] is nowhere near as healthy as it should be… despite the popular feeling that money is readily available, this is just not true. Private enterprise is still very conservative towards the cinema. It's not so much that it is concerned about the risk factor as that it just doesn't know movies. [A]lso, we are going through a difficult period economically. [T]raditionally, the sources of finance have been government organisations and distributors.[97]

McElroy also reflects on the lack of investment by American majors in Australian films and finding it 'unbelievable' given the success of films such as *Picnic at Hanging Rock*. Then the producer considers that the advantages of low-budget films 'may not be around much longer', given the budget increase of 50 per cent in the previous two years. McElroy concludes his reflection with a more positive note: 'The important thing about Australian cinema is the energy pumping out. The average age of people in the film industry is around 32–33. And because money is not readily available, every picture is given a lot of consideration'.[98]

At the time of production of *The Last Wave*, in 1977, the McElroy brothers gave their second interview with Scott Murray. The producers discuss the measures they adopted in the production of the film in terms of financial agreements with the AFC and with United Artists.[99] They stress the importance of having international stars in films that have to compete at an international level (a position opposed by Actors' Equity), and express their aspiration of making a film solely on the basis of private finance.

Jim and Hal McElroy explained how, in order to overcome disagreements and competition among producers, they were setting up an association of independent producers, in an attempt to find a unified voice[100] with which the AFC could deal. Mirroring a concern expressed by Patricia Lovell, the McElroys say that the association 'put a case to the AFC that independent producers are underpaid', considering the time invested and the risks involved. The association, continue the McElroys, 'has proposed that the salaries scale be significantly increased and instead of some producers rushing off to make another film just to make some money, we hope they will be able to stay on and responsibly market their films'.[101]

Film marketing represented another issue of concern for the McElroys. Intervening in the debate regarding the opportunity for government bodies to have their marketing branches, they maintain that financing and marketing should remain separated, unless the government bodies would like to produce their own films. Says Jim McElroy: 'If a state corporation sets up a marketing branch there will be a severe temptation on the part of producers to literally walk away from the responsibilities'.[102] In line with their previous interview to Murray, the McElroys conclude with a look at the future of film industry in Australia, which should 'embrace the entire entertainment concept'.[103]

The controversial relationship between the McElroy brothers and the AFC is also testified by two articles published by *Variety*. In the first, Jim McElroy expresses his hopes that the success of *Picnic at Hanging Rock* would help the Australian film industry to conduct itself in a more professional way and boost its international profile. Moreover, the producer predicts 'an increased power to individual producers to keep control of their own pictures'.[104] McElroy acknowledges that the Australian government is 'now looking at our films as commercial realities and appears to have finally realized that the producer is vitally important not only to the production itself but to the full marketing and distribution picture'.[105]

Jim McElroy, however, still expresses his bitter feelings towards the AFC, guilty of 'an over-inflated sense of self-importance',[106] and accuses it of having sold *Picnic at Hanging Rock* on the overseas market bypassing the producers of the film (Jim McElroy himself and his brother Hal). The Australia Film Commission's response was not to be awaited for long. The *Variety* issue of eleven days later reported the 'official response' of Alan Wardrope, the AFC's director of marketing and distribution. According to Wardrope, the McElroys' comments were 'characterised by inaccuracy' and coming a very long time after the 'alleged events'. It is worth reporting Wardrope's reaction at length:

> To suggest that the AFC has only just become aware of the importance of producers is naïve in the extreme and serves only to deny the track record of the AFC in assisting producers to get their projects off the ground and into production, and also to expose their finished product in the marketplace.[107]

Wardrope also stresses that the AFC has not only put more cash into producers' hands than any other financing group, but also has put up most finance in terms of marketing advances and completion guarantees. "[I]t falls to the AFC to come up with these funds so that the film may be completed and have a chance in the various international marketplaces."[108]

Herein, the AFC reinforces its role in controlling the marketing sector, which was precisely the area that, according to Jim McElroy, should have remained outside the AFC's control. Although the AFC proudly reiterates its role in boosting the possibilities of films on the international market, Jim McElroy had accused the AFC of impeding the films' chances internationally, by holding the rights of the movies on the international arena. James McElroy's bitterness over the AFC's handling of *Picnic*'s marketing has not subsided after more than 30 years. In a personal communication, the producer is keen to stress that

> The AFC's marketing was a disaster, but mercifully shortlived, except for the US. We managed to have the marketing returned to our control in the Rest of the World, but the AFC retained marketing in the US. They sold the film to a[n ineffective] company that went down… about a year later. There were some very shameful games played by certain parties at the time, over the control of marketing[109].

The controversy between the AFC and Australian producers highlights that in the period of the cinema revival, not everything went as smoothly as the appearances (and some critics) would suggest.

In their third interview with Scott Murray,[110] the McElroys look back at the year of the revival and discuss the status of the industry at the beginning of the 1990s. They discuss the 10BA scheme, pointing out that, at the time of the introduction of the scheme, they chose not to voice their concerns because of the enthusiasm that was surrounding the scheme, but they felt ready to talk about the tax legislation ten years later. According to James McElroy, the Australian film industry turned from a 'cottage industry into a business', although 'that business became too big, too many films were made and inflation took over'.[111] According to Hal McElroy, the scheme 'did give people lots of opportunities and we hoped, along with everybody else, that these opportunities would produce a second wave of actors, writers, directors, etc. but sadly it didn't'.[112] Scott Murray objects that a lot of talented new filmmakers came out of the 10BA, but according to the McElroys, they would have come out anyway, precisely because they were talented. 'The inescapable conclusion', continue the producers, 'is that there is an inverse relationship between the ease with which you can get money and the absence of genuinely resilient stars, directors and writers being thrown up'.[113] The strongest reservation against the scheme was that, due to the incentives for the production of films, too many bad films were made, which damaged the international reputation of Australian film in the United States, together with a bad handling of the marketing and pre-sales strategies.

The McElroys then express their views on the issue of 'productivity versus costs'. The producers reiterate their opinion that movies should be kept at a low budget because this is the only way to get money back at the box office. According to Jim McElroy, if a film is aimed at a national audience, $2 million is the ideal budget, 'as for the $10 million film, it must have a star and other international elements that will make it work globally'.[114] Looking back at the 1970s, the producers acknowledge that films were made for 'unrealistically low budgets'.[115] Keeping the costs of a film down is a necessity, to permit young filmmakers to enter the industry. One way to achieve a low cost is to shoot a film in a short period of time, which was becoming increasingly difficult in the 1990s, at the time of the interview. According to the producers, it is the efficiency that needs to be improved. Interestingly, the producers look at the American industry as an example: 'In America they have re-learnt the lessons we once knew but have now forgotten. [T]hat's how the American industry survived. They didn't say that everybody had to go on half salary; they said everyone is going to have to work faster and harder'.[116]

Scott Murray, recalling the 1977 interview, asks the producers about the role of the IFFPA.[117] According to the McElroys, the members of the association 'got caught up in 10BA and didn't pay enough attention to the very sorts of concerns we are talking about'.[118] Moreover, the extremely broad range of people involved in the association (from small-scale business to 'people making $12–14 million features') rendered its management difficult. Hal McElroy expresses his hope that

> [t]he harsher economic times are going to force people to… be more flexible and pragmatic. This so-called principle of defending Australia's cultural integrity has to be examined in the full light of the new economic dawn. I don't think it is appropriate for any industry in Australia to say that we are making something just for the Australians.[119]

Other than genuine interest in the future development of the Australian film industry and for its international visibility, Hal McElroy's comments could be attributed to a more personal interest: aiming the films at an international audience, a substantially bigger profit for the producers.

Examining the Actors Equity Policy, the McElroys express their concerns, highlighting the paradox born from what they define as the 'rush for cultural purity'. On one hand, the Australian producers are penalized for using overseas actors, but, on the other hand, there is an open-door policy of American film being made in Australia. The negative effects of this situation are that cast and crew get more money to work in an American film made in Australia than to work for an Australian film. Moreover, Australian productions are penalized for having foreign elements in the films, with the result that less Australian films are made by Australian people. Asked about the Australian Film Financing Corporation the McElroy brothers are more positive. They address the criticism about the scrutiny process to decide which film to finance, affirming that 'it is taxpayers' money and the AFFC has a legitimate right to commercially scrutinize projects in the market place'.[120]

The McElroy brothers were not the only ones to express concerns about the actors' guild. According to Bruce Beresford, the Actors Equity Policy played a part in his decision to move to Hollywood. Beresford said that the guild is 'xenophobic. They used to have a policy where you could bring in two foreign actors then they cancelled that'.[121] Moreover, the director adds that it was also difficult to bring in foreign technicians. Beresford affirms that he understand the reasons of the actors' guild, but argues that this attitude was damaging rather than benefiting the development of Australian cinema. He invoked a hypothetical company that could invest serious money for an Australian film, promising to employ '100% Australian technicians, 98% Australian actors' with the condition of having 'two foreign actors', conditions usually refused by the Australian Actors Guild.

These interviews highlight the problematic relationships between industry professionals and the AFDC and demonstrate that, despite its replacement with the AFC, not all the problems were solved, because certain long-standing issues were difficult to overcome. As a result, producers sought foreign investment, firstly in the form of distribution deals and then of entirely financing feature films.[122]

The 1980s

Susan Dermody and Elisabeth Jacka point out that the early 1980s represent the third period of the development of the Australian film industry. The introduction of the tax incentives at the beginning of the 1980s provoked the production of more action movies and a progressive reduction of 'period films', determining the idea of the loss of a unified project for Australian cinema in favour of a multitude of different cinematic projects.[123]

During the course of the 1980s, the private sector gradually replaced the governmental institutions in deciding which productions to finance, provoking a change in the type of film genres produced. Ocker genre films, based on a very stereotypical figure of the Australian male, and period films did not cease to be made but gradually yielded to action films that had high budgets, and their massive publicity campaigns significantly increased their box office results. Interestingly, Tom O'Regan affirms that the attitude of the producers had actually changed: instead of addressing new audiences, producers favoured the requests of the existing one.[124] If the policies of the AFC during the 1970s led to an international critical recognition of Australian cinema, the production of more commercial films took Australian cinema to the masses: films such as *Crocodile Dundee I* and *II* and the *Mad Max* trilogy enjoyed a great home and international success.

Tom O'Regan singles out *Mad Max* (George Miller, 1979), *My First Wife* (Paul Cox, 1984) and *Crocodile Dundee* (Peter Faiman, 1986), as the films which exemplify the trends and characteristics of Australian cinema during the 1980s. Although made before the tax incentives regime, *Mad Max* is significant because it enjoyed an international success without the showcase of an international festival such as Cannes. O'Regan, echoing Dermody and Jacka, points out that, with projects like *Mad Max*, the Australian film industry was shifting away from the values that had defined it in the previous decade, and had embraced the laws of the market as dictated by Hollywood, becoming one of the international providers of the global market.[125] According to O'Regan, *Mad Max* represents the Australian character to a lesser extent than ocker and the 'quality films' of the previous decade, and represents a return to genre cinema.

My First Wife, sustains O'Regan, represents the return to 'art film', and recalls European films for its urban setting. The film opposes the 'sensibility of the European emigrant to the philistinism of the modern Australia'.[126] Paul Cox's film represents the mid-life crisis of a married man and enjoyed success on the art circuits both at home and overseas. The third film singled out by O'Regan is *Crocodile Dundee*, a film that attempts to address simultaneously the American and the Australian public, being at the same time 'pure entertainment' but also representing themes close to Australian public, such as the rights of Aboriginals and the exploitation of uranium mines.

Interestingly, Jonathan Rayner also singles out Peter Faiman's film as one of the emblematic films of the 1980s, albeit for different reasons. According to Rayner, *Crocodile Dundee* and its sequel 'foreground the American influence on attempts to commercialize the output of the Australian cinema'.[127] Like *The Man from Snowy River* (1982), directed by the 'other' George Miller, *Crocodile Dundee* has its basis in the western, with the 'additional narrative element of Paul Hogan's outback hero being transported to New York'.[128] The similarities with Hollywood action films are enhanced in *Crocodile Dundee*'s sequel that simply 'increases the proportion of stunts and chases'.[129]

The Australian production context of the 1980s has affinities with the Hollywood production context of the same period that go beyond the American influence over the marketing strategies. Indeed, the introduction of new technologies such as home video had a similar effect in America and Australia, changing the viewing habits of the public. In Australia, it virtually eliminated cinema re-runs in favour of a more comfortable vision at home. In turn, this provoked the progressive disappearance of suburban drive-in cinemas, which gave way to bigger screens hosted in commercial malls.

The similarities between the Hollywood and Australian production context of the 1980s do not end here. In fact, although Hollywood was experiencing a progressive convergence between cinema and television, as the following chapter shows, the same happened in Australia. Tax incentives, in fact, favoured the production of television mini-series, some of which directed by filmmakers such as Noyce and Miller.[130] In the 1980s, television production was indeed becoming more prominent within the Australian context, cinema producers as well as directors manifested their interest in working in television, and their products were successful with both home and overseas audiences. In the aforementioned 1990s interview, producers Hal and James McElroy comment on their 'surprising move'[131] to television at the beginning of the 1980s, recalling the success of the series that they produced on American networks. Jim McElroy says:

> The Last Frontier was the first Australian-produced mini-series on American network television, and it won the year for network. That is a very considerable success. As well, *Return to Eden* was hugely successful in syndication in America and all around the globe. We then did a series on it, again successfully.[132]

A second public broadcaster in Australia, SBS-TV, was launched at the end of the 1980s, and it contributed to the distribution of foreign films in original language, giving producers and directors the chance to become familiar with non-English language cinemas. Alongside foreign films, SBS broadcast news, sport and Australian-independent features. According to O'Regan, the transformations occurred within the film and television industry in the 1980s affected the close relationship that Australian critics and intellectuals had with cinema. Critics felt disengaged by the transformation of cinema from a cultural product to a commercial industry.[133]

The phenomenon, that, in my opinion, more than any other characterized the cinematic production context of the 1980s and changed the perception of Australian cinema, rendering more problematic its definition, is the significant move of Australian filmmakers to Hollywood.

Australian filmmakers in Hollywood

As mentioned in the previous chapter, a significant number of Australian filmmakers arrived in Hollywood during the 1980s, some making a permanent move, others alternating American production with Australian films. I am aware that filmmakers' migrations to America during the decade does not only concern the Australian contingent, and that filmmakers of other nationalities moved to America in the 1980s; however, considering that in this book I have chose an Australian filmmaker as the case study of this phenomenon, in this final section of the chapter I principally concentrate my attention on the early American productions of the Australian directors and cinematographers.

The first director of the generation of the revival to reach Hollywood in the 1980s was Fred Schepisi. Arriving at feature filmmaking through television, in Australia Schepisi directed the semi-autobiographical *The Devil's Playground* (1976) and the controversial film *The Chant of Jimmie Blacksmith* (1978), a crude portrayal of the relationship between the aboriginal and the white population. The western *Barbarosa* (1982), his first American picture, was well reviewed by *The New York Times*' film critic Janet Maslin. Interestingly, the author affirms that Schepisi's 'foreignness… works to his great advantage', because the director has turned 'Texas into an exotic wilderness and used it to give the film's outlaw story its strangeness and beauty'.[134] Fred Schepisi continues to work in Hollywood, where he has directed successful films such as *The Russia House* (1990), starring Sean Connery.

Bruce Beresford became internationally known after the success of *Breaker Morant* (1980) and was sent several scripts from Los Angeles. While he was directing *Puberty Blues* (1981) he read Horton Foote's script *Tender Mercies* (1983). It is worthwhile to briefly examine the background history of the film, because it provides an insight into the first Hollywood experience of a different Australian director beside the main case study analysed in this book. *Tender Mercies* had been turned down by every American director to whom it was proposed, and Horton Foote, co-producer with leading star Robert Duvall, was advised to hire Bruce Beresford. The director was surprised that the producers asked an Australian to direct the film, because in his view there were a 'number of American directors who could do it fabulously well'.[135] Beresford was attracted by the script because of the very unconventional way in which it treated an American story, and he was aware the film would be difficult to make because it was 'very uncommercial'.[136] Nonetheless he accepted the direction and asked Russell Boyd to be his cinematographer.

During the production, Robert Duvall and Beresford had several disagreements and discussions about the approach to the film, and according to co-star Tessa Harper's account, in one occasion Beresford walked off the set, challenging Duvall to direct the film himself.[137] It is interesting to have Robert Duvall's views on the issue of an Australian directing an American film and on his relationship with the director. Duvall points out that it is better to have a 'talented guy from Sydney, Australia… than an untalented guy from Dallas, Texas', but acknowledges that he and Beresford did not have a very positive relationship. Duvall adds 'maybe these guys that come here and they don't have the final cut like they had in their own countries, plus they are on an unsure ground over here, anyway, and everything become very tentative, and the final result is not as good as what they did before from whence they came'.[138] On his part, Beresford declares that he understood that the actor had aspirations to direct, but concludes that he did not take much notice of Robert Duvall's suggestions.

The executives at Universal were not happy with the final outcome and decided to distribute the film only in three screens across the whole of America.[139] Despite such a scarce visibility and despite the fact that the movie was released one year before the Oscars season (in March 1983), the film, to the surprise of the cast and crew, received five nominations, winning two Awards.[140]

In 1985, Beresford directed the historical drama *King David*, a US/UK co-production with Richard Gere. After a brief return to Australia to make *The Fringe Dwellers* (1986), in 1986 Beresford went back to the United States to direct *Crimes of the Heart*, a comedy with Diane Keaton, Jessica Lange and Sissy Spacek. Towards the end of the decade, the Australian director made other two films in Hollywood, *Her Alibi* (1989), with Tom Selleck, and the Academy Award winner, *Driving Miss Daisy* (1989),[141] with Jessica Tandy and Morgan Freeman. Commenting on his move in 1983, Beresford briefly compares his experience as a filmmaker in Australia to his first impression as director of a Hollywood film. '[Making films in the US] it really wasn't vastly different from doing an Australian film',[142] says Beresford, and adds

> In Australia they second-guess you all the time. Everyone's hovering around, all the producers and studio executives, wanting to change this or change that. If you're directing here [in US] they don't come in and tell you how to direct it. Friends of mine, other Australians who have worked here, said they had exactly the same experience... In Australia the producer were always saying, 'We can't do this and we can't do that, we've got to save money here and there'.[143]

Other than presenting a contrasting picture to Robert Duvall's aforementioned opinion of national production contexts, this statement contrasts with the Australian experiences of other filmmakers, such as Weir, who repeatedly underlines, in his interviews, the positive and creative collaboration that he had with Australian producers. Interestingly, however, Beresford comments about his first American experience suggest that the director found Hollywood welcoming, echoing in this Weir's positive description of his own first experience in Hollywood.

Peter Weir, as already mentioned, moved to Hollywood in 1985. As I have shown in the previous chapter, Weir's *The Year of Living Dangerously* (1982) was the first Australian feature to be entirely financed by a Hollywood major. Weir was supposed to direct *The Mosquito Coast* as his first Hollywood project; however, the film was put on hold by Warner when Jack Nicholson, originally cast in the leading role, pulled out of the project. Before his move, Weir had already proposed to go to Hollywood twice: the first time in

1976, when he was asked to direct the screen adaptation of Stephen King's *Salem's Lot*, and he considered the proposal but eventually declined it;[144] and the second occasion was in 1979, when he signed a development deal with Warner Brothers to adapt for the big screen Colleen McCullough's best-selling novel, *The Thornbirds*, but a divergence of opinions with scriptwriter Ivan Moffat meant that he pulled out of the project[145] (the novel was subsequently successfully adapted for television by Warner).

After *The Mosquito Coast* was put on standby, Weir, determined to make his first Hollywood feature, examined three screenplays that had received the green light, including *Called Home*[146] which was later renamed *Witness*. Weir was assigned to the direction of the film after a meeting with Paramount executives and the leading actor Harrison Ford who was already cast.[147] Weir established a good working relationship with Harrison Ford, to whom he proposed the role of Allie Fox in *The Mosquito Coast*. With the perspective of having Ford as leading actor, Warner reconsidered the project. For his first two Hollywood features, Weir asked John Seale – who had collaborated with him in Australia on several films as cameraman and second-unit cinematographer – to be the director of photography. Despite Harrison Ford's presence and despite the fact that the script had been written by writer/director Paul Schrader, *The Mosquito Coast* was a failure.

Roger Donaldson is another Australian director who moved to the United States in the mid 1980s. In 1965, Donaldson emigrated in New Zealand, where, on the wake of the Australian government's involvement in the re-launch of the film industry in Australia, he lobbied the New Zealand government to create the New Zealand Film Commission (of which he was co-founder). In New Zealand, Donaldson worked for television before directing *Sleeping Dog* (1977), which represented an international breakthrough not only for Donaldson, but also for New Zealand cinema in general, being the first New Zealand feature to be released in the United States.[148] In 1984, Donaldson directed the Anglo-American co-production, *The Bounty*, with an all-star cast including Anthony Hopkins and Mel Gibson. The following year he made the drama *Marie* (1985), starring Sissi Spacek, Jeff Daniels and Morgan Freeman. Donaldson has enjoyed good success in his Hollywood career, directing films such as *Cocktail* (1988), starring Tom Cruise and Brian Brown,[149] and *Thirteen Days* (2000), starring Kevin Costner.

Among the directors of the revival, Philip Noyce is the last to have made the move to Hollywood. In Australia, Noyce worked as producer, writer and director, and obtained his first success with *Newsfront* (1978), which won several Australian Film Institute awards, including best film and best director. For Noyce, the transition to Hollywood was more gradual than for other Australian directors, because, before settling down professionally in America, he worked briefly in West Germany, where he directed *Tausend Augen* (1987). Noyce approached Hollywood cinema by directing an American-Australian co-production, *Dead Calm* (1989), a psychological thriller starring Nicole Kidman and Sam Neill; his first Hollywood feature is the action film, *Blind Fury* (1989). During his American career, Noyce has directed successful thrillers including *Patriot Games* (1992), starring Harrison Ford, and *The Bone Collector* (1999), featuring Morgan Freeman and Angelina Jolie.

Although for the majority of Australian directors their move to Hollywood became permanent, the case of John Duigan is different and, to an extent, less successful. Born in England and having migrated to Australia, during the 1980s Duigan wrote and directed several Australian films and television series. In 1989, the director had his first American experience with *Romero* that was independently produced by Paulist Pictures. Between 1989 and 1991, Duigan worked solely in Australia, and, in the late 1990s, he directed the English productions, *The Leading Man* (1996), with Jon Bon Jovi, and *Lawn Dogs* (1997). Duigan returned to Hollywood in 1999, to direct *Molly* (co-produced by MGM) starring Aaron Eckhart.

Gillian Armstrong had a similar career path, alternating Australian features with Hollywood productions. Armstrong attended the newly founded Australian Film and Television School, where she was mentored by Fred Schepisi, and was among the first group to graduate, in 1973. In the 1980s, she worked as director almost exclusively in Australia, and, in 1984, she directed her first Hollywood feature, *Mrs Soffell* (1984). *Mrs Soffell* can be read as a reflection on the female condition within a patriarchal society, and reprises a theme explored in the Australian films directed by Armstrong. Female gender and female heroine are also at the centre of other features directed by Armstrong in the United States, such as *Little Women* (1994) and *Oscar and Lucinda* (1997).

Considering the table of the films that Australian directors made in America in the 1980s, reproduced in Appendix II, two interesting factors emerge: first, that many had Australian cinematographers, and, second, the significant presence in the cast of actors born, or working, in Australia. The Australian directors of photography who moved to Hollywood during the 1980s began their American careers working with Australian migrant directors, thus establishing a good reputation within Hollywood. Indeed, as their work began to be known and appreciated, Australian cinematographers went on working with some of the more important Hollywood directors. John Seale, between *Witness*, his first film as cinematographer, and *The Mosquito Coast* worked on other three movies, including Randa Haines' *Children of a Lesser God* (1986). Seale then worked for John Badham in *Stakeout* (1987), Michael Adept in *Gorillas in the Mist* (1988), Barry Levinson in *Rain Man* (1988), before being reunited with Weir on *Dead Poets Society* (1990). In the 1990s and early 2000s, John Seale collaborated with Anthony Minghella in *The English Patient* (1996) and *Cold Mountain* (2003).

Russell Boyd, who also had collaborated with Weir on several occasions,[150] was called by Bruce Beresford to work on the director's first Hollywood feature, *Tender Mercies* (1983). The following year, Beresford was asked to direct photography for Gillian Armstrong's first US film, *Mrs Soffell* (1984). After the experience in America, during the 1980s Russell Boyd alternated Australian features (including Peter Faiman's *Crocodile Dundee*, 1986 and *Crocodile Dundee II*, 1988) with Hollywood ones (Norman Jewinson, *A Soldier's Story*, 1984; Ferdinand Fairfax, *The Rescue*, 1988; and John Cornell, *Almost an Angel*, 1990).[151]

Another Australian cinematographer who established a career in Hollywood in the 1980s is Donald McAlpine. In 1980, he directed photography for Peter Collinson's *The*

Earthlink, an American-Australian co-production with William Holden. In 1982, the cinematographer worked on Paul Mazursky's *The Tempest* (1982), starring John Cassavetas and Susan Sarandon, and in 1985 he collaborated with Beresford on the Anglo-American co-production *King David*.

Ian Baker was a fresh graduate of the Australian Film and Television School when Fred Schepisi called him to collaborate on his first American feature, *Barbarosa*. Baker established a long-lasting collaboration with Schepisi, working on *Plenty* (1985), *Icemen* (1984), *Roxanne* (1987) and *The Russia House* (1990). Geoffrey Simpson is another case of an Australian director of photography who collaborated with Australian directors in Hollywood. After works on several feature films and television in Australia, such as *Till There Was You* (1990), John Seale's first attempt as director, Simpson collaborated with the Australians Peter Weir (*Green Card*, 1990), Gillian Armstrong (*Oscar and Lucinda*, 1997) and Philip Noyce (*Dead Calm*, 1989, and *The Bone Collector*, 1999) and Roger Donaldson (*Cocktail*, 1993).[152]

The presence of Australian (and New Zealanders based in Australia) filmmakers and actors in Hollywood in significant, and in the 1990s, it has been enriched with the arrival in Hollywood of several successful Australasian performers (Nicole Kidman, Russell Crowe, Cate Blanchett, Miranda Otto, Heath Ledger, Eric Bana and Hugh Jackman) and directors (Peter Jackson and Baz Lurhmann).

Conclusion

By the time of Weir's arrival in the United States during 1985, the presence of Australian filmmakers was becoming more frequent, and their expertize was employed in both Hollywood and independent productions, and the films directed by Australian directors ranged from drama to thriller, from comedy to adventure. In other words Weir did not arrive in America as a perfect stranger. On the one hand, his Australian films were already being shown in American film festivals, whereas on the other hand, the increasing presence of Australian filmmakers meant that there were the premises for a promising Hollywood career for Peter Weir.

Moreover, Weir did not arrive in a vacuum: and this chapter has shown that Australian filmmakers in Hollywood were indeed collaborating with each other, and were able to cast Australian actors and actresses. This suggests the presence of a network, a 'community', of Australasian film professionals in Hollywood. Indeed, since their arrival in the 1980s, Australian filmmakers and actors have continued to collaborate with each other (Peter Weir's *Master and Commander*, with the Australian cinematographer Russell Boyd and the Australia-based New Zealand actor, Russell Crowe, is a recent example). A thorough analysis of this phenomenon, however, goes beyond the scope of this book, and constitutes an interesting avenue for further research. Another factor that emerges from this chapter regarding the immediate passage of Weir to Hollywood is that he worked right from the beginning with high profile collaborators, and important and powerful stars, such as Harrison Ford. As is demonstrated in the following chapter, dedicated to an analysis of Weir's most significant films, the director has maintained a similar approach throughout his Hollywood career.

Notes

1. The term 'revival' was first used in the early 1980s and has since been adopted by scholars of Australian cinema. However, athough there is agreement among scholars that a revival of the Australian cinema industry has taken place, there is neither a clear definition of what the revival is nor a general agreement as to when it actually started or, indeed, ended. In 1980, David Stratton postponed the revival by five years, referring to the period from 1970 to 1979 alternatively as 'the new wave' and the revival of Australian cinema. In 1983, Graham Shirley and Brian Adams entitle 'The Revival' the section of their book dedicated to the period from 1965 to 1975. Dermody and Jacka put the period from 1970 to 1984 under the heading, 'Industry Revival', and, in 1987, Brian McFarlane talks of the 'revival of the Australian film industry in the 1970s'. See David Stratton, *The Last New Wave. The Australian Film Revival*, London: Angus & Robertson, 1980; Graham Shirley and Brian Adams, *Australian Cinema. The First Eighty Years*, Sydney: Angus & Robertson and Currency Press, 1983, 215–279; Susan Dermody and Elisabeth Jacka, *The Screening of Australia. Anatomy of a Film Industry. Volume 1*, Sydney: Currency Press, 1987; and Brian McFarlane, *Australian Cinema 1970–1985*, London: Secker & Warburg, 1987.
2. Graham Shirley and Brian Adams, *Australian Cinema.*
3. David Stratton, *The Last New Wave.*
4. Tom O'Regan, *Australian National Cinema*, London and New York: Routledge, 1996, 45.
5. Ibid., 305.
6. Ibid., 54.
7. Ibid., 61.
8. Ibid., 63.
9. See Brian McFarlane and Geoff Mayer, *New Australian Cinema. Sources and Parallels in American and British Film*, Cambridge: Cambridge University Press, 1992.
10. Jonathan Rayner, *Contemporary Australian Cinema. An Introduction*, Manchester and New York: Manchester University Press, 2000.
11. Andrew Higson, *Waving the Flag: Constructing a National Cinema in Britain*, Oxford: Clarendon, 1995, 5, cited in Jonathan Rayner, *Contemporary Australian Cinema. An Introduction*, Manchester: Manchester University Press, 2000, 3.
12. Ibid., 2.
13. Natalie Brillion, 'Mexicans with Parkas and Mobile Phones: Transnational Cinema at Hollywood's Edge', *Screening the Past*, March 13, 2006, http://www.latrobe.edu.au/screeningthepast/19/mexicans-parkas-mobiles.html (last accessed 3 April, 2008). The following quotes all refer to this article.
14. Brillion refers to 'the populist white Anglo-Celtic dominant conservative discourse where myths such as egalitarianism, anti-authoritarianism... and mateship; and icons such as the Anzac, digger pioneer, bushman, larrikin... are articulated'. Brillion, 'Mexicans with Parkas

and Mobile Phones', 206.

15. Brillion points out that the marketing and the perception of the film varied greatly depending on the context of reception. In Australia, Fox accentuated the brand 'Australian' (emphasizing the involvement of Baz Lurhmann, Nicole Kidman and the Sydney studios) and its participation in the production of great Australian films, and marketed the film as Australian in Europe and at film festivals. In America, on the contrary, given the association of the film with runaway Hollywood productions, its Australianess was downplayed and the idea of an 'all American' film was used to market *Moulin Rouge*.
16. See Tom O'Regan, 'The Politics of Representation: An Analysis of the Australian Film Revival', PhD thesis, Griffith University, 1985, http://wwwmcc.murdoch.edu.au/ReadingRoom/film/PolRep/ch3.html (accessed 2 July, 2007).
17. Susan Dermody and Elisabeth Jacka, *The Screening of Australia. Volume 1*, 17.
18. See Brian McFarlane, *Australian Cinema 1970–1985*, 20–21.
19. Ibid., 21.
20. Ibid.
21. See Graham Shirley and Brian Adams, *Australian Cinema*, 242.
22 See Brian McFarlane, *Australian Cinema*, 21, http://www.sensesofcinema.com/contents/02/22/chapman.html (accessed 8 October, 2005). *Sense of Cinema* is an online journal supported by the Australian Film Commission, Film Victoria and the University of Melbourne.
23. Tom O'Regan, 'Profilo storico e nuove tendenze del Cinema Australiano' (Italian translation by Luigi Giacone), in Gian Piero Brunetta (ed.), *Storia del cinema mondiale*, vol. IV, Torino: Einaudi, 2001, 1037–1098, at 1045.
24. Graham Shirley and Brian Adams, *Australian Cinema*, 247.
25. See Tariff Board Report, in Graham Shirley and Brian Adams, *Australian Cinema*, 247.
26. The Royal Commission Report had the aim to 'inquire into and report upon the moving-picture industry in Australia' up to 1927, but its recommendations, including the introduction of a quota system for Australian films, were not fully followed. Ibid., 76.
27. Ibid.
28. Graham Shirley and Brian Adams, *Australian Cinema*, 249.
29. Ibid., 251.
30. Ibid.
31. Tariff Board Report, 36, quoted in Graham Shirley and Brian Adams, *Australian Cinema*, 269.
32. Susan Dermody and Elisabeth Jacka, *The Screening of Australia. Volume 1*, 168.
33. James McElroy, personal communication, 30 November, 2010.
34. *Report of the Interim Board of the Australian Film Commission* (1975) in Shirley and Adams 1983: 270.
35. James McElroy, personal communication, 30 November, 2010.
36. See Graham Shirley and Brian Adams, *Australian Cinema*, 271.
37. See Susan Dermody and Elisabeth Jacka, *The Screening of Australia. Volume 1*, 168.
38. In fact, James McElroy clarifies that the SAFC was not producer of *Picnic*. The film producers were James and Hal McElroy with Patricial Lovell as Executive producer. James McElroy, personal communication, 30 November, 2010.
39. Ibid., 180.
40. James McElroy, personal communication, 30 November, 2010.

41. The film was actually financed before the government announced the tax changes; however, film budgets had begun to increase before the taxation system was in place (the average budget had gone from $600,000 in 1987 to $2 million in 1982).The film cost $2.6 million. See Susan Dermody and Elisabeth Jacka, *The Screening of Australia. Volume 1*, 182.
42. Graham Shirley and Brian Adams, *Australian Cinema*, 253.
43. See *Sydney Morning Herald*, 2 March, 1971, cited ibid.
44. An Australian art film has, according to the authors, a 'frequent first-person point of view, the interiorisation of dramatic conflict, the stress on characterisation rather than plot' and draws on 'high literature tradition rather than popular fiction'. Susan Dermody and Elisabeth Jacka, *The Screening of Australia. Volume 1*, 31.
45. Ibid.
46. Ibid.
47. Ibid.,197.
48. See Susan Dermody and Elisabeth Jacka, *The Screening of Australia. Volume 1*, 197–198.
49. Ibid.
50. Among the films partially financed by the EFTE are Peter Weir's *Homesdale* (1972), Bruce Petty's *Australian History* (1971), Phil Noyce's *Good Afternoon* (1972), Gillian Armstrong exhibiting her first short film *The Roof Needs Mowing* (1971). See http://www.sensesofcinema.com/contents/02/22/chapman.html (accessed 8 October, 2005).
51. 'An Overview of Government Inquiries into the Film and Television Industry', Policy Unit Executive Branch, Australian Film Commission, May 1985, i.
52. The overview does not enter in the detail of what these areas are. 'Towards a more effective Commission: The AFC in the 1980s. October 1979', in *An Overview of An Overview of Government Inquiries into the Film and Television Industry 1971–1985*, 21.
53. Ibid.
54. Ibid.
55. Ibid., 22.
56. 'ABC/AFC Working Party on ABC Purchasing Policy', in *An Overview of Government Inquiries*, 53.
57. 'ABC/AFC Working Party on ABC Purchasing Policy', 54–55.
58. Ibid., 55.
59. Ibid.
60. Ibid., 56.
61. In 1976, Columbia partly financed David Waddington's *Barney*, in 1977 United Artists granted Hal and James McElroy, producers of Peter Weir's *The Last Wave*, the 'the largest sum *ever offered* to an Australian producer *in advance* for the distribution rights' (Scott Murray, 'Hal and James McElroy. Producers', *Cinema Papers*, no. 14, October 1977, 149) and in 1982 Weir's *The Year of Living Dangerously* was the first film entirely financed by a Hollywood studio, MGM.
62. Actors' Equity is a film union that was very influential during the period of the revival and was against the employment of international actors in Australian films, to safeguard the rights of local actors and actresses. See Susan Dermody and Elisabeth Jacka, *The Screening of Australia. Volume 1*, 205–206.
63. 'Cultural Activities Review. Australian Film Commission, August 1984', *An Overview of Government Inquiries*, 68.
64. For administrative reasons, this division did not take place.

65. 'Cultural Activities Review', 68.
66. Ibid., 72.
67. Ibid.
68. Ibid.
69. Peat Marwick Mitchell Services were commissioned for the inquiry of the AFC's activities, the ABC/AFC Working Party reviewed the acquisition policy of the ABC, and the Policy Unit of the Executive Branch of the AFC was responsible for the 'Cultural Activities' review.
70. Below referred to simply as Interim Report.
71. Interim Report, 4.
72. Ibid., 2
73. Ibid., 4.
74. Ibid., 2.
75. Ibid., 3.
76. The questionnaire was submitted to 293 producers; to 'investors contemplating entry' into film industry investments, 25 casting agencies (10 responding), and companies involving 'film processing, editing and mixing services'. See Interim Report, 2–3.
77. See Interim Report, 6.
78. Interim Report, 6.
79. Interestingly the only film, in the period 1980–81, that commenced principal photography prior to the announcement of the tax incentive scheme was Peter Weir's *Gallipoli* (Interim Report, Appendix 3). The film was financed on the basis of the previous legislation. Indeed, *Gallipoli* had, at the beginning, financial problems, because of the estimated budget of $3 million. Subsequently, the newly formed production company of Rupert Murdoch and Robert Stigwood, which was in search of a 'flagship movie to launch their film partnership', invested in the project so that it could go ahead. Thus, *Gallipoli* was funded under the old system, but with the substantial aide of private investment. See Dale Pollock, 'Weir Escalates Aussie Film Invasion', in *Los Angeles Times*, 23 August, 1983, 31.
80. Of 293 producers to whom the survey was sent, 38 per cent responded.
81. Interim Report, 9.
82. Ibid.
83. Ibid., 9.
84. Ibid.
85. Interim Report, 10.
86. Ibid.
87. Ibid.
88. Cover letter of the Interim Report, by Danny Collins and Pom Oliver, addressed to the President of the Film and Television Production Association of Australia and to the General Manager of the Australian Film Commission, 15 January, 1982.
89. Susan Dermody and Elisabeth Jacka, *The Screening of Australia. Volume 1*, 215.
90. Ibid.
91. Ibid.
92. Scott Murray, 'Informal discussion with Jim and Hal McElroy and Peter Weir', *Cinema Papers*, n. 1, January 1974, 20–21.
93. The McElroys underline the importance of keeping the cost of movies low (less than $250,000) and say that for every four dollars spent at the box office, the producers get one dollar back.

94. Scott Murray and Antony I. Ginnane, 'Producing Picnic. Pat Lovell', *Cinema Papers*, no. 8, March–April 1977, 298–301, at 377.
95. Ibid., 299.
96. The involvement of Lovell in *Picnic at Hanging Rock*, indeed, was broader than finding the investors for the film. Lovell had the idea of adapting Joan Lindsay's novel *Picnic at Hanging Rock*, she was the first to option the book and proposed to Peter Weir the direction of the film. At a later stage, she sought the collaboration of more experienced producers, the McElroy brothers.
97. Anon, 'Jim McElroy', in *Films and Filming*, vol. 23, no. 6, March 1977, 36.
98. Anon, 'Jim McElroy', 36.
99. They asked the AFC to guarantee an overdraft to cover the payment from United Artists. The latter offered the McElroys 'the largest sum ever offered to an Australian producer in advance for the distribution rights'. One of the novelties introduced in the production of *The Last Wave* was that the film was 'partly bank financed' by the Commonwealth Bank of Australia (which required the guarantee from the AFC). See Scott Murray, 'Hal and James McElroy. Producers', 149.
100. The Independent Feature Film Producers Association (IFFPA).
101. Ibid.
102. Ibid., 183.
103. Ibid., 150.
104. Stephen Klain, 'McElroy's Pleasure: Australians Recognize Value of the "Producer"', *Variety*, 10 January, 1979, 4.
105. Ibid.
106. Ibid., 64.
107. Wardrope also denies that the AFC ever gave a six-month option on *Picnic*. See Anon, 'Aussie Film Commission Defends "Picnic" Handling Attitude Towards Prods', *Variety*, 22 January 1979 (page not available).
108. Ibid.
109. James McElroy, personal communication, 30 November, 2010.
110. Scott Murray, 'Hal and Jim McElroy', *Cinema Papers*, n. 79, May 1990, 14–17, 66–70, at 14.
111. Ibid.
112. Ibid.
113. Ibid.
114. Ibid., 15.
115. Ibid.
116. Scott Murray, 'Hal and Jim McElroy', 16.
117. International Federation of Film Producers Associations, later renamed SPAA (Screen Producers Association of Australia).
118. Scott Murray, 'Hal and Jim McElroy', 16.
119. Ibid., 16–17.
120. Scott Murray, 'Hal and Jim McElroy', 68.
121. Gary Crowdus and Gupta Udayan, 'An Aussie in Hollywood: An Interview with Bruce Beresford', *Cinéaste*, vol. 12, no. 4, 25.
122. Peter Weir's *The Year of Living Dangerously* was the first 'Australian' film entirely produced by a US major, Metro Goldwin Mayer.

123. See Tom O'Regan, 'Profilo Storico e nuove tendenze del cinema australiano', 1072.
124. See ibid., 1071.
125. See ibid., 1074.
126. Ibid., 1076 (translation mine).
127. Jonathan Rayner, *Contemporary Australian Cinema*, 19.
128. Ibid.
129. Ibid.
130. Such as *The Dismissal* (1983), *Cowra Breakout* (1984) and *The Last Bastion* (1984).
131. Scott Murray, 'Hal and Jim McElroy', *Cinema Papers*, no. 79, May 1990, 13.
132. Ibid., 70.
133. See Tom O'Regan, 'Profilo Storico e nuove tendenze del cinema australiano', 1073.
134. Janet Maslin, '*Barbarosa*, Australian-directed Western', *The New York Times*, July 25, 1982, http://movies.nytimes.com/movie/review?Res=9B04E7D71038F936A15754C0A964948260 (accessed 22 September, 2007).
135. Bruce Beresford in Anchor Bay Entertainment, 'Miracles and Mercies', *Tender Mercies* DVD Interviews, 2002.
136. Gary Crowdus and Gupta Udayan, 'An Aussie in Hollywood', 23.
137. See Tessa Harper in Anchor Bay Entertainment, 'Miracles and Mercies', *Tender Mercies* DVD Interviews, 2002.
138. See Robert Duvall, ibid.
139. See Horton Foote, ibid.
140. *Tender Mercies* was nominated for best director, best picture, best song, and won the awards for best actor and best original screenplay. See http://www.imdb.com/title/tt0086423/awards (last accessed 28 June, 2008).
141. The film won the awards for best picture, best actress, best makeup, and best non-original screenplay.
142. Gary Crowdus and Gupta Udayan, 'An Aussie in Hollywood', 23.
143. Ibid.
144. Personal communication, 12 March, 2006.
145. See Stephen Farber, 'Natural Dangers. A Conversation with Peter Weir', *New West*, 11 November, 1979, 100. See also my interview with Peter Weir, 12 March, 2006.
146. See Earl Wallace and Pamela Wallace, *Called Home*, at the Margaret Herrick Library, 23 March, 1983; see also the cover letter to the script presented by Philip Gersh to Jeff Katzenberg, Paramount internal communication, 5 August, 1983, at the Margaret Herrick Library.
147. Personal communication, 12 March, 2006.
148. The film was positively reviewed on *The New York Times*. See Janet Maslin, 'Sleeping Dogs', *The New York Times*, 28 February, 1982, http://movies.nytimes.com/movie/45162/Sleeping-Dogs/overview (accessed 24 September, 2007).
149. *Cocktail* was the eighth top grossing film of 1988.
150. Boyd directed the photography of Weir's *Picnic at Hanging Rock*, *The Last Wave*, *Gallipoli* and *The Year of Living Dangerously*.
151. Since 1992, when he worked on Ron Shelton's *White Men Can't Jump*, Boyd has been permanently working in the United States.
152. Australians are not the only non-American cinematographers to have gone to Hollywood in the 1980s. I can also mention, for instance, the West German Michael Ballhaus, who directed

the photography of John Sayles' *Baby it's You* (1983) and James Foley's *Reckless* (1984). Working in several France/Germany co-productions, Ballhaus moved permanently to the United States in 1986, when he directed the photography of Prince's musical, *Under the Cherry Moon*.

Chapter 4

Four Key Steps from Australia to Hollywood

Introduction

The previous chapter has been dedicated to an analysis of the Australian production contexts at the time of Weir's professional growth and move to America. In this chapter, I analyze how the Australian and the Hollywood production contexts affected Weir's work and filmmaking. I consider how they have informed and determined Weir's – and his collaborators' – choices during the pre-production and production stages of four key films: *Picnic at Hanging Rock* (1975) and *The Year of Living Dangerously* (1982), produced in Australia; *Witness* (1985) and *The Truman Show* (1998) made in Hollywood.

I investigate which are the main differences and similarities in Weir's filmmaking in the two production contexts, looking at the production history of these films and carrying out a textual analysis to examine how filmmakers' choices are transferred onto the screen. I have chosen to take into consideration, in my analysis of the films, the opinion of professionals directly involved in the making of the films. I have conducted interviews with Peter Weir, director of photography Russell Boyd – who has worked with Weir in both Australia and Hollywood – and Philip Steuer, production supervisor of *The Truman Show*.

The analysis of the films will be done considering not only my investigation of the Australian and Hollywood production contexts, but also the transnational context within which Peter Weir operates. I will, therefore, take into account to what extent the theories on transnational cinema, which I have highlighted in the second chapter of this book, can apply to the four films, and, ultimately, I will investigate if Weir can indeed be considered a transnational director.

Weir's career spans over 40 years in which he has made several documentaries (when he was a young filmmaker), fourteen feature films, two short films and one feature length television production. I have chosen to analyse four films that, in my opinion, are relevant in mapping the different stages of development of Weir's career. In the chapter dedicated to the Australian production context, I have mentioned that the eminent Australian film scholars Dermody and Jacka indicate *Picnic at Hanging Rock* (1975) as the film which started the Australian film revival, and one of the defining films of the AFC genre; other film critics have since agreed on this evaluation. Such unanimous critical acclaim, in my view, could not have been ignored when selecting the films to analyse in this chapter.

Picnic is, indeed, indicative of the aesthetic sensibility that was predominant at the time; its, as it were, 'visual quality' was the result of specific filmmaking choices regarding photography, casting and filming locations. *Picnic*'s aesthetic is in line with, or rather, informed the other films of the genre (such as, to give one example, Gillian Armstrong's *My Brilliant Career*, 1979) and responded to the specific demands of the Australian Film Commission (AFC) that was, as aforementioned, focused on improving, through film productions, the image of Australia abroad.

The next two films that I am analysing, *The Year of Living Dangerously* and *Witness*, effectively mark the passage of Peter Weir from the Australian to the Hollywood production context. They were made in the space of three years between 1982 and 1985, a relatively short period of time that allows a better comparison of the two contexts. Despite being the last film that Weir realized in Australia, *The Year of Living Dangerously* shares many characteristics with Hollywood films. I aim to investigate the particular position that *Year* occupies in Weir's career and ask to what extent it can be considered, as scholars do, an Australian film.

Witness is the first film made by Weir in Hollywood and this alone justifies its inclusion in this chapter. Its position in Weir's body of work, in fact, raises a series of questions related to the challenges that a different production context posed to Weir, in terms of choices and way of working. I will investigate how Weir got involved in the making of *Witness* and the importance that its success had for the director's American career.

Lastly, I have chosen *The Truman Show* (1998) as my fourth case study, because it is indicative of the status reached by Peter Weir in America, in relation to its success with the public and his position in the industry. Firstly, it is the Weir's highest grossing film to date and featured in 12th position in the table of the Year's highest domestic grossing films (topped by Spielberg's *Saving Private Ryan*), ranking above Nora Ephron's comedy *You've Got Mail* (in 14th position, with Tom Hanks and Meg Ryan), Campbell's *The Mask of Zorro* (in 19th position, with Antonio Banderas and Catherine Zeta-Jones), Columbus' *Stepmom* (in 20th place, with Julia Roberts and Susan Sarandon) all films featuring some of the most popular stars of the decade. Secondly, Weir's involvement in the project (originally to be directed by Andrew Niccol) is revealing of the established position that the director achieved within the Hollywood production context.

The road to Hollywood

In 1976, Warner Bros. wanted to adapt Stephen King's book *Salem's Lot* for the big screen and approached Stanley Kubrick to direct. At the time, however, Kubrick was working on *The Shining* and turned down the proposal. Nonetheless, Kubrick was evidently interested in the idea, because he suggested the studio to contact the young Australian director Peter Weir.[1] Kubrick had never met Weir, but had seen *Picnic at Hanging Rock* and thought him suitable as director of the film; Warner executives followed Kubrick's suggestion and contacted Weir. It is worth reproducing at length Weir's recollection of the events:

> I considered it, spent some days thinking about it, an agent approached me and said 'my God! You realize this is a very big break for you, you have only made two films' and I said 'I read the book and I just didn't respond to it', and the agent said 'just do it, it will get you started to do what you want to do next, this is a career opportunity, and if you walk away from this and go back to Australia, you will never be asked again'[2].

This extract from my interview with the director shows that Weir carefully considered the proposal. Continues Weir:

> The executives – John Calley was the head of production – were also very seductive and charming, and it was very tempting. I was welcomed into a kind of club, 'the club of that day' which was a very exciting period, as you know, mid 70s. And I was wavering, 'should I make the step, and I was not sure, and I thought I am not strong enough, I don't know enough'.[3]

Hence, Weir had been 'tempted' to go to Hollywood nearly ten years before his actual move, but many issues were to be considered. Weir was conscious that going to Hollywood could have been a turning point of his career, as his agent reminded him,[4] but at the same time could have been the point of no return in case of a negative outcome. Weir knew the risk of not being asked again in case of refusal, but thought that this risk would have been even more real in case his first film in America was a failure. These contacts between Hollywood studios and Peter Weir – ten years before to his actual move – show that Hollywood went to Weir as much as Weir went to Hollywood, and demonstrate that, when the director eventually moved to America, he was not unknown to Hollywood producers.

I argue that Weir, by not accepting Warner's offer, has given demonstration of being a very cautious and astute professional: cautious because he was aware that having up to that moment directed only two feature films he had not yet acquired the necessary skills to compete at Hollywood level; astute because he had realized that the Australian production context was the ideal place to obtain such skills. As my chapter on the Australian film industry has shown, the working conditions of 1976 were indeed very favourable for the development of a young filmmaker into a fully skilled professional.

The Australian government was eager to sustain – through grants – emerging talents such as Weir (provided that their film met given criteria) and, as Dermody and Jacka point out, the mid-1970s were precisely the moment when the Australian film industry was leaving, as it were, its childhood and was entering adulthood. Moreover, producers were getting more experienced and so were other professional filmmakers, such as directors of photography. Therefore, Weir considered his options and decided to continue his formation in a production environment that was very protective of this generation of young filmmakers.

In Australia, Weir not only enjoyed the financial backing of the Australian government, but also the support of a network of filmmakers – fellow directors such as Beresford and Noyce – who were growing together professionally and were ready to participate in each other's films and share professional advice and labour. Benefiting from such a thriving working environment were, in fact, not only directors, but also directors of photography, editors and cameramen, who enjoyed the best possible training and worked for each of the main film directors.

In 1976, Peter Weir decided to stay in Australia because he was well aware that the Australian production context would provide him with the best possible training and prepare him for his future move to Hollywood. By staying, he wanted to give himself the best possible chance of succeeding once the step towards Hollywood was taken. When he was asked to go to America the first time, Weir did not feel ready because, as he explains in my interview, he had only done two feature films:

> I didn't know what I was doing very much, I think two feature films. I was just working on intuition and a little bit of knowledge and bluffing it and not in command of the craft, not experienced enough to deal with these very seductive people; they were very charming, they [would have] dinners and [invited me to] come and meet stars.[5]

This passage suggests that Weir was able to look at his career from a wider perspective and could figure himself in the Hollywood environment, where he would have to deal with big names and canny executive producers. The two features that he mentions are *The Cars that Ate Paris* (1974) and *Picnic at Hanging Rock* (1975). If it is true, that after directing *Picnic*, Weir still felt that he did not quite have the necessary skills to make his move to America; it is also true, as the following analysis shows, that, with *Picnic*, Weir not only established himself as one of the main directors of the revival, but also reached international recognition.

The first step of Weir as transnational filmmaker: *Picnic at Hanging Rock* (1975)

Picnic at Hanging Rock is the defining film of Weir's Australian period for a variety of reasons: it is the film that consecrated him as one of the key directors of the Australian revival that made him internationally famous and attracted the interest of international film critics towards Australian cinema in general and himself in particular; it is also the first project that was financed by the AFC, which inherited the movie from the Australian Film Development Corporation (AFDC). As I have discussed in the chapter on Australian cinema, the AFC sought to revitalize the image of Australian culture and character that had been damaged by the films of the ocker genre. As a consequence, the commission selected for funding films that had given characteristics, including a polished aesthetic quality and tended to favoured adaptation of classic Australian novels.

AFC films are sophisticated costume dramas that, as Dermody and Jacka point out, share a common visual quality: 'The cinematography is dedicated to the glories of the Australian light, landform and vegetation, often with clear traces of a romantic... school, Australian post-impressionism. The approach of the camera is functional rather than expressive. [The films have] lyrical pans across picturesque landscape or beautifully dressed interiors'.[6]

The film opens with a series of images that recall landscape paintings, impression enhanced by the stillness of the images and by the misty clouds that surround the titular Hanging Rock (Image 1). This still can be compared with Louis Buvelot's *Between Tallarook and Yea*, painted in 1880 (Image 2). In this painting, the mountain skyline

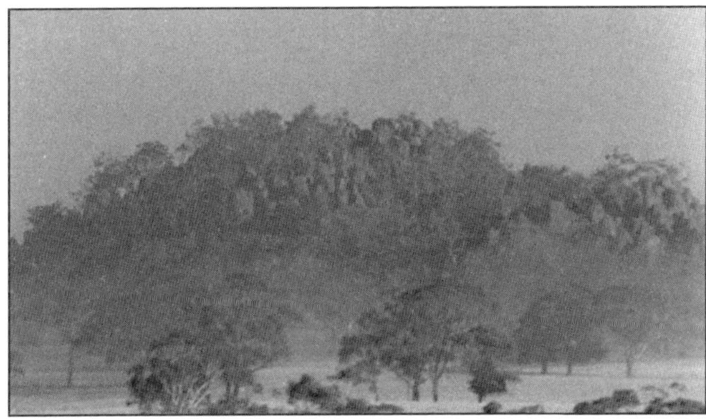

Image 1. *Picnic at Hanging Rock* (1975)
© James McElroy

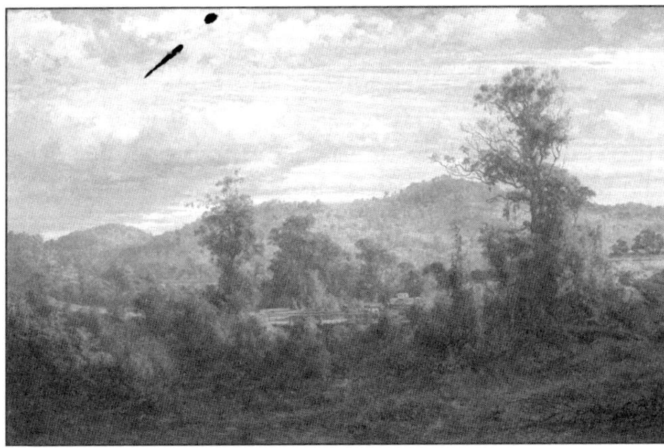

Image2. Louis Bouvelot. Born Switzerland 1814, arrived Australia 1865, died 1888. *Between Tallarook and Yea* 1880. Oil on canvas 106.7 x 167.7 cm. National Gallery of Victoria, Melbourne. Gilt of Stanford, 1902

constitutes the guideline for the eye of the viewers. As in the movie's still frame, the vanishing point of the picture is the slightly off-centred highest peak of the mountains. According to Tim Bonyhady, Buvelot's paintwork is relatively broad and 'the main features of the landscape – sunlit gum trees, background hills and rough pastures with cattle at water in a shadowed foreground – are common place'[7]. Some of these elements are clearly recognizable in *Picnic's* still frame (images 1 and 2).

The AFC demanded a certain 'visual quality' from the films that it decided to finance. However, the Commission did not actually give a definition or an indication of what was meant by 'visual quality'. Herein, I do not aim to attempt to give such definition, but I examine the ways in which the filmmakers responded to such requirements. *Picnic at Hanging Rock* was the first of such films. It is somehow a paradox that Weir's iconic Australian film was not an original idea of the director, but of new film producer Patricia Lovell. In 1971, Lovell read Joan Lindsay's novel *Picnic at Hanging Rock* and thought that it would make a good film.[8] However, a few years passed before it was possible to transfer the book onto the big screen. At the time, Lovell was a journalist for ABC, was interested in cinema and had been encouraged to go into film production.[9] Between 1971 and 1973, Lovell saw Peter Weir's short film *Homesdale* (1971) and thought that he would be the right director for *Picnic*.

Lovell acquired the book's rights, commissioned a script to David Williamson and contacted Weir to propose the direction to him.[10] According to David Stratton, Weir (demonstrating awareness of the issues concerning film production as well as those regarding the creative process) was doubtful that Lovell had the necessary experience of raising enough funding to produce the film. Therefore, he suggested Lovell bring into the project the McElroy brothers, more experienced producers with whom he was working on *The Cars that Ate Paris*.[11]

Patricia Lovell's search for funding was far from easy. At the first approach, the AFDC turned down Lovell's request for financial backing. In the second occasion, the AFDC considered the proposed budget of AUD 442,000 too expensive[12] and made a counter proposal of AUD 380,000.[13] In the meantime, the project suffered another blow. David Williamson, one of Australia's leading scriptwriters, dropped out because of other commitments and suggested the producers take on board Cliff Green. Finally, in September 1973, Patricia Lovell received AUD 1500 from the AFDC to pay for the first draft of the screenplay. Despite this good omen, the gestation of the film continued to be problematic. In January 1974, the McElroys, unhappy with the script and frustrated by the lack of substantial progress, withdrew from *Picnic*.[14]

Weir, in the meantime, had completed, with Peter Green, a first draft of the script, and was profoundly unhappy about the situation. He understood that without the experience of the McElroys the future of the film was in jeopardy. Eventually, the director managed to persuade Patricia Lovell to recall Jim and Hal McElroy into the project.[15] Even with the McElroys back on board, the problem of finding the financial backing of the film remained unresolved. Lovell and the McElroys undertook further negotiations with the

AFC (which had in the meantime replaced the AFDC), which agreed to back one-third of the film on condition of having some private investment. The producers then approached British Empire Film, which, at first reluctant, finally agreed to back another third of the film: at this point, only one-third of the budget remained to be covered.[16]

The McElroys and Lovell decided to turn their attention to a regional film body, the South Australian Film Corporation,[17] a choice that would have an impact on some creative decisions during the pre-production and production of the film. In order to grant their money, in fact, the South Australian Film Corporation (SAFC) imposed on the filmmakers certain conditions. First, the majority of the locations and facilities had to be in southern Australia; second, the actors interpreting minor characters had to be cast from within Southern Australia;[18] third, the SAFC asked to have a degree of creative control on the film.

In order to ensure the latter condition, the SAFC's John Graves was appointed as executive producer, with – crucially – a 'watching vote'. This meant that the SAFC was involved not only financially, but also had a say in the creative decisions. In other words, John Graves would be constantly present on the set and his suggestions would have to be taken into consideration. To avoid having three producers, Lovell took the credit of executive producer, and in January 1975, '*Picnic* Production' was renamed 'Sugarfoot Company'.[19]

Once the film funding was secured, the next task facing the producers and the director was casting. For the role of Mrs Appleyard, the school's headmistress, Weir and the McElroys initially approached Vivien Merchant. The actress agreed to star in the film, but, at the moment of shooting, was no longer available to travel to Australia. The British Rachel Roberts was then approached to play Mrs Appleyard but she too was not initially available. Fortunately, she became available in time for the beginning of principal photography.

As I have analysed in the chapter on the Australian production context, the casting of international stars was a controversial point within the Australian film industry, because on the one hand, in order to relaunch the national cinema, it was important to have a star internationally recognizable, but, on the other hand, the actors equity stressed the importance of having Australian cast in order to protect the right of Australian actors. In the case of *Picnic at Hanging Rock*, Weir and the producers were adamant that the role of the school's headmistress, who represented the English educational authority, should be played by a British actress.[20]

Indeed, the presence of British actresses in the film (not only Rachel Roberts, but also Vivean Gray and Helen Morse), was a box office draw as far as English and also European audiences were concerned. However, the producers and the director balanced the decision of casting British stars with the casting of Australian actresses. In the meantime, Peter Weir and Patricia Lovell had been travelling across Australia auditioning several girls for the roles of school pupils,[21] and all the schoolgirls were selected from a group of Australian girls and actresses. *Picnic*'s principal photography commenced at the beginning of February 1975, and continued for six weeks. During the shooting, Patricia Lovell and the McElroy brothers were constantly on the set and took part in creative decisions.[22]

Picnic answered the AFC's requirements to the extent that Dermody and Jacka regard it as the cornerstone of what they call the AFC genre. The film was adapted from the eponymous novel by Joan Lindsay, and Peter Weir, director of photography Russell Boyd and Weir's wife Wendy Stites (responsible for the consume department)[23] translated, as it were, the AFC's demand for aesthetic quality in the decision to give *Picnic* a pictorial feeling.[24] The overall yellowish tone of the film was influenced by Australian impressionist paintings. For the look of the school girls, Peter Weir and Russell Boyd were inspired by the painting of the pre-Raphaelites. Weir, interviewed by Sue Mathews, recalls the difficulties of the casting:

> I knew how [the girls] had to look from photographs and paintings. The hard part was finding them. Between Pat Lovell and me, we saw a couple of hundred girls in various States, but by chance we found this particular face, this pre-Raphaelite, nineteenth-century look, only in South Australia[25].

Dante Gabriel Rossetti's *Portrait of Fanny Cornforth* and a close up of Miranda show, indeed, many similarities (Images 3 and 4). There is a physical resemblance between Sara and Fanny: they have the same hair colour, style and a similar fair complexion.

Cinematographer Russell Boyd, who received the British Film Academy Award for the photography of the film, explains how he rendered the look of the film: 'in order to capture a bit of the golden effect of the light that Australians [painters] were working in at the time, I used a net over the lens during the entire picture, which I dyed with a yellow dye'.[26] To capture the particular light of the *Picnic*'s sequence, adds Weir, shooting 'was done over a period of a week for one hour only, I think between twelve and one, when Russell [Boyd] found the light was at its most interesting. [R]uss's [*sic*] insistence that we shoot only at that hour to capture that look, which became a key element of the film'.[27]

There are a couple of scenes, in the film, which resemble tableaux vivant. The first is when the *Picnic* party sits on the rock to have lunch, rightly before Miranda asks permission to explore the rocks. The second is during the exploration, when Miranda and the other girls graciously lie on the ground in an almost synchronic movement. The girls' bodies against the background of the rocks resemble motionless shapes, which the camera explores in some detail, panning on the girls' bare feet, white dresses and hair spread on the rocks. The evocative soundtrack that combines pipe and classical music gives to the whole scene a dreamlike feel that is a recurrent trait of *Picnic*.

In this scene, the camera lenses have substituted Michael's voyeuristic gaze: when the party led by Miranda leaves the *Picnic*'s site, it catches the attention of Michael, a young, aristocrat Englishman who follows them in the early moments of their exploration. In Michael's (and the spectator's) eyes, Miranda stands out from the other girls. She is often

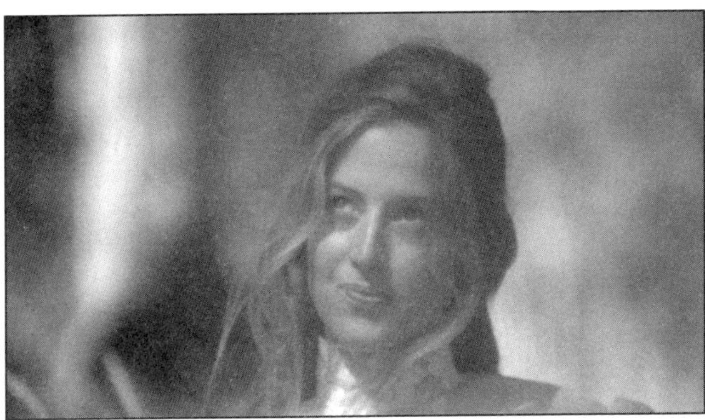

Image 3. Miranda.
Picnic at Hanging Rock (1975)
© James McElroy

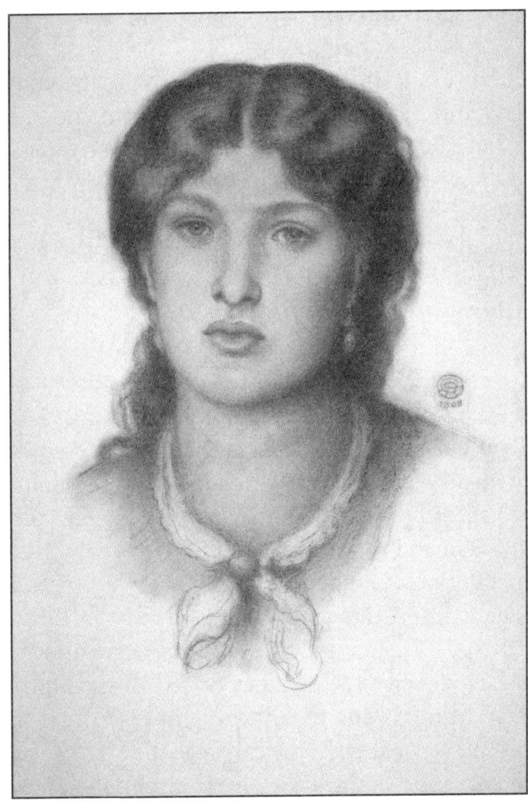

Image 4. Dante Gabriel Rossetti,
Portrait of Fanny Cornforth (1865).
© Birmingham Museum &
Art Gallery

surrounded by a glow, rendered by a very subtle backlight; her white dress reflects the sunlight brightening her face; her gracious movements are poignantly enhanced by slow motion and her young features are highlighted by short focus medium close ups: all these elements combined contribute to give her an almost hieratic look. It is no surprise that Mrs De Poitiers, the only one who seems to show some emotion at all after the girls are missing, compares Miranda to a 'Botticelli Angel'.

Michael's gaze gives way to an interpretation of the film that goes beyond its being a period drama. *Picnic*, indeed, is also a film with a soft-pornographic undertone, a dimension that has been marginally explored by critics, who dwell rather on the homosexual connotations of lesbian love in the film. The film has also been read using a feminist theoretical approach and it is arguable that there is a certain fetishism of female garments since the beginning of the films.[28] The opening montage shows the girls all lined up to lace each other's corsets, excited at the prospect of the trip. The girls carry an aura of sensuality that increases as the film progresses. They read love letters and recite love poems, carefully pressing garden flowers to preserve their beauty, an image that suggests the desire to preserve their youth. The fetishism of women's clothes is also evident when Mrs McCraw is reportedly spotted without her skirt[29] and Michael finds a piece of lace which leads to the rescue of Irma, who is missing her corset.[30]

The length of the girls' dresses hides their bodies but captures all the same the imagination of Michael and Albert (Michael's friend and stable boy): the latter compares their body shape to an hourglass and his 'crude' remarks are reprimanded by Michael. The Australian, whose feelings have been hurt, responds: 'I say these things, you think them!' Such exchange is representative of the contraposition between the austere and formal British culture and costumes and the more exuberant and less formal Australian attitude. Michael embodies the English aristocracy of the time: he is formally dressed and his manners are impeccable. Albert, on the other hand, represents the less formal and exotic (in the eyes of the British) Australian costumes: he is rough and uneducated, but has a common sense that is missing in the English boy.

This hiatus between the values of the mother country and the ones of colony is an underlining theme not only of *Picnic*, but also characterizes other films of the revival.[31] The austerity of Appleyard College, its heavy Victorian and quite decadent décor (heavy mahogany furniture, flower themed wallpapers), the formality of the daily meals, are contrasted by the exuberance of the schoolgirls, whose excited whispers and chattering resonate against the empty high-ceilinged rooms of the building.

The Victorian educational institution is embodied by Mrs Appleyard, who is always dressed in black and whose hair is impeccably adjusted. The only concession that the headmistress allows in the film is when she tells the girls that they can remove their gloves during the trip to the Rock. The hastiness with which they do so is interesting if compared with the deliberate slowness when Miranda and the others remove their stockings on the rocks, a slowness that enhances their sensuality. In the carriage, the girls are still innocent, but the exploration to the rock marks a sort of rite of passage from childhood to a promised, but never fulfilled, adulthood. Such passage is symbolized in the slow motion crossing of the creek, accompanied by the main music theme of pipe and classical music.

Bruce Smeaton's originally composed music and Gheorghe Zamfir's pipes accompany the journey to the rock, enhancing the sense of mystery, anticipation and anxiety that characterizes the central part of the film. The same theme returns when the girls explore the rocks: combined with a low angle 360° panning shot, the music conveys the overwhelming force and the magnetic attraction that the rocks have on the girls; the two have now become an indivisible entity.

The unbalanced contraposition between human will and the forces of nature is another underlining theme of the film. Nobody seems able to resist the power of the rock: when Michael goes in search of Miranda, he is at first very confident (not to get lost, he marks his passage like Orpheus in the labyrinth), but gradually he is overwhelmed by the mysterious force and has barely the strength to crawl on the ground.

Picnic is also a mystery. In order to get the spectator into the correct mood from the beginning of the film, Peter Weir decided to insert the unsettling sound of an earthquake to accompany the opening stills of the rock:

> Very early, [I] put [the sound of] an earthquake in there. I thought there must be certain primal sounds that we carry in our genes somewhere that are from the experience of the world, an earthquake for one, that is to say the ground unstable beneath you is terrifying, so I put the sound of an earthquake in here and there, but made sure it only just registered on the soundtrack so you wouldn't think 'What's that noise?' 'Oh that sounds like an earthquake' but that at least in a good theatre with a good sound system you could have an experience of some unease.[32]

Coupled with the still images of a rather misty rock, the overall effect is, indeed, quite unsettling. Such rumbling sound is repeated twice in the film, always accompanying the ominous clouds that gather around the rock, which transmit to the spectator the feeling that something unpleasant is going to happen.

Later in the film, when Michael goes in search of Miranda, the rock echoes his voice; this effect conveys the sense of mystery of the place: the rock provides more questions rather than giving the solution to the girls' disappearance. This sense of mystery is in strong contraposition with the bright sunshine and this contrast enhances the attractive power of the rock on the viewers and girls alike.

Miranda seems conscious of her fate from the beginning. The film opens with Miranda's voiceover quoting Edgar Allan Poe: 'What we see and what we seem are but a dream, a dream within a dream'[33]. Later, she tells Sarah 'you must learn to love somebody else… I will not be here for long'. In this scene, Russell Boyd captures her image reflected by two mirrors: Miranda is going out of other people's reach: she is becoming a projection, a mirage. Michael is the one who experiences the ultimate hallucination, in his dreamlike visions of Miranda.

The author of *Picnic at Hanging Rock* novel, Joan Lindsay, had reservations over the way in which her work was adapted and accused Weir of changing the tone of the book. However, such reservations were put aside after the film enjoyed great success with the public and the critics.[34] The film was promoted by the Greater Union Organisation, with the tagline 'a recollection of evil',[35] which, in my view, captures only in part the essence of the film.

Picnic was released on 8 August, 1975, and, in November of the following year, was screened at the Chicago International Film Festival, where it had mixed reviews.[36] *Picnic* was distributed in the United States by the Atlantic Releasing Corporation and was widely released in America in February 1979; as Peter Weir explains, the American audiences did not appreciate the lack of solution to the mystery,[37] and possibly, this could have been a contributing factor to the film's failure at the American box office. Conversely, it enjoyed a positive reception from the public when it was screen in European art houses. *Picnic* made a total gross of AUD 1,576,175.[38]

Despite its failure at the US box office, *Picnic at Hanging Rock* is the film that positioned Weir on the international map and can be considered the first step to Weir becoming a transnational director. Until *Picnic*, Weir was virtually unknown abroad. Or, if he was, he was known as the director of the dark horror film *The Cars that Ate People*. This was the US version of Weir's first feature film, *The Cars that Ate Paris*, which was released in the United States in September 1979, only two months before *Picnic*'s first screening in the United States and seven months after its wide US release. *The Cars that Ate People* was a heavily edited and dubbed version of the original; the action was moved to a suburban American town, the actors were dubbed with American accents and the film was marketed by the American distributor New Line as a horror film. After these interventions, *The Cars that Ate People* turned out to be a complete box office disaster.

Conversely, *Picnic* rendered overseas public and critics – including US critics – aware of the changes that the Australian film industry was undergoing at the thematic and aesthetic level.[39] Moreover, *Picnic*'s success on the European market was a demonstration that the structural changes that the Australian film industry was undertaking had an impact not only at the level of domestic success of the films, but also at the level of their international success. In other words, it is possible to affirm that *Picnic* put Weir on the world map not only in his own merit, but as part of a the larger phenomenon of the Australian revival.

As aforementioned, *Picnic*'s aesthetic quality, considered within the aesthetic values of the revival films, paved the way for the future positioning of Weir's and his fellow Australian directors within the Hollywood panorama. I argue that with *Picnic*, Weir began his journey to acquiring the status of transnational filmmaker, because it was the first film that made him known internationally and earned him critics' recognition. But what exactly is a transnational filmmaker and can the theories on transnational cinema examined in the first chapter of this book be applied to Peter Weir?

In order to answer these questions, it is important to return to the notion of transnational cinema. According to Higson, any national cinema has to look beyond its national borders and confront itself with the reality of other national cinemas. I have previously addressed the issue of the nature of Australian national cinema, highlighting both the migration of Australian filmmakers abroad and the early signals of a reversal (the return of Australian stars and filmmakers to Australia, as in the example of the recent production *Australia*).

As shown in Chapter 1, the first necessary criterion identified by scholars to define a film as transnational is its subject matter: those films that treat transnational subjects such as diaspora and displacement can be considered transnational. The second criterion is that transnational cinema should be made by a transnational filmmaker. The problem is, however, that scholars do not specify if this second criterion is as necessary as or is an *alternative* to the first. In my opinion, either of the two criteria is sufficient to have transnational cinema.

However, at this point, it becomes necessary to make a clearer distinction between *transnational cinema*, *transnational films* and *transnational filmmakers*. I argue that, in order to have transnational cinema, it is necessary to have *either* a transnational filmmaker *or* a transnational film. It is possible to have transnational cinema when a film's content is transnational even if the filmmaker is not transnational. As I have shown in the first chapter, scholars agree that a transnational film is a film which deals with issues of migration, displacement and diaspora. More complex is the matter of what a transnational filmmaker is, and, most importantly, the issue of whether Weir is a transnational filmmaker or not.

In my opinion, it is necessary two consider the issue from two points of view: the production of the films made by the given director and their content. Going back to the theme of the film analysed in this session, *Picnic at Hanging Rock*, I have shown that the schoolgirls protagonist of the film experience a double sense of alienation and indeed a form of displacement: on the one hand, they do not fit within the Victorian education establishment of Appleyard College, and, on the other hand, they struggle to come to terms to the obscure forces of nature that will ultimately claim three of them. Although *Picnic's* subject matter cannot be called transnational, it certainly shares some of the characteristics of transnational cinema.

As well as not being transnational for its content, the production history of *Picnic* shows that it is a fully Australian film having being produced, directed and shot entirely within the Australian context. However, *Picnic* is a film that has some, if not *trans*- certainly *inter*national characteristics, such as the aforementioned presence of international stars such as Rachel Roberts, Vivean Gray and Helen Morse.[40] The presence of international stars in national films was not a novelty and served to enhance the worldwide marketing possibilities of those films. Indeed, *Picnic* shares this characteristic with other national films that were released in Hollywood at the time which had either international, or internationally famous, actors and/or actresses.[41] In the rest of this chapter, I will analyse the production and aesthetic of the remaining three films that I have selected, investigating if they can be seen as transnational, beginning with *The Year of Living Dangerously*.

The Year of Living Dangerously (1982): an Australian film?

Like *Picnic*, *The Year of Living Dangerously* had several years of gestation before it was finally shot. Unlike *Picnic*, it was Peter Weir's idea to adapt C.J. Koch's eponymous book into a film. Weir optioned the book's rights in 1979 and he began work on the script with David Williamson (who was on this occasion able to stay on the project). Williamson was well known in the Australian film industry, having worked previously on films such as Tim Burstall's *Stork* (1971) and Weir's own *Gallipoli* (1982). The presence of the writer, as I show below, was to be used as a box office draw for the Australian audiences.

The Year of Living Dangerously tells the story of Guy (Mel Gibson), an Australian journalist on his first assignment abroad: to report about the political situation in Indonesia during the last year of Sukarno's regime. Guy befriends the dwarf photographer Billy (Linda Hunt), who has a network of important friends, and eventually manages to get Guy an interview with the leader of the communist party. Both Billy and Guy fancy Jill (Sigourney Weaver), a British diplomatic attaché.

Weir reports that, during a conversation on the set of Gallipoli, he proposed the role of Guy to Mel Gibson. Even though the pair had developed a good relationship, Gibson's initial response was negative, because he considered Guy's character too different from himself. Weir, however, reassured the actor: he was going to change the novel's character and make it less elegant and more aggressive, so the actor accepted the part.

Alongside Williamson's collaboration, Gibson's casting was the second crucial decision for the eventual success of the film both at home and abroad. Although born in the United States, Mel Gibson, in fact, grew up professionally in Australia, and, at the time, was known as an Australian actor; his role in George Miller's *Mad Max* (1979), had granted him a wider recognition and popularity with overseas audiences.

In December 1981, Jim McElroy, producer of the film, concluded a deal with MGM for the production and distribution of *The Year of Living Dangerously*:[42] the studio agreed a budget of $5.5 million US dollars.[43] Shortly afterwards, Freddie Fields announced that *Year* was going to be his first project as MGM's president: it was the first time that a major American studio fully financed an Australian film.[44] MGM's move had very significant consequences on the development of Weir's career, because it meant that, by the time he went to Hollywood, he was known by Hollywood studios and prepared to work within the American industry, having already worked with (and for) Hollywood executives. Considering the impact of MGM's backing of the film, it is important to give due credit to producer Jim McElroy for making the deal possible. McElroy's role is a further demonstration of the importance, for Peter Weir's career, of having had the right support from the Australian production context.

After casting Gibson and Weaver, Weir and his collaborators had to find a suitable actor to play the part of the dwarf photographer Billy. Following a series of unsuccessful auditions with male actors, Weir suggested to Linda Hunt that she should play the part. According to the director, this request was made only half-heartedly and as a sort of joke, because Weir was afraid that Hunt might be offended, and he was expecting the actress to decline. In fact, Linda Hunt was at first very sceptical and asked if the role could be rewritten for a woman. However, this would have meant the redrafting of the entire script and falling six months behind schedule. Weir was impressed by the actress' audition and by the feminine sensibility that she would put into the character. Eventually, Hunt agreed to play the part as it was in the script. Linda Hunt's audition was also attended by an MGM representative, who gave the green light to the casting.[45]

The Year of Living Dangerously is set in Indonesia in 1967, the last year of Sukarno's regime; even though the political situation at the time of filming had improved, it was still impossible, for the crew to obtain a permit to shoot on location. Producer Jim McElroy thought of Malaysia as alternative site, but after scouting some locations, he soon realized that, in the country, there was no local expertize in filmmaking. Eventually, the crew agreed to shoot in the Philippines for the economic advantages that they offered.[46]

The principal photography of the film started in March 1982 and continued for twelve weeks.[47] While shooting in the Philippines, Weir and the crew were caught amongst a demonstration of 25,000 people outside the American Embassy in Manila. Weir filmed some of the demonstration and inserted some of the footage in the film. However, the situation was extremely unstable and the crew received a threatening letter that demanded filming stop and the crew leave the country. Weir consulted with his collaborators and decided to pull out of Manila a week earlier than scheduled; filming was completed in Australia.[48] During the shooting, producer James McElroy complained about Metro Goldwyn Mayer pressure to keep the budget down. The final cost of the film, indeed, shows that MGM's concerns were well-founded: the film was $120,000 over budget, costing $6 million.[49]

At the beginning of 1983, Peter Weir and Mel Gibson toured the United States and Canada to promote *The Year of Living Dangerously*.[50] The film had a mixed reception from the American critics[51] and provoked a debate over the authenticity of its portrayal of the social and political situation in Sukarno's Indonesia.[52] Peter Weir received the Palm D'Or as Best Director at the 1983 Cannes Film Festival,[53] and, the following year, Linda Hunt won the Oscar as Best Actress in a supporting role. The film had a discrete success with the public and made more than $10 million dollars in the United States.[54]

Year is, to a certain extent, a political film, because it takes a stand against a dictatorship and denounces the living conditions of the poor people of Indonesia. However, political issues never take centre stage in the film, but remain as background for the narration of the protagonists' personal dramas. Indeed, the film is centred on the love story between Guy and Jill, and on Guy's friendship with Billy, who becomes his mentor and guide. In the film, Guy has at first to decide between professional duty and friendship, and then between love and career. *The Year of Living Dangerously* is adapted from C.J. Koch's novel of the same title and adopts an interesting perspective on the lives of western journalists in Indonesia: they appear more preoccupied with exploiting the local sex industry than with portraying objectively the difficult situation of a country torn among Sukarno's supporters, the communist party and Muslim militarists.

The story is told by alternating Billy's point of view with the view of the omniscient narrator. At the beginning, the unfolding events are narrated through Billy's internal voice over, accompanied by the ticking sound of his typewriter (which is a characteristic sound associated with Billy through the film). Billy introduces the character of Guy as if speaking directly to him: 'you are an enemy here, Hamilton', warns the photographer. Billy, in fact, is used to compiling files about the people he knows, keeping clippings and photos, and defines himself 'a master on the quiet page'. 'Just as I'm master', continues Billy's voice over, 'in the dark room, stirring my prints in the magic developing bath. I shuffle like cards the lives I deal with'. In the end, however, Billy's manipulation of other people's lives backfires against him.

In the film, the character of Billy is the one that undergoes the deepest transformation. At the beginning, the photographer idolizes Sukarno, to the point that he loves impersonating him, wearing similar attire: hat, cane and dark sunglasses. It takes two-thirds of the film for Billy to open his eyes to the real living conditions of Indonesian people. Only after the death of his adopted child, in fact, Billy begins to question Sukarno. The photographer, used to making night visits to the slums, makes a last visit in the daytime. The sunlight reveals the full extent of the poverty in Jakarta and quite literally opens Billy's eyes: he sees the miserable conditions in which people live with a new perspective.

Afterwards, Billy wanders around the streets of Jakarta and looks up at a poster of Sukarno. The low/high angle shot/reverse shot shifts the relationship between Billy and Sukarno. Billy, who once used to climb on Guy's shoulders dressed as Sukarno, therefore reaching the dictator's height does not stand any longer at the same level. Sukarno's cruel face, framed with a low angle, literally looks down on Billy, framed with a high angle. Unfortunately, is now it is too late to do anything about the situation: 'what then must we do?' Billy types obsessively at the machine. The dwarf pays the consequences of his misjudgement with his own life: he is thrown out of a skyscraper window for exposing a banner against Sukarno that the dictator does not even have time to see.

Billy's presence continues to be felt even after his death. He is present in his photographs, and in particular he is present in Guy's mind when he lies helplessly on the bed after being hit on the head by a soldier while trying to flee the country. Guy imagines Billy's voice as if carried by the creaking sound of the wind blowing through the bamboo forest that surrounds Billy's bungalow. The noise of the wind is associated with Billy's character from the beginning of the film. When Billy takes Guy to his bungalow for the first time, they walk down a narrow path. The creaking bamboo makes Guy wonder about the 'weird noise'. Billy explains: 'is the bamboo. But there is a spirit here, I hear him outside at night. He came inside one night, and spilled some bottles of developer'. Guy asks if Billy really believes 'that stuff' and Billy confirms: 'absolutely, old man, the unseen is all around us, particularly here in Java'. With this comment, the noise of the wind becomes something non-human, mystical.

When Guy and Jill go to Billy's bungalow waiting for their friend, the bamboo creaks in the same manner, but this time it is unnoticed, because for Jill it is a familiar sound, and for Guy is not 'weird' anymore, because it defines the place where Billy lives. Towards the end of the film, the creaking sound of wind blowing through the bamboo is heard once more. Billy has been killed and Guy has been seriously wounded. He lies on the bed, helpless, sweating heavily with his eyes blindfolded. A fade out marks the passage of time and the film cuts to a low angle close up on bamboo penetrated by faint rays of light.

The camera zooms almost imperceptibly on Guy's face and Billy's voice over merges with the noise of the creaking bamboo. Guy, in a delirium, calls Billy's name and imagines his voice: 'Krisna says to him, all is clouded by desire, Arjuna... as fire by smoke, as mirror by dust. Through this it blinds the soul'. With this scene, the noise of the bamboo has completed its ontological circle. Billy had initially dissociated the noise from its source, making it the sound of a spirit. After his death, the blowing wind returns to being just a natural sound (the characters do not even notice it). In this last instance, however, the noise of the bamboo is once more associated with a spirit. But not just any spirit. It becomes Billy Kwan's spirit, a spirit of a man that is no longer alive but who still projects all his charismatic force on Guy's imaginations, a spirit that is still giving moral lessons to the journalist, whose soul is metaphorically and literally – blinded.

Billy is the only character in the film who is introduced without any sort of mediation. As aforementioned, Guy is introduced by Billy's voiceover, whereas Jill is first seen in a picture on Billy's bedside chest of drawers. Sigourney Weaver's character is very feminine, in sharp contrast with the rather masculine Ripley whom she played in Ridley Scott's *Alien* (1979). Jill is a sensual girl for whom men frequently fall: a French journalist was engaged to her, Billy proposed to her and Guy falls in love with her. Peter Weir has repeated in several interviews that *The Year of Living Dangerously* is a romance; indeed, the film was marketed as such with the tagline 'a love caught in the fire of revolution'. Year's poster is also quite revealing. In the background, Gibson is passionately kissing Weaver, while in the foreground, Gibson *à la* Bogart stares at the viewer with a cigarette in his hand.[55]

Nonetheless, the romance between Guy and Jill is downplayed, and the love scenes are never explicitly shown: love is treated delicately. The couple kiss three times during the film: at the ball, on a staircase outside Guy's hotel room and during the final airport sequence. In each occasion, the characters are to one side of the frame or filmed from a distance. When Jill and Guy kiss on the staircase, they are framed to the left hand side of the frame and even after the camera zooms the frame composition remains unbalanced; in the final scene, their kiss is shown with long to medium long shots. In my interview, Weir explains the type of tension that he was trying to create:

> In *Living Dangerously* Mel Gibson and Sigourney Weaver were having trouble getting this sort of tension between them, and having trouble even kissing, it was very awkward, and each was blaming the other and a way privately to me, you know, because the screen kissing are a very special thing. So I put up *Notorious*, for them to watch, with Cary Grant and Ingrid Bergman: the way they circled each other, the way they kissed,

> and the way they looked at each other. So there were the three of us really studying something very basic, learning still.[56]

When Guy walks towards the plane in the concluding scene that has been compared with the end of *Casablanca*, oriental gamelan music is played, a last reminiscence of the world that he is living behind. Gamelan music defines the city of Jakarta. In the opening credit sequence, it accompanies a show of the quintessential Indonesian form of art: the ancient shadow play called 'Wayang Kulit'. It is worth noticing that the choice of opening the film with the Wayang Kulit did not appear in the initial draft of the screenplay, which opened directly with the arrival of Guy Hamilton at Jakarta airport. This scene, according to the second draft of the screenplay, was still to be accompanied by 'the faint menacing tempo of Indonesian gamelan music [which] drifts through the heavy night air'.[57] In the final version of the film, however, the arrival of Guy at the airport is, as aforementioned, introduced instead by Billy's voiceover.

In changing the opening of the film, two significant choices have been made by the scriptwriters Peter Weir, Alan Sharpe, David Williamson and Christopher Koch: having the Wayang as opening sequence, they set immediately the tone of the film, evoking in the viewer the mood and philosophy that pervades the entire feature. As Billy Kwan explains to Guy:

> If you want to understand Java, you have to understand the Wayang, the sacred shadow play. The puppet master was a priest. That's why they call Sukarno the great puppet master, balancing the left with the right. Their shadows are souls, and the screen is heaven. You must watch their shadows, not the puppets.[58]

Secondly, deciding to accompany Guy's introduction to the viewer with Billy's voice over rather than with music, the filmmakers establish Billy as one of the central characters, if not *the* central character of the film. Like Sukarno manoeuvres the political life of Indonesia, Billy tries to manoeuvre the lives of his friends. When Guy discovers his own file, he suspects Billy of being an agent for either the FBI or for the PKI (Partai Komunis *Indonesia*, Indonesian Communist Party), and the good relationship he has with Billy begins to crack.

Alongside the romance between Jill and Guy, the relationship between Billy and Guy constitutes, in fact, the backbone of the film and its development is significantly portrayed by camera angles and frame composition. When Billy and Guy meet for the first time, the camera angles reflect their respective points of view: a low angle shows Billy's perspective and a high angle shows Guy's. Such points of view, however, do not reflect the relationship between the two characters: Guy is on his first overseas assignment and does not have connections, whereas Billy, on the contrary, has the right contacts and knows how to twist the circumstances in his favour. The latter therefore, occupies a more prominent position between the two. As the friendship between Guy and Billy consolidates, the camera angles and the frame composition change and begin to reflect this unbalanced relationship, and often Billy occupies a higher position than Guy within a frame.

Two-thirds into the film, however, the relationship definitely cracks: Billy feels betrayed because Guy has used information he has received confidentially and Guy understands that he has been manipulated by Billy. At this point, the camera angles and frame composition return to the initial, and more natural, perspective, where Guy's point of view dominates over Billy's. It is worthwhile to compare and contrast more closely two scenes that exemplify the shifting balance in Guy/Billy's relationship, the first occurring at the beginning of the film, the latter occurring towards the end.

In the first scene, Guy is at the desk in his hotel room, with his back to the camera and Billy enters from the backdoor. Billy walks towards Guy and occupies a predominant position in the frame. Billy asks Guy if he got an interview and he answers that Sukarno does not concede interviews to western journalists unless they have contacts. The camera follows Guy as he stands up, and cuts on Guy who, now looking down on Billy (off screen) says 'what do you want me to do? Shoot myself?' Guy complains that if he does not get an interview soon, they will send him back to Sydney's newsroom. The camera follows Guy as he walks back to the desk. At this point, Billy appears in the frame on the left hand side. Guy sits down at the desk, at the right side of the frame, his back to the camera.

Billy sits on the desks, now appearing the taller of the two: 'If you could get any interview you want… excluding the one with Sukarno, who would it be?' Guy, in a position of inferiority, looks up at Billy: 'The leader of the communist party'. Billy, looking down on Guy, replies: 'I'll get it. I can get you to him tomorrow'. Guy says 'he doesn't give interviews'. Billy: 'he does when he needs to. He is a friend of mine. I've already spoken to him about you'. The camera closes up on Billy as he says: 'if you want it, it's yours'. Guy looks intently at Billy, who continues 'it should make quite a stir internationally. If you can get me to Aidit', says Guy, 'I'll give you all the film work you can handle. Exclusive'. Billy, smiling, answers 'that's great old man. That's what I've always wanted, a real partnership'.

Billy gets off the desk and the camera precedes him as he walks away: 'We'll make a great team old man. You for the words, me for the pictures'. The camera zooms in on Billy who looks back at Guy (off-screen). At this point, Guy has assumed a secondary position both in the frame and in the relationship. Billy: 'I can be your eyes'. Guy, smiling, looks puzzled, while Gamelan music starts.

An even more explicit representation of Billy's dominance is the scene when, during the PKI's demonstration, Billy asks Guy to lift him on his shoulders to film the crowd. Guy's gesture symbolizes his acknowledgement of Billy's status. The image of Billy on Guy's shoulder (Image 5) recalls Bernard of Chartres' aphorism (quoted by John of Salisbury): 'We are like dwarfs standing upon the shoulders of giants, and so able to see more and farther'.[59]

After the little slum boy whom Billy had 'adopted' dies, Billy wanders the streets of Jakarta and then confronts the journalists accusing them of exploiting the poverty of Indonesian. Billy runs away from the journalists' bar, and Guy runs after him, while

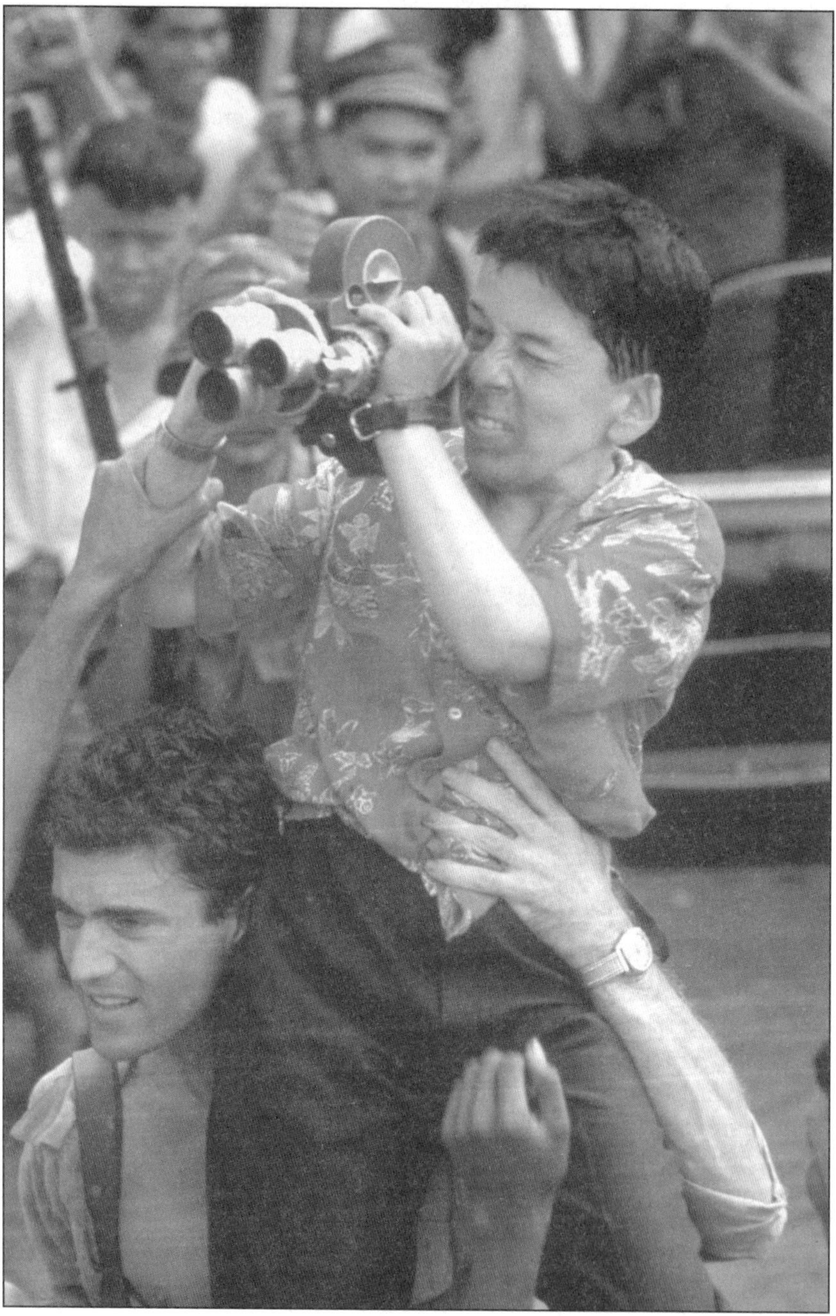

Image 5. Guy carries Billy on his shoulders. *The Year of Living Dangerously* (1982), © Warner Bros.

suspenseful music intensifies. Billy finally stops and the two characters are framed in a long shot. Guy shouts: 'What the hell is the matter with you?' Billy: 'What do you want?' Guy circles around Billy, assuming a dominant position and behaviour. In the background, Sukarno posters are covered by PKI graffiti, revealing Indonesia's political contradictions; poor people sit with their backs to the wall, with lit fires to cook food.

'You made the broadcast', accuses Billy, and the suspenseful music gets eerie, repeating the same chords. 'I didn't source that back to Jill'. 'It doesn't matter', Billy replies 'that is not the point'. As Guy circles around Billy, his head goes out of the frame (the audience cannot see Guy's face, just as Billy cannot unless he raises his head): 'Yes, it is the point', says Guy. 'When this thing breaks, it could change the political shape of South East Asia. How far are my loyalties to Jill supposed to go?' Billy replies 'I would have given up the world for her. You won't give up one story'. 'It's not just a story! dammit! It's *the* bloody story. Can't you understand this?'

On the last sentence, the camera reverses to a medium close up of Billy, now looking up at Guy 'Don't you understand? You've lost Jill'. Billy moves towards Guy and the camera cuts to a medium shot of the two, Guy on the left, Billy on the right side of the frame. 'What? What have you told her? You told her something'. Billy is still standing on the right side of the frame, as he says: 'I gave her to you and now I'm taking her back. Do you understand?' Guy looks incredulous. 'What? You gave her to me? For Christ's sake! You mad little bastard!' Sukarno's picture, looms in the background, as the fire casts shadows and lights on Guy's face (the whole scene is shot with low key lighting, with a blue tone). Guy continues: 'You think you can control people's lives just because you got 'em in your bloody files?' (see Image 6)

Billy walks toward the camera, at the far right of the frame. Guy, in the background, is now out of focus. 'I believed in you, I thought you were a man of light. That's why I gave you those stories you thought so important. I made you see things. I made you feel something about what you write. I gave you my trust. So did Jill. I *created* you!' At this point, the music fades as the camera cuts back to Billy's close up. Billy walks towards Guy, circles him, then walks away. In this scene for the first time since their initial encounter at the airport, the camera emphasizes the difference in Billy's and Guy's height. The camera angles and the frame composition indicate that Guy is finally conscious of the power that Billy had on him and takes control of his life back.

This confrontation between Billy and Guy is accompanied by oriental music. In the film, the score changes depending on the situation it is associated with: as aforementioned, Indonesian characters are more directly connected with oriental music, westerners are associated with rock music played in the journalists' bar and at the English Embassy ball. In one instance, Guy and his colleague Curtis are alone in a club and the radio plays a rock song. Curtis, who is drunk, starts dancing with a local beauty, only to be interrupted by an official who asks them to leave under the threat of a gun. This scene is an example of how sound is used to emphasize the contrast between two very different cultures and ways of thinking. While the Westerners considered rock only a form of entertainment,

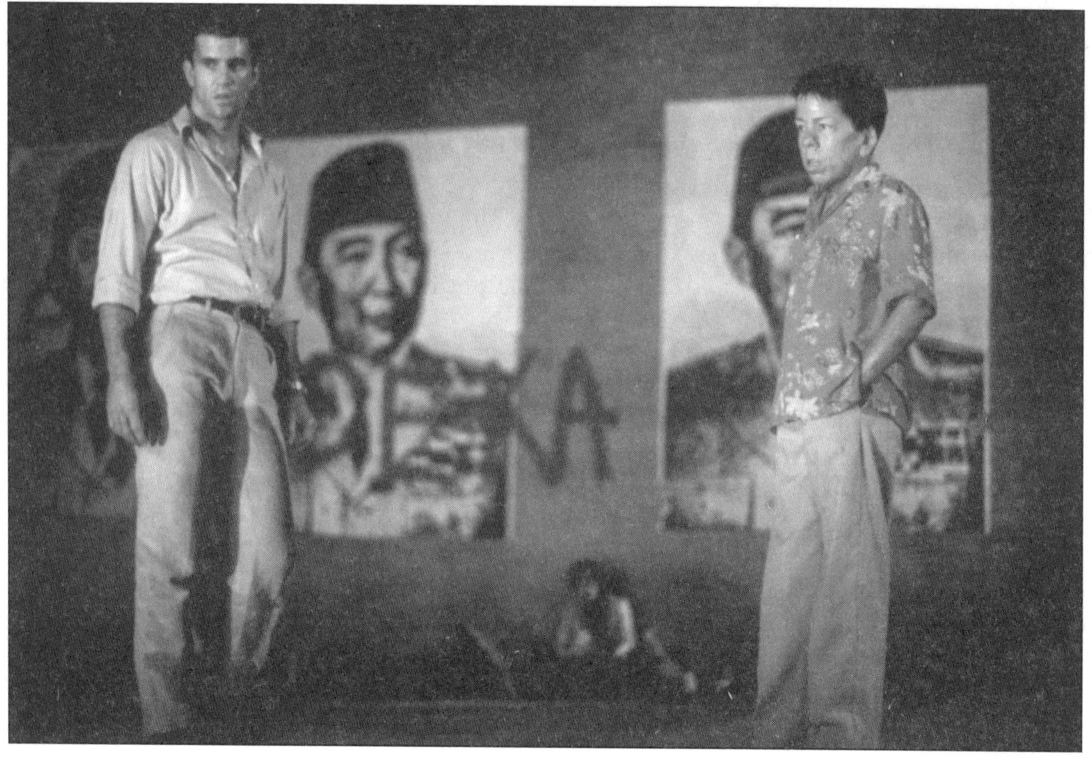

Image 6. Guy confronts Billy. *The Year of Living Dangerously* (1982), © Warner Bros.

the local authorities see it as a threat, a symbol of US imperialism. Rock music is also associated with the idea of love and attraction. It is dancing to a rock song that Jill and Guy first realize that there is more than just friendship between them.

Like the music, the colour palette and lighting of the film also change depending on the location. The colour red dominates the restaurant where the foreign journalists usually gather, lit with a very dim light that creates an ideal setting for dubious activities among the clientele. A sharp contrast marks the difference between the poorest and the richest areas of Jakarta: bright colours dominate the households of the Westerners' residences,

Sukarno's palace and the British Embassy; on the contrary, the slums have a soft-colour palette. The proximity of a stagnant canal, the darkness and the constant cries of babies reflect the squalor of the area.

The Year of Living Dangerously is a crucial film in Peter Weir's career, because it begins to mark the director's transition from Australia to Hollywood. With *Gallipoli*, Weir already had the chance of working with an American producer (Francis O' Brien); with *Year* Weir worked for a Hollywood studio and under an American employer. As aforementioned, during the 1970s Weir had a development deal with Warner Brothers, but his first American experience was postponed. The fact that Weir made *Year* for a major Hollywood studio meant that, by the time he moved to America, he was already known within the Hollywood film industry. Producers had the chance of appreciating his way of working, his ability of directing major stars and of drawing from his cast performances worthy of an Academy Award. I argue that *The Year of Living Dangerously* is the real turning point of Weir's career.

Although critics generally consider *The Year of Living Dangerously* an Australian film, this claim is questionable, because if there are valid arguments to consider it an Australian film, equally there are valid reasons to consider it a Hollywood movie. In the latter respect, *Year of Living Dangerously* set a precedent in the history of the Australian cinema industry, because it was the first film to be entirely financed by a Hollywood major studio, Metro Goldwyn Mayer. It also has two American stars, Sigourney Weaver (famous for her role in *Alien*) and Linda Hunt, who won an Oscar for her performance.

Considering the points in favour of *Year* as an Australian film, it has an Australian director, an Australian producer, an Australian cinematographer (Russell Boyd), an Australia co-writer (David Williamson), and an Australian star (Mel Gibson grew up professionally in Australia and at the time was still considered an 'Australian' actor).

Considering *Year* as a Hollywood film it is possible to see that it has some of the characteristics of 1980s Hollywood productions: it is a package film,[60] it is produced by a Hollywood major and has two major stars. Finally, when compared with Australian budgets of the time, *Year* is a big budget film. *The Year of Living Dangerously* was aimed at both the Australian and at the American market, and fitted in the Hollywood context as part of the cycle of films that Claudia Springer defines 'Third World Investigative Films'.[61] In the early 1980s, in fact, Hollywood showed a particular interest in producing films preoccupied with Third World issues, including Roger Spottiswoode's *Under Fire* (1983), Oliver Stone's *Salvador* (1986) and Roland Joffé's *The Killing Fields* (1984).[62] Critic Vincent Canby adds to this list *Missing* (Costa-Gavras 1982) and *Gandhi* (Richard Attenborough 1982).

As this book has shown, the growing financial commitment of Hollywood studios to the production of Australian films[63] was due to the introduction of tax concessions, and, according to Dermody and Jacka, was aimed at 'producing films, made in Australia, for their own [Hollywood] markets'.[64] This observation is important when related to the Hollywood production of *The Year of Living Dangerously* in view of Weir's future career, because it indicates that, according to Hollywood producers, a film directed by Weir would have a market in the United States. For these reasons, *The Year of Living Dangerously* is a key film to understand why Weir was immediately accepted, and then successful, in Hollywood.

Since As *The Year of Living Dangerously* has both characteristics of films made in Hollywood and of films made in Australia, it is poignant to argue that it is a *transnational film*. The film fits within this category not only for its production history, but also for its subject matter. Indeed, looking at Weir's production more widely, *Year* is the only film that fully answers to the characteristics of transnational cinema as described by scholars. In fact, it is the only film in which the protagonist experiences a sense of displacement across two different national contexts and not, as happens in the other films directed by Weir, within one national context.[65]

Applying Elmer and Gasher's concept on foreign location shooting,[66] which has been outlined in the first chapter of this book, *Year* can, furthermore, be considered from both an Australian and a Hollywood perspective. Firstly, the film ought to be seen as a 'foreign service production', because it is a Hollywood production that brought Hollywood money to the local industry (by employing local crew and partly a local cast); on the other hand, looking at the film from a Hollywood perspective, *The Year of Living Dangerously* ought to be considered a 'Hollywood runaway production', in which a Hollywood studio used money on local facilities and hiring a local director, whilst maintaining an eye on the home market by framing the subject matter within a popular Hollywood cycle of the time and, most importantly, by having a romance between a major Hollywood star (Weaver) and an emergent, but known to the American public, 'Australian' star (Gibson).

Secondly, considering Ezra and Rowden's view that transnational cinema is the cinema that is made by transnational filmmakers and that has transnationalism as its object,[67] I argue that *Year* certainly has this second characteristic. As the chapter on transnational cinema has shown, scholars agree that a film with transnational subject matter deals with diasporas and/or displacement across different borders. Considering Guy Hamilton, he experiences the ultimate displacement of having to live in a different country, and to adapt to a different culture, but he also experiences a form of displacement within his own circle of friends, since he does not fit with the values and style of life of the other foreign correspondents who live in Java.

The fulfilment of the first criteria used by scholars to identify transnational films (that they should have a transnational director), would imply defining Weir as a transnational director. After having analysed two productions of the Australian period (my observations on *The Year of Living Dangerously* remaining valid), a more complete answer to this question requires the analysis of the other two films which have singled out in this chapter, *Witness* and *The Truman Show*, both made in Hollywood.

Hollywood up close: *Witness* (1985)

After *The Year of Living Dangerously*, Peter Weir was due to direct the Warner Bros' production *The Mosquito Coast*, but a successions of events meant that he directed *Witness* as his first American film. At first, *The Mosquito Coast*'s postponement appeared to be both a negative event and a bad omen for the beginning of Weir's Hollywood career. Considering the story of his career with the wisdom of hindsight and given the opposite fortune of *Mosquito* (a failure) and *Witness* (a success), I argue that had Weir directed *Mosquito* first, the story and the development of his American career would have been very different and might not have been as successful. The pre-production histories of the two films are inextricably linked.

During *The Year of Living Dangerously*'s shooting, Sigourney Weaver brought to Peter Weir's attention Paul Theroux's recently published novel *The Mosquito Coast*, because she thought it a good subject for a cinematic adaptation.[68] Producer Jerome Hellman, in the meantime, had purchased the book's rights for $250,000, and commissioned a script to Paul Schrader.[69] In 1983, Hellman asked Warner Bros' president Robert Shapiro to produce the film; the latter agreed to finance the development of the screenplay and gave Hellman the go-ahead to find a director.[70]

Schrader developed the first draft of the script, and, together with Hellman, flew to Australia to meet Peter Weir to propose he direct the film. After a week of discussions concerning the book and the script, Weir accepted.[71] Weir went to the United States to scout possible locations in New England, and to meet writer Paul Theroux. According to the director, during their first meeting, Weir warned Theroux that he had a problematic history with writers.[72] However, '[Theroux's] attitude [was] totally different', admits the director, 'he said that I had to take it away, make it mine, and that he'd be happy to comment on any drafts'.[73]

Weir and Hellman approached Jack Nicholson to play the leading role, and the actor initially accepted, but eventually did not star in the film. There are different versions surrounding Jack Nicholson's involvement in the film. According to *The Los Angeles Weekly*, Jack Nicholson was eager to play the role of Allie Fox, but producer Jerome Hellman felt that he would have dominated the project. According to Weir's version, Jack Nicholson had difficulty filming in Belize because he feared he would not be able to follow the matches of the Los Angeles Lakers, even though the production would have accommodated the actor's needs. In any case, Weir sustains that Nicholson was no longer available by the time the film received the final green light. Weir got the news while he was in Los Angeles and ready to start filming.[74]

The second major setback to the film's pre-production happened when Robert Shapiro was replaced as head of Warner. Jerome Hellman submitted the project to the new executive, but he – considering Jack Nicholson's absence – was not interested in the film.[75] It was early 1984, and Peter Weir and his producer realized that the picture had to be postponed for another year. While Hellman started looking for another producer for the film,[76] Weir was left without a project.

In the meantime, the genesis of *Witness* had already begun. In 1983, the wife of screenwriter Earl Wallace, Pamela, had the idea of developing a script narrating the story of a cop who falls in love with an Amish woman.[77] Earl Wallace and William Kelley sent a first draft of the script, entitled *Called Home*, to several producers: Edward Feldman agreed to pay for a rewrite of the script[78] and had the idea of casting Harrison Ford in the leading role. The actor, contacted, found the script very interesting:

> It was the kind of film which I thought was about 90% there, which is a much higher grade that I give most film scripts when I first get them. But I felt that, if we didn't have a really good director, it wouldn't gain anything – in fact, it would most likely lose something in the translation.[79]

With the backing of Feldman, Earl Wallace and William Kelly sent a draft to Paramount, which, at this stage, ended with Rachel killing the corrupt policeman and Swann (as the protagonist was initially called) leaving the Amish community.[80]

In August 1983, Paramount's analyst Dan Brown advised the studio's executive Jeff Katzenberg to consider the script for production,[81] and in March 1984, Edward Feldman and Harrison Ford discussed a possible director for the film. According to Pat Broeske, Ford 'compiled a list of directors he wanted to work with. Weir was among them'.[82] Contacted, Peter Weir accepted within three days.[83] In my interview, Weir recalls the event that led to his hiring as *Witness* director. It is worth reporting the account in its entirety.

> When [*The Mosquito Coast*] collapsed [because] they just couldn't get the money, I went back home and I was so ready to go and make a film in America that I called my agent and I said… 'I want you to send me green lit projects'. [H]e sent me three and I said I would pick one, I will try and imagine it is the 1930s or 40s and this is a studio assignment, I wanted to break my own way of making films with all this kind of artistic integrity, I wanted a job. I was so anxious to get out of Sydney. So three scripts arrived… one had the awkward title of *Called Home*. [And] I read it and I thought there is something in this, it is a little bit obvious, but this is for free no question, so I rang my agent back and I said I would be interested in it.[84]

This passage suggests that at this stage of his career, Weir felt professionally ready to make the move to America and that he was extremely frustrated by the negative developments of *The Mosquito Coast*. The director was keen to move to America to the point that he would make changes to his way of working: while in Australia Weir was used to choosing his own projects (either writing original scripts or adapting novels that captured his imagination), he would accept to work on a project originated by somebody else. 'To be honest', says Weir, 'I took the assignment because I decided it was a good idea not just to make films which obsessed me. [I] wanted to be like those directors in the '40s who took assignments from their studios and got on with them'.[85]

In these passages, Weir gives the idea that he wants to appear as being always in control of the situation: he does not affirm that, in order to work in Hollywood he *had* to accept a change in his way of working. On the contrary, he stresses that he *wanted* a change in his way of working. In my interview, when asked about the challenges that he had to face going to Hollywood, Weir says, 'I didn't have any bad stories in Hollywood because I was always very clear what I was going to do even before I have final cut in my contract, so I wouldn't have to compromise. I wouldn't be afraid and compromise'.[86]

However, Weir, in order to work in Hollywood, *did have* to compromise. He had to change his way of working not only accepting what he calls 'a studio assignment', but also relenting his control over the actors casting. In Australia, Weir always had a say in the casting process that was done in collaboration with the producers. In the case of *Witness*, however, the decision to cast Harrison Ford in the leading role had already been made by the studio. When Weir received *Called Home*'s script, however, he was not yet aware of the presence of Harrison Ford. 'They told me', says Weir, '[that the leading actor] was Harrison Ford and I said 'oh no, not really Harrison Ford, oh my God, that is a huge star!' I hadn't really thought about that'.[87] The casting of Ford was a decision that would prove crucial not only for the film, but also for Peter Weir's future career in Hollywood.[88] In my interview, Weir recalls first meetings with Ford and Paramount's executives as follows:

> I flew to Los Angeles and met with the producer [and] Harrison, in the studio and it all went forward, because we all got on. But I was very clear with the executives, after having Harrison who is a pretty shrewd character and very careful. So he wanted to know how I saw this script and I wanted to know how he saw it. I didn't want a movie star trouble. So we met up at his home in the mountains and our comments on the scripts as we sat down to talk were very similar where we saw problems and where we saw virtues and then he excused himself to go to his office. He really rang his agent to say this guy has passed the test and I rang my agent to say that I really liked Harrison we could work together.[89]

By establishing a positive relationship with Ford, Weir showed to Hollywood executives that he was capable of working successfully with not only big, but also problematic stars (Ford was notoriously a difficult and demanding actor to work with,[90] and in the mid 1980s he was at the peak of his career). Below, I will return to the importance of the positive relationship between the director and Ford for Weir's career.

During *Witness* pre-production, Weir met not only with Harrison Ford and Edward Feldman, but also with Paramount executives to discuss the film's story. It is worth reporting at length Weir's account of the meeting:

> I came to the studio and there was Jeff Katzenberg, the head of the studio, his boss Michael Eisner, and… Barry Diller, so I didn't realize who these people were then, let alone what they became, but they were all in this room with my agent and myself and they were all very smiling, and of course Harrison was probably the biggest star in the world then. [Katzenberg] said 'Well Peter, Harrison likes you, we like you, like your films so let's go make a movie'. I said 'So you have no further questions' and they said 'No'. I said 'I do'… 'Oh what is that?' 'I want to be clear that this is my first film here, I want you to be very clear and understanding of how I am going to do it'. They said 'Yes'. So I said 'I would like to take ten minutes right now and tell you the story in person, because I think if I tell you the story you will get a better picture than the screenplay' and Jeff [Katzenberg] said 'Let me get this clear, you want to pitch us a story that we are offering you?' and I said 'Well not pitch it, I just want to tell it'.
>
> So I stood up like a performance and sort of told the story. We began with rolling fields of wheat or some crops and out of it comes people dressed in what is clearly 19th century clothing, it is a period film probably 19th century, carriages, a house and then on the screen we would put 'Pennsylvania, 1984' and I saw them lean forward and listen. So I quickly told them and as I was telling it I realized there was some big holes in the script but covered them over with talk and at the end they did say that was wonderful. It gave me a better picture, I think some in the room had not read it so it was actually the first time they had heard this story.[91]

This account is particularly significant, because, if on the one hand it reinforces the idea that the director was keen to give the impression of himself as being always in charge of every situation, on the other hand, such attitude also reinforces my view that Weir is a very self-conscious director, aware of his own limits and capabilities, and that he, in his Australian career, had acquired the necessary skills to deal with film industry personnel at the higher levels, and was now ready to engage with Hollywood professionals on the same level. After the meeting, Ford and Paramount gave the final approval to Weir's appointment as director.[92]

Weir chose Australian John Seale, who had worked for him as cameramen,[93] as cinematographer, and *Witness*' principal photography commenced on 27 April, 1984.[94] The film was shot on location in Philadelphia and Lancaster, Pennsylvania,[95] was completed one day ahead of schedule and was released in America in February 1985.[96] The local Amish community reacted to the film with a combination of curiosity and concern about the authenticity of the way in which their costumes and traditions were portrayed. For these reasons, some leaders of the community refused to see the movie. In response to these concerns, Paramount's representatives said that the film 'respect[ed] the Amish ways'.[97]

Witness presents two main themes, the clash of an individual against a hostile society and the difficulties of love between people belonging to different social environments. John Book (Harrison Ford) is a Philadelphia cop who finds himself stranded within an Amish community and falls in love with Rachel, a young widow (Kelly McGillis). Paramount executives were wary of the risk that such an unusual plot could alienate Hollywood audiences, but decided to take it, considering the driving presence of Harrison Ford.[98] *Witness* is, indeed, a film that defies some Hollywood conventions, especially for its unhappy ending.

Witness' story unfolds between the 'urban jungle'[99] of Philadelphia and the solar landscape of Pennsylvania Dutch County. The difficulty, according to Weir, was 'to have that [Amish] element in a contemporary film as a choice people are making now, an hour out of Philadelphia, three hours from New York'.[100] To mirror the differences between an urban way of life and the eighteenth century Amish lifestyle, director of photography John Seale uses two different styles of photography. Robert Birchard points out that '[for] John Seale *Witness* provided a unique photographic opportunity and he took full advantage of the possibilities. The cold, hard-edged and claustrophobic city is contrasted with the warm, open and peaceful life of the Pennsylvania Dutch County'.[101] Nick Roddick also gives credit to Seale's work: '*Witness* is strong on mood, largely thanks to John Seale's brave and intelligent cinematography, which is as little daunted by excess of darkness as by excess of light'.[102]

The colour palette, the set design and the photography of the two settings differ significantly: in the country, there is a bright sunlight and natural colours are predominant. Inside the Amish's houses, the brown shades of the wooden furniture dominate. The Amish costumes are inspired by Flemish paintings,[103] and in particular, as Seale points out the works of Jan Vermeer, who always,

> has a single window light source on the left but you never see outside the window because it is always a bit of an odd angle. [S]o we ended up putting windows on the left and, coincidentally, when we tested Kelly (McGillis), we found out that the left was her optimum side.[104]

Indeed, the image of Rachel in the barn (Image 7) has similarities with Vermeer's painting *Kitchenmaid* (Image 8), from the position of the light source, to the dress.[105]

In contrast, Philadelphia is characterized by an overall darker atmosphere that pervades not only the night-time sequences but also the police station. The interior of the station is lit by artificial light that gives the environment an impersonal feel, in contraposition to the warm interiors of the Amish farms. It is interesting to notice that, at the beginning of the film, the gradual passage between the two realities is marked not only visually, but also aurally. When Eli drives Rachel and Samuel to the city, the first signal of twentieth century American lifestyle is the sound of the off screen traffic that overwhelms the clattering of the horse shoes on the tarmac. When a long shot reveals the source of the noise, the audience sees an enormous truck trailing behind the much slower carriage, and a conspicuous queue of cars behind it. Later, the carriage stops at a traffic light, its shiny rear reflectors the only concession to American twentieth century rules: the sight of the carriage in the middle of a small provincial town symbolizes the contrast between the two ways of life in one simple but cleverly constructed shot.

The city of Philadelphia is first seen through the eyes of young Samuel, with the camera placed at the boy's height in order to enhance the majestic proportions of the train station. When the boy looks up at the statue of the angels, a juxtaposition of high/low angle shot/reverse shot, combined with a melodic and intense music, reflects Samuel's marvel and helps the audience to identify with the overwhelming feeling that the boy is experiencing. This feeling is enhanced by a slow zoom out that terminates with a bird's-eye-view, showing Samuel lost in a sea of strangers in the disproportionate station hall. At which point, Rachel comes to the boy's 'rescue' before he witnesses the gruesome murder that commences the whole story.

After the boy has witnessed the killing the police are called to the scene and John Book's silhouette precedes his first appearance in the film. The development of the characters during the film is marked by their costumes' changes. At the beginning, Book is wearing a suit with the defining props of his job well visible (a gun under his armpit and a badge on his belt). In the early part of the film, he is portrayed as a sturdy policeman and this trait of his character embodies the tough side of Harrison Ford's complex persona, the one that spectators had mostly experienced in *Star Wars*' Han Solo and in *Blade Runner*'s Rick Deckard.

After he is shot, John Book takes refuge in the Amish community. Since his clothes are drenched with blood Rachel gives him her late husband's clothes, a plain looking black suit (that has hooks instead of buttons because 'buttons are vain'). At first, Ford/Book looks very uncomfortable in the black Amish clothes and provokes a laugh in both Rachel and the spectators: his clumsy bearing makes him stand out among the other Amish, who giggle at him. The Amish's costume that Book wears embodies the more amusing and softer side of Ford's persona, one that emerged during the *Star Wars* trilogy and that characterized the *Indiana Jones*' protagonist.

Witness, in my opinion, has the merit of adding a new edge to Ford's persona: the serious, romantic and thoughtful lover. I am aware that one could argue that the character of Han Solo already had a romantic side. However, Solo was a flatter character than John Book, and, in the trilogy, Ford was more believable as an action hero than as a lover. *Star Wars*' script, in fact, did not leave enough space for the development of Ford's persona: *Witness* completes a development that *Star Wars* had only started. John Book is a more thoughtful lover than Solo; he can be serious as well as romantic, and, most importantly, he is capable of renouncing his own happiness in order to not destroy the life of the woman he loves.

The transition from tough cop to tender lover is marked by the demise of his cop clothes for a simple patched blanket, which Book wears as a sort of mantle while waiting for the Amish outfit: the blanket leaves him bare-chested and makes him vulnerable to Rachel's gaze. Later in the film, Ford reciprocates such a gaze, at first through a mirror and then standing directly before a naked Rachel. In this scene, the film cuts from the full

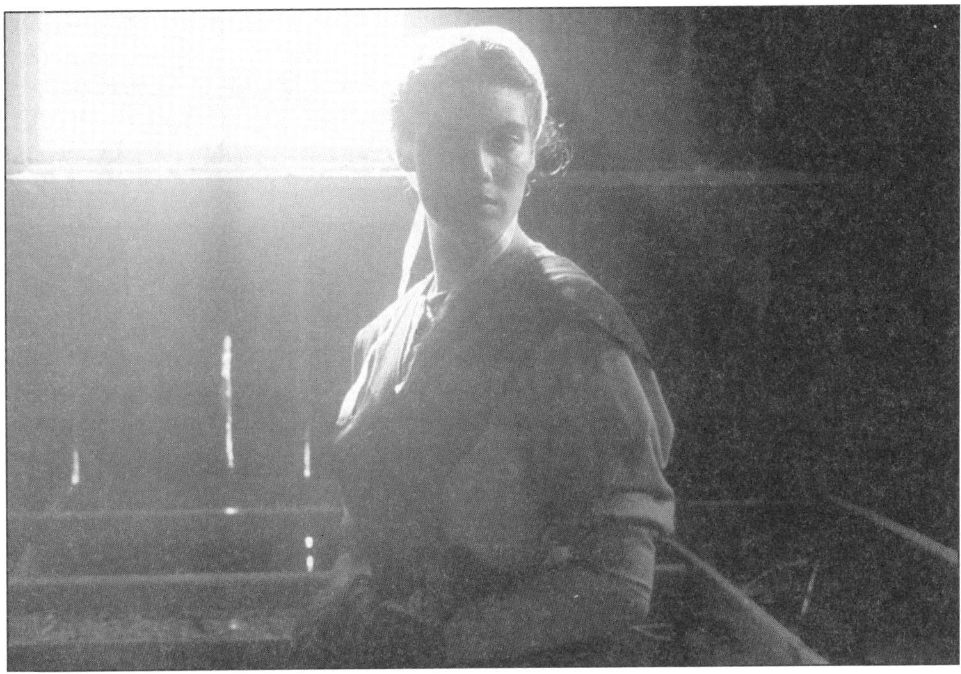

Image 7. Rachel. *Witness* (1985), © Paramount

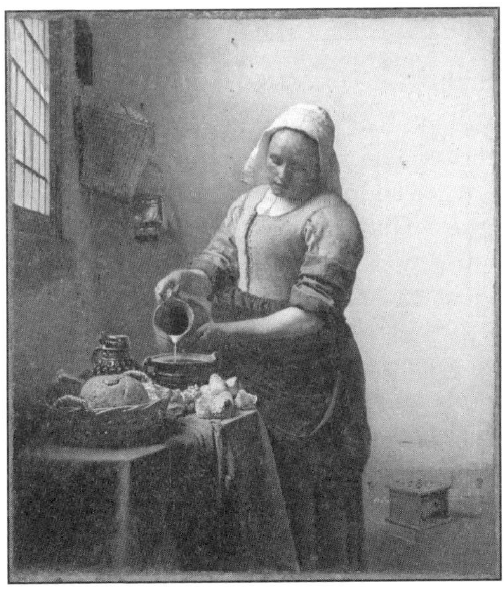

Image 8. Johannes Vermeer, *Kitchenmaid* 1685 (est.) © Rijksmuseum, Amsterdam

body shot of a Rachel to the full body shot of a clothed Book, and then to a juxtaposition of medium close ups and close ups shot/reverse shot of the two characters. No words are exchanged, only intense looks that are sustained for several seconds while both characters assess the situation and decide against making love. The following day, Book tells Rachel: 'if we had made love last night, I would have had to stay, or you would have had to come with me'.

The development of Rachel's character is marked more subtly by her use of accessories. When her character is first introduced, she is dressed in black mourning clothes, with a black head cuff. Her costume and demeanour are as sombre as any of the other Amish, who are mourning the death of Rachel's husband. As the story unfolds, however, Rachel's behaviour changes; during her first encounter with John Book she is reluctant to even speak to him: she sees him as evil because of the gun that he is always carrying around. After he is shot, however, her attitude changes and she begins to see him as a man and, after tenderly caring for him, she develops feelings. At this point, Rachel begins to questions the rules of the *ordnung*[106] and the ways of the Amish.

There are two scenes that are particularly indicative of the development of Rachel's character from an impeccable Amish widow, to a defiant woman and finally to a reluctantly (re)conformed Amish woman. After a very romantic dance in the barn with John Book to the notes of Sam Cook's *What a wonderful world*, she is confronted by her father, who warns her that 'there has been talk' and that she is running the risk of being shunned by the community. This would mean that her father could no longer share meals with her or worship with her. In this scene, Rachel progressively moves away from her father and raising her voice protests that she has 'committed no sin', that she is not a child any longer, and that she can make her own decisions. The fact that she is not wearing her head cuff symbolizes her temporary estrangement from the community.

The second scene is even more significant and occurs towards the end of the film. A long shot shows Rachel standing in the middle of the empty kitchen, framed by the doorway, in semi-darkness, with her hands behind her back in an act of resignation. However, the mise-en-scène conveys contradictory information. On the one hand, the maximum depth of field allows the audience to see all the details of the room, making her an integral part of the house, and by extension, of the community. On the other hand, the fact that the woman is framed in the doorway suggests that she feels trapped in the community. The semi-darkness also indicates that she is torn between following the light of her love and the idea of going back to what she feels is the darkness of her conformed existence. A reverse shot shows her father at the opposite end of a corridor, standing in almost total darkness. Rachel asks him if John is really leaving and why, because he is going back to nothing. He replies that he is going back to his world where he belongs, 'and he knows it', says Eli, 'and you know it too'.

Before going back to her customary way of life, however, Rachel has one final moment of defiance. She notices Book working outside and she deliberately removes the white head cuff, which is shown abandoned on the floor with an indicative high angle shot. A cut shows Book turning towards the window. At this point, a non-diegetic music starts and a series of shot/reverse shots show Rachel and Book walking and then running in each other's arms. At first, a series of long shots reveals the distance that divides them, then the camera goes from medium close up to the close up of their embrace and kiss, whilst the music reaches its peak. Like previously, no words are exchanged in the whole scene and again no dialogue marks their last encounter the following day. Book is standing in the porch, facing the vast empty road that leads away from the farm. Rachel is at first framed by the window, then by the doorway. The two exchange a prolonged look while the camera, once again, passes from long to medium shot and to close ups. John looks at the field and then turns towards her one last time, before finally leaving in his car.

In the last few sequences of the film, Book has gone back to his old clothes and looks relaxed and comfortable while Rachel is last seen without her head cuff. However, the ending leaves no doubt that a love story between the protagonists is impossible. The final extreme long shot shows Book's car heading away and Daniel, an Amish who had long set his mind on marrying Rachel, approaching the farm. Unlike Rachel, Book had understood from the beginning the impossibility of their love, he has always known that he could not have hidden indefinitely in the Amish community and was aware that his Philadelphia life would, as some point, reach him in Eli's farm.

In the latter part of the film, in fact, Schaefer (Joseph Sommer), McFee (Danny Glover) and another officer – responsible for the opening murder – arrive in the community. A long shot shows a car in the distance approaching the farm, accompanied by the same suspenseful music that preceded the murder. The figures of the three men approaching the farm in the morning haze slowly fill the frame. This scene shares some characteristics of gangster movies (the car, the rifles, the frame composition, the three-men-formation walking deliberately slowly). The music continues to intensify as Schaefer and McFee search for Book, while the now shining sun is reflected by the white-painted wooden farm, creating a sharp contrast not only with the sight of the gunmen, but also, and more importantly, with the earlier low-key lighting of night scenes of violence in Philadelphia's night clubs area. In the sequence, the pace of the montage increases as the gunmen enter the house and ask Rachel for Book's whereabouts.

The final confrontation takes place in the sty and in the barn, and has all the ingredients of a cop action film: suspenseful music, the, as it were, 'hide and seek' exchange between the prey and the predator, who call at each other from behind sheltered positions; the unarmed 'prey' who can rely only on his intelligence to lure the armed, but slow, 'predator' to his own death (in this case by suffocation under the pressure of the entire corn stock of the barn); an armed exchange that terminates with bodies shattered against walls. In the initial draft, this scene was absent and Peter Weir was in favour of ending the film only with the final verbal confrontation between Schaefer and Ford in front of the watching Amish community.

The studio, however, felt that the subject matter of the film could potentially estrange audiences, even with the presence of a big draw such as Harrison Ford. Paramount's Dan Bronson, referring to the script, comments:

> I like this… almost in spite of myself. [T]he marketing problems are enormous, I'm not sure how you get a mass audience into the theatres to see something like this, but I suspect that once you got them there, they'd stay. [I]t's exciting and it's moving, and it might be worth the risk – a risk reduced but not eliminated by the presence of Harrison Ford.[107]

Producer Edward Feldman persuaded Peter Weir to add more action to the ending, in order to render it more appealing to Hollywood audiences. Says Feldman: 'the thing about Peter Weir is that with him one bullet is enough. [P]eter has always had wonderful emotional moments in his pictures, but nothing physically ever happens, it's always cerebral'.[108] This comment is revealing on the one hand of the perception that Hollywood had of Weir at the time, an as it were, 'director of emotions', and, on the other hand, shows once more that Weir had to compromise some of his choices in order to comply with the new demands of the Hollywood industry.

Together with *The Year of Living Dangerously*, I argue that *Witness* is the other crucial film of the director's career for a variety of reasons. It is Weir's first American film, and this alone would make it a defining film in Weir's production. Secondly, the good relationship that Weir established with Harrison Ford, combined with Ford's fine performance in the film, showed that Weir was able to bring the best out of stars not only in Australia, but also in Hollywood. Moreover, the film was successful not only with the public – it made $4,500,000 domestically in the first three days[109] and had a US gross of $65,000,000[110] – but also with the critics, receiving positive reviews in the United States, especially Los Angeles (albeit with some negative reviews by New York critics).[111] In May 1985, *Witness* was presented at the Cannes Film Festival out of competition[112] where it was positively received by both the public and critics.

The film's success helped Weir to establish a high profile in Hollywood from the beginning. The fact that the film received several Oscar nominations (including Best Director) raised Weir's status within the Hollywood studios. Although in my interview the director affirms that *Witness* was 'more Hollywood than *Mosquito Coast*. *Mosquito Coast* had that kind of independent film feel. It was my style of the day, *Witness* was outside of my style it was a genre picture, melodrama'.[113] *Witness* is an atypical Hollywood film. It has characteristics of several Hollywood genres: of a cop film (that features good and bad cops); of a thriller (the audience is compelled to ask how the protagonist will unmask the culprit); of, to a certain extent, an action film (not only for the shooting exchange at the end) and of a romance (the impossible love story). *Witness*' ending, however is, arguably, not a characteristic trait of a Hollywood film, or is its setting within an Amish community. Despite – or because of? – its ending, the film was appreciated by the public and very well received by critics.

Witness is an unusual Hollywood film also because it has retained some of the aesthetic characteristics of Weir's Australian productions, notably the type of polished and, as it were, lyrical photography of the Amish county, photography that, to a certain extent, recalls Russell Boyd's work in *Picnic at Hanging Rock*. I have already mentioned that John Seale, cinematographer of *Witness*, had worked with Weir and Boyd in several of Weir's

Australian films, and I have highlighted as well how *Picnic* was inspired by the art of the Pre-Raphaelites and of Australian Impressionism, whilst the visual look of the Amish setting in *Witness* was inspired by Flemish painting.

Considering this comparison, however, it could equally be argued that, rather than defining *Witness* as a film with an Australian visual quality, *Picnic* could just as well be considered a film with a Hollywood visual quality. In this respect, it is possible to see that Weir could be considered a transnational director not only because he has successfully worked in two different production contexts, but also because, within these two contexts, he has produced films which share similar aesthetic characteristics.

Furthermore, *Witness*, as aforementioned, presented to the Hollywood public a different Harrison Ford, introducing a well-rounded character with a stronger dramatic edge and it is not a coincidence that the actor was nominated for an Oscar. The relationship between Weir and the actor was crucial to the success of the film and for the future of Weir's career. Interviewed by Bygrave, Weir expressed his relief at the fact that Ford shared some of his concerns over the script: 'The concerns I had about the original script – which was very good by the way – fortunately turned out to be the same concerns Harrison [Ford] felt'.[114] It is significant to notice that Weir uses the word 'fortunately'. What would have happened if Ford did not share the same concerns that Weir had? Weir was obviously concerned about the quality of his working relationship with an actor of Ford's calibre and felt that to establish a good relationship with Ford was very important. Weir's words raise another issue. In case of a disagreement between Weir and Ford, which of the two would have had the final word?

Considering briefly their position in Hollywood – Weir was a newcomer, Ford was a star at a peak of his success and his presence was a draw for audiences – I argue that Ford, and not Weir, would have had the final word. In other words, *Witness* could have been made without Weir but it could not have been made without Ford. Weir, the director, was replaceable, Ford, the star, was not. The relationship Weir had with Ford was also crucial for the making of *Mosquito Coast*, which after Jack Nicholson was no longer in the project, was at a standstill. Ford's positive answer to Weir's request to play the leading role allowed the film to go ahead. Weir's capability of establishing a good relationship with his leading actors and his reputation for being able to work with 'troublesome stars', contributes to explaining why Weir was hired to direct projects, such as *The Truman Show*, that were originally to be directed by others. In my interview, I asked cinematographer Russell Boyd to describe Weir's relationship with his collaborators:

> Peter's key feature to my mind is his complete regard for all those around him. He does have the intensity of a director who takes his work very seriously and yet he always has humour and compassion. I can't remember when he may have raised his voice on the set.[115]

Boyd's words suggest that Weir establishes working relationships based on mutual trust and respect. The relationship between Ford and Weir, in many ways, mirrors what happened in *The Truman Show*: the positive relationship established with Jim Carrey played a fundamental role for the fortunes of the film.

Big money, big stars: *The Truman Show* (1998)

In October 1993, New Zealander Andrew Niccol sent *The Truman Show*'s script to producer Scott Rudin, who found it original. Rudin bid $1.5 million for its purchase and presented the script to Paramount,[116] with Niccol attached to direct. However, the studio expressed concern, because Niccol was, at that stage, a scriptwriter newly arrived in Hollywood, with little experience as director of commercials in London.[117] However, Niccol was confident that he could handle the 'jump from TV to the big screen'.[118]

In 1994, Scott Rudin had the idea of casting Jim Carrey, who had only featured in comedies, for the more serious role of Truman.[119] The actor agreed with Paramount a salary of $12 million, but demanded a rewriting of the script. He waited for a rewrite of the script for a month and a half, at the end of which he had a telephone conversation with Scott Rudin that, according to Variety, ended in 'a screaming match about when the rewrite… would be delivered'.[120]

Annoyed by such delay, Jim Carrey threatened to accept another project if a rewrite was not ready within a few days. And so he did, signing a $20 million deal with Universal to star in the comedy *Liar Liar*.[121] The studio had – wrongly – assumed that Carrey would 'hold himself off the market until the "Truman" rewrite came in'.[122] In the meantime, Paramount had to hire Michael Leeson to do another rewrite, for, according to Variety, a 'hefty fee'.[123] According to the trade journal, the situation was so difficult that Paramount's representatives held meetings with Carrey's representatives to try to save the project. Eventually, Jim Carry rejoined the project, but he was not comfortable with the idea of having a first time director. In my interview, producer Philip Steuer confirms

> They [Paramount executives and Scott Rudin] attempted to make it with Andrew [Niccol], and [m]aybe Jim Carey would not approve anymore. There were some issues and it was deemed it would have been better to get a bigger… a more experienced director. [Andrew Niccol] was determined. It was such a phenomenal screenplay, like one of the best I have ever read actually. So it had a lot of heat on it in town and Andrew attached himself to direct. At that point I do not think he had done *Gattaca* yet. He was a sort of an unproven entity… and I think the studio was nervous with such a big budget and a big movie star.[124]

At this stage, *The Truman Show* was at a standstill and Scott Rudin thought of Peter Weir as a possible director.[125] Weir was positively surprised on hearing that Carrey was cast in the leading role,[126] and, after meeting the actor, agreed to direct. According to *The Los Angeles Times* 'Paramount… was upset with [Carrey] and reportedly had even considered forgoing the project until Weir expressed interest, [t]hat essentially saved the project and made the wait for Carrey worthwhile'.[127] Why did Weir's interest in directing the film save the project?

Jim Carrey, before being hired for *The Truman Show*, had had enormous success in comic roles (*Dumb and Dumber*, 1994, and *Ace Ventura*, 1994) and was attracted to the more serious role that the character of Truman offered, but, as Steuer points out, he was not comfortable at being directed by a first timer. On the contrary, Carrey welcomed the idea of being directed by Peter Weir, because of the director's experience, and most importantly, because of his record with Robin Williams, whom Weir turned into a dramatic actor in *Dead Poets Society* (1989).

In my interview, Philip Steuer points out that Niccol was eager to direct, but according to the producer, he later recognized that Weir was the right person for the project. 'He was paid very handsomely to do [the script]', says Steuer, 'but I think once he got Peter on he realised [that] the movie was going to be in good hands'.[128]

After Weir's involvement in the project, *The Truman Show* had to wait for one more year before going into production, due to Carrey's commitment with *Liar Liar*. In the meantime, Weir worked on 14 drafts of the script with Andrew Niccol;[129] according to Steuer, the relationship between the director and the screenwriter was very positive.[130] In August 1996, Richard Rothschild and Philip Steuer, contacted by Edward Feldman, entered the project as co-producer and production supervisor respectively.[131] *The Truman Show*'s principal photography commenced in Seaside, Florida, on 9 December, 1996.[132] I asked Philip Steuer to describe the atmosphere on the set and in particular, the relationship between the director and Jim Carrey. Says Steur:

> The relationship was actually really good, [e]veryone had a lot of respect for Peter Weir including Jim Carrey, who was very well behaved. [I] think he [Carrey] was a bet of Peter. It was a very hard movie to shoot because where we were shooting in seaside world, the weather always changed, and we were constantly battling out and, you know, figuring a way to shoot every day. Every day was a challenge. But everyone, everyone got along very well.[133]

Steuer remarks on Jim Carrey's good behaviour are a further evidence of Weir's ability of dealing with difficult and demanding actors (Carrey is, like Ford, a difficult and demanding actor to work with, as the events leading to his involvement in *The Truman Show* confirm). Director of photography Russell Boyd, in my interview, confirms Weir's ability of establishing a good relationship with the cast: 'the actors', says the cinematographer, 'always respond knowing they are working with someone great and mostly consider it an honour to be directed by him'.[134]

Despite Weir's positive attitude towards his cast, however, not all the actors initially involved in *The Truman Show* completed the shooting. In March 1997, Dennis Hopper dropped out of the project for 'creative differences' after only one day of shooting.[135]

Edward Feldman received a call from a Creative Artists Agency agent who suggested casting Ed Harris for the role of Christof, which only required ten days of filming; Harris was cast after a meeting with Weir.[136] *The Truman Show*'s principal photography was completed on 21 April 1997.[137]

I argue that, among all the films directed by Weir in Hollywood, *The Truman Show* is the most difficult to classify within a genre, being a drama with elements of science fiction, but also, as I analyze below, a thriller; 'Reality TV movie' is an appropriate definition given by an anonymous internet user.[138] *Truman* was shortly afterwards followed, in this peculiar category, by Ron Howard's *Ed TV* (1999), with the difference that while *Truman*'s protagonist is unaware of the broadcast, the protagonist of Howard's film volunteers to be filmed 24 hours per day.

The Truman Show is also a film about Truman's coming of age from innocence to awareness. Truman is the only authentic and unaware protagonist of a 24/7 live television show in which everyone else is an actor. The film represents – and denounces – the ultimate form of a degenerated Big Brother. The film has more than one level of interpretation, and could be seen, as does Jonathan Rayner, as a 'nostalgic evocation of a non-existent idyllic past [the 1950s]'.[139]

Reality-TV, strict surveillance and identity theft are themes that Hollywood has explored repeatedly in the late 1990s. Another 1990s film that explores the extreme effects of surveillance and technology is *The Net*, directed in 1995 by Irwin Winkler. In *Truman*, the predictability of the characters' every action and behaviour recalls the endless repetition of the same day in Harold Ramis' *Groundhog Day* (1993). Interestingly, speaking in 2005, the actor Noah Emmeric (who plays Truman's friend Marlon) points out that the film was 'on the forefront in addressing [surveillance and similar] issues'[140]. *The Truman Show*, indeed, can also be read as a commentary on television production and on the dangers of pushing forwards its limits.

The Truman Show is also a meta-film or a 'show-within-a-film', where everything is double. On the one hand, there is the film directed by Peter Weir, whereas on the other hand, there is the show created by Christof; the two have separate credits. The film opens with a montage of interviews with the members of Christof's cast, after which the show's credits appear; the credits of Weir's film only roll in the end, indicating that Weir's *The Truman Show* includes, but is not limited to, Christof's '*The Truman Show*'. The actors also have a double role; each actor of Weir's film plays an actor of Christof's show, who in turn plays a different role in the fictitious life of '*The Truman Show*': Truman's mother, wife, friend and so forth.

The film also has two sets of cameras. The cameras of the film directed by Peter Weir, in fact, include but at the same time are distinct from the cameras of the show directed by Christof. The first can be defined the 'conventional cameras' that use conventional angles and frames, the second are mostly hidden cameras. Weir explains the use of hidden cameras in the film:

> I began to do it by suggestion, so there was a reference for it, via all sorts of wide angle lenses and cameras in odd positions unusual for a dramatic movie. We would also shoot through oval or circular 'masks', to give you the feeling that these hidden cameras are built into various part of the landscape.[141]

To convey the idea of the controlled environment in which Truman lives Weir worked closely with Peter Biziou, Dennis Gassner and Wendy Stites (in the capacity of visual consultant). Says Gassner '[the cameras were] scattered through town for surveillance purposes. This concept became inherent in all of the design elements of the film'.[142] Indeed, with a closer analysis, it is possible to identify these cameras, disguised in wheel bins, placed above advertising boards, disguised as features of the town obelisk. The latter, says Gassner, 'was representing an art piece… as well as acting as a sentry'[143] for the Christof production company Omnicom.

Although camera angles and architectural features help the audience from the beginning to identify the hidden cameras, the full scale of the artifice is revealed only half way through the film, after Truman's father is reintroduced in the show, when a television special explains the nature of *The Truman Show* revealing a network of hidden cameras records and broadcasts Truman's life live 24/7.[144] In the special, the audience is informed about Truman's previous life with a series of flashbacks, from the death of his father, which is evoked by the sight of the sea, to Truman's encounter with Lauren/Sylvia, the only character of the show who tries to warn him about the reality of his situation.

The climatic encounter between Truman and his father constitutes the disruption in Truman's linear narrative,[145] and is carefully staged – live – by Christof, who commands the camera angles and movements as well as the music levels, in a self-conscious reference to the work of filmmakers. The television commentator plays the role of the omniscient narrator for the benefit of the audience. The latter too is double: on the one hand, there is the, as it were, 'real audience' of Peter Weir's film; on the other hand, there is the audience of Christof's '*The Truman Show*'. This is a meta-audience that parodies and exaggerates the reactions of the 'real audience'. This audience is spread across the world: 'in Japan, Taiwan,… Europe and the Middle East'.[146]

In the first scene after the show's credits, a low angle shot presents the protagonist's routine: greeting neighbours with his own trademark 'good morning' trying to escape from the Dalmatian's effusions and taking the car to go to work: such routine is interrupted by a reflector literally coming out of the blue (sky): this is the first clue that Truman is given about the true nature of his life. As the story unfolds, strange happenings continue to multiply (the neighbours moving in a loop, the behind the set gimps through the back of a fake lift, the radio's broadcast that follows Truman's movements) and Truman becomes more suspicious of his predicament. While the protagonist is gradually made aware of the reality of his situation, the audience is immediately partaken in the revelation that Truman's life has been staged for the benefit of a 24/7 live television show which has been running for 10,009 days.

Weir and Niccol's decision to reveal the artifice from the beginning introduces an element of suspense to the film that can, therefore, be considered not only a, 'reality-TV' film, but also as a thriller that has the type of suspense which was favoured by Hitchcock. The latter believed that, in order to have genuine suspense (as opposed to the surprise proper of the whodunits), the audience must be presented with all the facts and that the spectator should have greater knowledge of the events than the protagonist. By employing this narrative technique, the spectator of Hitchcock's films is encouraged to ask a crucial question 'how will the protagonist manage to catch the real killer?' as opposed to 'who is the killer?'

Suspense, according to Hitchcock, is characterized by anxiety: the greater the identification with the protagonist the greater the anxiety, and the greater is the relief when the truth is finally discovered.[147] It is possible to apply this line of reasoning to *The Truman Show*: the audience knows from the beginning that Truman is the only authentic character in the show, and, through identification, is induced to ask two crucial questions: 'when, and how, will Truman find out that his life is not authentic?' and 'how will he react once he discovers the truth?'

When Truman begins to have the first suspicions, he changes his routine, becoming, as he puts it, 'spontaneous' and 'unpredictable'. Instead of entering the insurance company's building like he does every day, he makes a 360° escape through the revolving doors, walks among the traffic creating havoc, drives at fast speed[148] and so forth. The changes in his routine are marked by the music score. Truman's routine is always accompanied by the same allegro piano music that conveys the impression of a carefree existence. However, in all the circumstances when Truman acts in an unpredictable way, the piano is replaced by fast tempo suspenseful music, which increases the curiosity and anxiety of the spectators. Commenting on the use of music in the film, Philip Steuer recalls: 'When we were [running the] screen dailies every night, Peter [Weir] would play music. He chose the sort of music he'd thought that he would use and a lot of it ended up in the movie, it was pretty remarkable'.[149]

The film has a very distinctive polished photography; the constant sunshine reflected by the white façades of the identical houses reinforces the idea that Seahaven is, indeed, meant to look like a set.[150] To render the visual look of Seahaven, Dennis Gassner and Wendy Stites were inspired by the characteristic and unique architecture of the Florida town of Seaside, which the art department had only to emphasize to create 'the ideal setting for Seahaven'.[151] I asked Philip Steuer who had the idea of having a constant sunshine in the film: 'that was a choice of Peter, because it was supposed to be a very artificial looking. Obviously, the movie is about a controlled environment, so it was very important to have sunlight at all times for the day scenes'.[152] Peter Biziou and Peter Weir underline how the glossy visual look of the film was influenced by television commercials, to reinforce the idea that everything, in Truman's world, is for sale,[153] 'from the actor's wardrobe to the homes they live in'.[154]

The actors' clothes (Merly's dresses and shoes) and their props (Truman's suitcase and hat), but also the diegetic rock and roll music played at the high school party, compared with other elements (the modern car that Truman drives, for instance), raise the issue of the period in which Christof's television show – as opposed to Peter Weir's film – is set. Weir's film is, in fact, arguably set in a period contemporary to its late 1990s release, as the type of technology employed to make the show (the lunar studio, the hidden cameras), reveal. However, the time setting of the television show is not clearly definable. While the costumes and the music are 1950s,[155] the cars, the lawnmower, the vending machines definitely belong to the 1990s. It is, therefore, possible to argue that the show is deliberately set in an indefinable time, because time, in Seahaven, is of no importance. Truman has never visited any other world than his own and does not know the difference between a contemporary style of life and 1940/50s America. In other words, Truman does not have an idea of how the real world is meant to look like, and, for him, it is perfectly normal, to make one example, that the posters displayed in a travel agency should discourage a costumer from travelling rather than lure him into visiting paradisiacal locations and that a 1940s fashion style should go alongside 1990s cars.

Every element in *The Truman Show*, is carefully studied and has a particular relevance. Truman's own name can be broken down as 'true man' but this name has a double meaning. Truman was named by Christof, with the intention of making a 'True Man' of him; on the other hand, 'true man' can be read as an indication that Truman is the only authentic person of *The Truman Show*. When, at the end of the film, Truman says to Christof 'nothing was real' the show creator answers '*you* were real!'[156]

The protagonist's name is not the only significant one in the film. Christof's name has, in fact, clear biblical connotations, because it contains the name of Christ; moreover, the location of his headquarters in the lunar studio[157] make him close, in the audience's imagination, to a sort of ancient deity, and give him the best possible view (a God-like view) of the whole of Seahaven; finally, he refers to himself as 'the creator' of the show (the verb 'to create' is, indeed, often associated with God).

Towards the film's end, moreover, Christof's voice comes directly from the sky, in a scene that evokes biblical images and their filmic representations, such as, for example, *The Ten Commandments* (Cecile B. De Mille, 1956). Christof's is the more significant voice within the film: his is the voice of the *deus ex machina* of the whole show, and is both diegetic and, most importantly, non-diegetic (when he dictates instructions to the characters through a hidden earplug). In the final sequence of the film, Christof's God-like voice comes directly from the sky and tries to persuade Truman not to leave the show.

Christof guides not only the actions, but also the thoughts and the words of the show's main characters. After Truman has had a row with Meryl, Marlon is urgently sent to Truman's house and takes him to their favourite getaway place on the uncompleted freeway bridge. Truman reveals his fears of being part of something big and that 'everybody seems to be in on it'.[158] The following passage of the screenplay is revealing of how the filmmakers convey Christof's image – of authority, reassurance and total control – through camera movements, montage and actors' performances (facial expression and of tone of voice)

EXT. FREEWAY. NIGHT.

...

MARLON

I know that feeling when it's like everything's slipping away and you don't want to believe it so you look for answers someplace else. But, well, the point is, I would gladly step in front of the traffic for you.

INT. CONTROL ROOM. NIGHT.

CHRISTOF stares intently into camera, holding his distinctive earpiece to his head. Beside him, his ever present assistant, Chloe.

CHRISTOF

(hushed tones)
And the last thing I'd ever do is lie to you.

EXT. FREEWAY. NIGHT.

MARLON

(staring into Truman's eyes)
And the last thing I'd ever do is lie to you.
(pause)
Think about it, Truman, if everybody's in on it, I'd have to be in on it too.
I'm not in on it because there is no it.[159]

In addition to controlling the lives of the people who 'live' in Seahaven, Christof also has the power of controlling the weather conditions. When Marlon and Truman are contemplating a perfect sunshine, Marlon comments that the 'big man' has a beautiful paintbrush. Whereas Truman naturally thinks that his friend is referring to God, Marlon is aware that the perfect sunset is nothing more than a scenario carefully set up by the show's own 'god', Christof. Seahaven's sunset has a pictorial quality, which is also traceable in the final sequence of the film, when Truman sails towards the horizon. It is worth quoting at length Weir's description of how it was made:

> [The tank at Universal's][160] had the permanent sky and the water. It immediately occurred to me [that] we must have a staircase up into the sky and a door: it will be so visually interesting. [A]s much as possible I try to strip the artifice away, I try not to

make it clever, but simple and natural. It is for the audience to make all the connections: there is a studio, it has a sky wall, the boat hits the sky, there must be a door for the technicians, he goes up the steps, the steps must therefore go into the sky so no one would ever notice from a distance if he ever sailed in a boat. So everything was to feel delightfully right as you watch the film. I do not need to impress the audience. [I] just want them to say 'what a great story'.[161]

Surrealist paintings can indeed be seen as a source of inspiration for the visual look of the last sequence. In my interview, I asked Philip Steuer if the final sequence had been inspired by a painting; the producer observes: 'certainly it has that appearance, and I think it was just the oddity of reaching the end of the set, and this is just a strange story. There is a sort of Magritte'.[162]

Indeed, the influence of the painter is particularly evident in the scene when Truman's boat hits the faked horizon, which closely resembles Magritte's *Le Seducteur* (Image 9): the two images share numerous similarities: they are framed in the same way, with the sky taking two-thirds of the picture, the boat sails in the same direction, and the colour palette is dominated by blue and by the different shades of white.

The Truman Show was widely released in the United States on 5 June, 1998 and received good reviews from the American critics.[163] The film, as aforementioned, is Weir's highest grossing film to date (it grossed $125,603,360 in the United States), therefore is somehow a paradox that, on the film's release, Weir, Scott Rudin and Paramount's executives were worried that the film, which cost $60 million, would not perform well at the box office.[164]

The Truman Show's clever marketing highly contributed to its success. Paramount, indeed, exploited the *Truman* phenomenon on different media, with a campaign that, in its means and diffusion, bears similarities with the way in which *The Blair Witch Project* was marketed the following year (1999). Both films were promoted on the internet exploiting the 'reality' factor. The viewers of *The Blair Witch Project* were led to believe that the film was based on real footage, whereas the public of *The Truman Show* was encouraged to support a campaign to free Truman. In June 1998, in fact, Paramount created the website www.freetruman.com, 'to propel the mission of the fictitious Truman Liberation Front'.[165]

The Truman Show's success arrived at an important time for Weir's career, because it came five years after his last feature, *Fearless* (1993) and almost ten years after Weir's last success with the public, *Dead Poets Society* (1989). In my interview, I asked Philip Steuer how he would position *The Truman Show* within Weir's production. 'I am a huge fan of Peter Weir's work', comments the producer. 'I think the movie stands up with any of these films actually, his better films like *Witness*, *Mosquito Coast*, *Fearless* and *Picnic at Hanging Rock*'.[166]

Although I have identified clearer transnational characteristics, both from the point of view of production and from the point of view of content in the previous three films analyzed in this chapter, it is more difficult to find transnational traits in *The Truman*

Show. Considering the film's subject matter, it is possible to argue that, once again, Peter Weir was involved in the direction of a movie in which the main protagonist experiences a sense of alienation and displacement. I am aware that this characteristic does not make *The Truman Show* a film with a transnational content *per se*, because, unlike the protagonist of *Year*, Truman does not live in a country different from his country of origin, but, nonetheless he lives in a 'foreign' country, a fictitious America that only resembles 'real' America. Equally, *The Truman Show* is, production-wise, the least transnational of the four films, having been entirely produced by a Hollywood studio and featuring an all American cast. In the closing section of this chapter, I compare and contrast the four productions analysed.

Picnic, Year, Witness and *Truman*: comparing and contrasting

In this chapter, I have chosen to analyze *Picnic at Hanging Rock, The Year of Living Dangerously, Witness* and *The Truman Show*, because of the particular position that they occupy not only within Peter Weir's career but also within their respective production

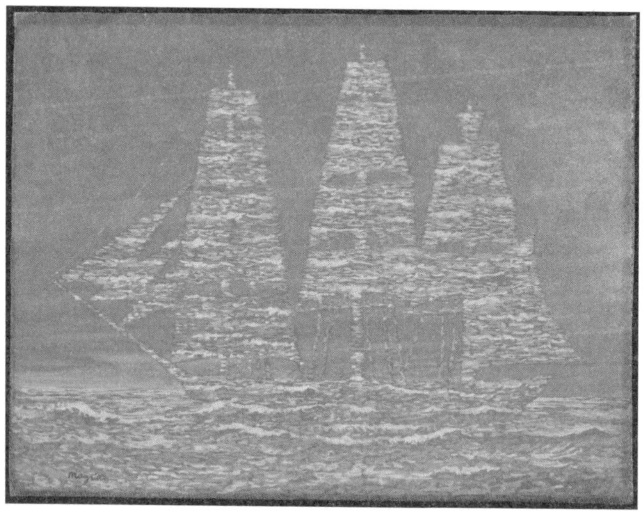

Image 9. *Le Seducteur*, 1960 (gouache & w/c on paper) by Magritte, Rene (1898-1967)
Private Collection/ Photo © Christie's Images/The Bridgeman Art Library
Nationality/Copyright Status: Belgian/in copyright until 2038

contexts. A comparison among these four films shows that Weir was, to some extent, already a 'Hollywood director' when he moved to America: Weir's Australian productions already had, in fact, some of the qualities of Hollywood productions of the 1980s and he was already used to working with Hollywood producers and to adopting Hollywood ways (such the marketing of his films as package films).

Picnic at Hanging Rock has been regarded by critics as one of the most iconic films of the revival and shares its aesthetic qualities with other films of the period genre that also had to comply with the requirements of the AFC. The film is representative of a cinematography that is characterized, as aforementioned, by natural lighting, 'lyrical pans' and the depiction of beautiful landscapes, as Dermody and Jacka describe. It is also the film that has allowed Weir to be known in international art house circuits and by the overseas, particularly European, public, in part because of the employment of international stars such as Helen Morse and Rachel Roberts, and in part because of its circulation in European art house circuits and international festivals.

Like *Picnic*, the Hollywood produced *The Year of Living Dangerously* is reflective of the production context within it was made, and fits within the cinematic context of its time. *Year* is part of the so called cycle of 'Third World investigative films', and, moreover, has been conceived, alongside many Hollywood films of the 1980s as a package film. *Year*'s transnational nature is due to the fact that the film is at the same time an Australian feature, featuring an 'Australian' star and having Australian crew *and* a Hollywood production, which attracted American money into the Australian film industry thanks to the long-sighted intervention of producer Jim McElroy. As *Picnic at Hanging Rock* features international stars, so *The Year of Living Dangerously* features international names such as Sigourney Weaver (American) and Mel Gibson (considered Australian). *Year* was also designed to appeal to both a home and an international market. *Year* appeals to Hollywood audiences because it is, ultimately, a romance between the two major stars, with the added elements of a cliché (somehow unlikely) happy ending.

Like *Year*, *Witness* has been produced by a major Hollywood studio (Paramount), features a major star (Harrison Ford) and has been designed to appeal to a Hollywood audience, with a storyline which had to comply with Hollywood demands. *Witness* is the film that completes Weir's entrance into the Hollywood production industry and signals a significant change in the director's way of working: in order to work in Hollywood, Weir had to join a project after important decisions (the casting of lead actor) had already been made; he had, as he puts it, to accept a 'studio assignment',[167] and, importantly, he had to 'pass the Harrison Ford test' before being accepted as director.

Weir's first Hollywood film shares several similarities with both *The Year of Living Dangerously*, and, as I show below, *Picnic*. As aforementioned, Weir was not an unknown director by the time he arrived in America: when Paramount executives hired him to direct *Witness*, they did it with the awareness that Weir and his collaborators would give to the film the distinctive 'visual quality' which was proper of the Australian films of the revival. Paramount executives were aware that *Witness*' setting among – and representation of –

the Amish community was a delicate subject and they wanted to transfer Amish costumes and life on the screen in a way that was not only accurate (as Hollywood filmmakers could have done) but also poetical, and an Australian director and cinematographer, thanks to their type of background and, as it were, 'aesthetic school' could guarantee.

The producers were indeed aware that Weir and cinematographer John Seale would bring their, as Dermody and Jacka say it, 'lyrical' photography to the film, as they had done in their previous Australian productions (*Picnic*, but also, to make another example, *Gallipoli*). Indeed, John Seale's photography of the Amish county in *Witness* has common points with Russell Boyd's photography of *Picnic* (a pictorial look and an overall feeling of a bucolic atmosphere). This aesthetic approach was considered by Paramount and Feldman as fitting the kind of look that *Witness*' story and setting demanded.

I have argued that *Year* already had elements of Hollywood films, in its packaging, in its being financed by Hollywood, and also, it is important to add, in its ultimately being a romantic story. However, *Witness* has retained some of the characteristics of Weir's Australian films (aesthetically and story wise), that in turn have been influenced by the Australian production context. If *Witness* is a Hollywood film as far as its production and its stars, this is less so for its subject matter and, in particular, its ending. It is true that Weir had to negotiate the ending having to put more action in the film, but it is also true that, had it followed the expectations of Hollywood audiences, the film should have ended with John Book staying in the Amish community or Rachel leaving it. Applying this argument to *The Year of Living Dangerously*, one sees that, had it followed conventions more typical of art house films, it would not (necessarily) have had a happy ending.

With *The Truman Show*, Weir joined a trend of reality television films that was taken on by Hollywood with, for example, *Ed TV* (however, as aforementioned, the idea of the big brother 'watching over you' was not new to Hollywood). *Truman* has the characteristics of a blockbuster film (big marketing campaign supported on the internet, presence of a huge star). *Witness* showed that Weir readily integrated in Hollywood thanks to his previous experience in Australia and *Truman* shows that Weir, in the late 1990s, had established himself as Hollywood director recognized by the public, the fellow filmmakers and the Hollywood establishment. An indirect confirmation of Weir's recognition is Philip Steuer's comment regarding his placement of *The Truman Show* alongside the likes of *Picnic at Hanging Rock*.

The analysis of *The Truman Show* shows that, by the late 1990s, Peter Weir had reached the position of an established Hollywood director to the extent that Jim Carrey, one of the biggest and better paid stars of the period (and, possibly to this day), chose Weir to direct the film that was intended to change his career's path. With *Truman*, Carrey wanted to prove to the Hollywood industry and to the public that he was capable of sustaining the leading role in dramas as well as comedies, and that he should not been pigeonholed as a great comedian, but seen as an all-round actor.

Weir had put himself in the position to be chosen as the director of the film thanks, as aforementioned, to his previous experience with Robin Williams, who successfully played his first dramatic role in *Dead Poets Society*. As in the case of *Witness*, Weir was selected and chosen by both the studio and the leading actor to direct the film, and he enjoyed, as Philip Steuer points out, a good relationship with Carrey.

The analysis of these four films and their production context highlights more similarities than differences among them. In both contexts, Weir had to address the demands of producers, with the difference that in Australian he had also to answer to the aesthetic and thematic concerns of the Australian government, whereas in Hollywood these were the demands of studio producers.

In my interview, I asked Russell Boyd if he had found working with Australian producers different to working with American ones. At that stage of my research into this book, I was supposing that the Australian and the American contexts would have more differences rather than similarities. Boyd, however, highlights significant similarities between American and Australian producers:

> [In America] there are plenty of independent producers who work a lot like their Australian counterparts. They are usually attached to the director from the beginning, including script development and the raising of the finance. The studio producers are usually more budget oriented and are directly answerable to the studio regarding how the budget is spent. Often a film has an independent and a studio producer.[168]

I am aware that it is possible to affirm that Australian producers were, at the time of Weir, all independent; however, as I have shown they too had to be answerable: instead of to the studio, they had to answer for their decisions to the national financing bodies and various other investors.

Another similarity it is possible to identify between Weir's Australian and American working experience, is that the director has worked with stars in both Australia and Hollywood, and has had a positive relationship with his collaborators in both contexts; he asked some of his Australian collaborators (such as John Seale) to move to Hollywood in order, I argue, to maintain certain continuity both aesthetically and in terms of working environment.

Looking at the subject matter of those four films, it is possible to argue that, to a certain extent, the protagonists all experience a sense of displacement, but, rather than across national boundaries, there are displaced *within their own national context*. In fact, the four films analyzed in this chapter (and also those that I have not singled out, as critics have highlighted)[169] share a representation of a person that does not fit within his or her context, but do not deal with transnational issues. In this respect, therefore, Weir should not be considered a transnational filmmaker.

However, if being a transnational filmmaker signifies being able to work successfully in two production contexts, than Weir *is* a transnational filmmaker, being simultaneously an Australian *and* a Hollywood director. He has been an agent *and* a product of the Australian production context of his time, and, on the other hand, he has now become, as this chapter has shown, an established Hollywood director. In Australia, he represented the national cinema worldwide, and in Hollywood he fully fitted within the industry and the establishment.

I have argued that a filmmaker can be considered transnational even if s/he does not make films with a transnational subject matter, as long has s/he has worked within, and in particular across, two different production contexts within two different countries. Herein, I would like to add another element that, in my view, defines a transnational filmmaker. In order to reach a full transnational status a filmmaker, in my view, has to be well known – if not successful – beyond his or her own national context, to the public and to the critics alike. In other words, in my view it is important to have recognition at international level in order to be regarded as transnational.

A filmmaker who is well known within his or her own national context and has only made one feature film abroad, then returns to produce films at national level, cannot be considered transnational, because s/he did not have the time and opportunity to grow professional roots in a different production context. In the case of Peter Weir, he responds to this additional criterion, which makes him closer to being defined a transnational director.

Moreover, not only he has worked in two different contexts, but he also works *across* two different production contexts. As he says in my interview and as Russell Boyd confirms, Weir does often work on the pre-production and/or post-production of his films in Australia. Says the director: 'sometimes I would work with a writer in Australia. In *The Truman Show*, I worked with Andrew Niccol on rewrites by fax, we would fax drafts to each other over nine months'.[170] In fact, although working within Hollywood as a mode of production, Weir never moved to Hollywood as a physical location. And this both complicates and reinforces the idea of Weir as a transnational filmmaker. In my interview, I asked the director why he decided to remain living in Australia.

> I began to realize', says Weir, 'that as more films are made in America or American financed or based, that by living out of the country and by having up to two years at a time away from the country, kept the country somewhat, what some might say, foreign. And I like that, I liked it to be each time I would go to make a film I was going back to this rather strange and mysterious country that interested me. Whereas if I had lived there it would have become more familiar and you would pick up on an American way of being'.[171]

While in this passage Weir considers his decision as a choice *not to live* in America, his decision can also be looked on as a decision *not to leave* Australia: his ties with his home country are so strong that, although he has been working in Hollywood for the past 27 years, he has decided to remain living in Australia, unlike other filmmakers who chose to move permanently to the United States. Therefore, I argue that Weir is a, as it were, 'part-time transnational filmmaker': not only does his home country remain his place of residence, but he has also maintained working ties with it. Weir, in fact, works on the post-production of his films in Australia, and, as mentioned in my interview, even includes a clause in his contracts in this respect.[172] It is worth considering Weir's take on the relationship between nationality and cinema:

> [directors such as Zhang Yimou] didn't ask to be born Italian or Australian or whatever they just happened to be, they didn't even ask to be an artist or whatever, and so they try and make sense of it all enter the great stream of creativity, in which nationality is simply lines drawn on a map, they are just tribal groupings or whatever they are and particularly in a modern world with so much froth.[173]

At this stage, I asked Weir if he was referring to cultural transnationalism. Says Weir:

> Yes. And then the great stories of betrayal, of love, of revelation of the search for meaning and spiritual religious things, these belong to all cultures. [This] is very much to do with the national boundaries of that country that produces that individual. But in the world of the arts it is a common heritage.[174]

The film's story is, for Weir, more important than the production context. Interestingly, in my interview, Weir also quotes Alfred Hitchcock saying the 'film is another country', endorsing the idea that films (and art) are a 'common heritage' and the expression of cultural transnationalism. At the same time, for Peter Weir, the director's name is more important than his or her nationality.

Looking at the credits of the films that Weir has directed in Australia,[175] it emerges that he loves to work with a close group of collaborators in his films, including his wife Wendy Stites (in different capacities),[176] cameramen John Seale, director of photography Russell Boyd, editor William Anderson, composer Bruce Smeaton. In Hollywood, Weir changed some of his collaborators, but maintained the habit of working with a restricted group of people, such as composer Maurice Jarre and editor Thom Noble, and even worked in more than one instance for the same producer, as in the case of Edward Feldman, who before *Truman* had worked with Weir in *Witness* and *Green Card* (1990). In my interview, I asked Russell Boyd to describe the collaboration between Weir and his crew. Says Boyd:

> Wendy [Weir] possesses quite exquisite taste and has a lot of influence in the look of the film, particularly in the design, the colours and the costumes. John [Seale] was a fabulous operator, I think he still operates a lot of his films, and I actually learnt a lot from him. We worked together on a lot of early Australian films. The working relationship could probably described as all of us having faith and trust in each other.[177]

In Hollywood, Seale was asked by Weir to be cinematographer on *Witness* and the subsequent *The Mosquito Coast* (1986) and *Dead Poets Society* (1994). After the latter film, however, Weir decided to change cinematographer for each film, and this is, in my view, one of the significant differences between his Australian and Hollywood works. It is worth quoting at length what Peter Weir said in my interview about the reasons for this choice:

> I think the only time I wonder about [working with the same collaborators] is do you get too comfortable? Sometimes I have made a change because I have felt we are too familiar after the three or four films and that I want a new sensibility in with the collaborator, the same as I wouldn't want to make every film with the same actor, because I think there is some kind of tension with somebody when you don't know each other too well, that can contribute and can cause sparks, good creative sparks. On the other hand, sometimes you don't want those sparks, you are creating those sparks as the director and you really want to not have to worry about the camera, because you know you have your old collaborator there, you know Johnny Seale, Russell Boyd and we can talk in short hand to them. So I think it is a little mix of the two, I think there is a certain, when I moved I went from Russell to John, as John went from operator to lighting camera man and then from John I decided I would virtually have a different camera man from each film and you know that is what happened, then sort of surprised myself by going back to Russell [Boyd in *Master and Commander*], and I am sure it surprised Russell.[178]

Indeed, Weir went back to Russell Boyd for *Master and Commander. The Far Side of the World* (2003) a film that required a visual quality, or a 'light and a feeling' as the director puts it.[179] This old collaboration continued in Weir's last film to date, *The Way Back* (2010) a film in which the landscape is an integral part of the story, which Boyd, once again, maximizes with his 'pictorial' photography. That suited the Australian cinematographer. I have already discussed the implications of such a change, pointing out that this constituted the real compromise that he had to make in order to work in Hollywood.

Conclusions

In this chapter, the textual analysis and investigation of the production history of the four films has highlighted how the Australian and Hollywood production contexts (in the shape of the AFC, Australian producers the McElroys, Hollywood producers and studio executives) have influenced and informed the choices of Weir and his collaborators on multiple levels. The films casting (*Witness* and *Picnic*), aesthetic (*Picnic* and also *Witness*), financing (*The Year of Living Dangerously*, marketing (*The Truman Show*) and the success of the films have all been influenced by the production contexts in which the films were made.

The comparison between the four films analyzed in the last chapter has highlighted more similarities than differences in Weir's Australian and Hollywood production, similarities that are present across the various stages of filmmaking, pre-production, production and post-production but are especially evident in the production phases of the films.

Beside those similarities, I have highlighted that the move to Hollywood meant, for Weir, to have to adjust to a different way of working (accepting studio assignments rather than choosing his own projects and not participating in the casting process), but, on the other hand, the production history of the films shows how in neither context was he in complete control of his work, having to give account for his creative and financial choices to producers, studios, and in Australia, to the government. Ultimately, I have argued that Weir should be considered a part-time transnational filmmaker, because he has continued to live *and* to work across two different production contexts.

I asked Russell Boyd if he had found any differences in Weir's way of working in Hollywood as in comparison with Australia, the cinematographer commented:

> Peter now [2006] seems quite a bit more sure footed and confident with his filmmaking and storytelling than twenty years ago, although he always had dozens of great ideas about how he wanted to go about a scene to give himself maximum flexibility in the editing room.

As there is a gap of more than 20 years between Boyd's last collaboration with Weir in Australia on *The Year of Living Dangerously* (1982) and his work on the Hollywood *Master and Commander* (2003), Boyd is in the best possible position to assess both any changes in Weir's way of working across the two contexts and also Weir's development as director. The fact that he has not noticed substantial differences between Weir's way of working in Australia and in Hollywood, make it possible to affirm that Hollywood has not really changed, but rather has matured, Peter Weir.

Indeed, the reason why Weir was readily accepted in Hollywood is because the two production contexts and their products are less different than it might be assumed (in my analysis of the respective contexts, I have shown how the Australian industry, in the 1980s, was getting closer to the Hollywood one). Weir's success in Hollywood was also due to the fact that, as highlighted in this chapter, when he arrived in America in 1985 he was known on the international film festival circuit, both in Europe, and, most importantly in this context, in America.

Weir was known not only to Hollywood producers, but also to a niche Hollywood public, who was familiar with Weir's Australian productions that had seen distribution in America (*The Cars that Ate Paris*, *The Last Wave*, *Picnic at Hanging Rock* and *The Year of Living Dangerously*), and to American critics, that were aware of the revival of Australian cinema and were familiar with the work of Peter Weir. I have argued that Weir can be considered rather than an Australian or a Hollywood filmmaker, a transnational filmmaker, because he has been an integral part of two production contexts. This chapter has shown that the films that Weir has produced in Australia and in Hollywood share more similarities than differences, reinforcing my argument that Weir was successful and readily accepted in Hollywood because he was, in some respects, already a 'Hollywood director'.[180]

Notes

1. Weir refers to Kubrick as 'an unmet' friend, and admits to being very indebted to him as a source of inspiration. See Thomas, Kevin, 'Peter Weir Climbs Hollywood Beanstalk', *Los Angeles Times*, August 30, 1979, 21.
2. Personal communication, 12 March, 2006.
3. See Ibid.
4. I am aware that the agent was all but impartial in his strong suggestion to Peter Weir, having all to gain from promoting his client among the Hollywood directors. In the 1980s, in fact, agents were assuming an increasing importance to the point that, for instance, Michael Ovitz of the CAA had a position 'at the very top of the Hollywood's power elite'. See Paul Grainge, Mark Jancovich and Sharon Monteith, *Film Histories. An Introduction and Reader*, Edinburgh: Edinburgh University Press, 2007, 484.
5. Personal communication, 12 March 2006.
6. Susan Dermody and Elisabeth Jacka, *The Screening of Australia. Anatomy of a National Cinema. Volume 2*, Sydney: Currency Press, 1988, 33–34. A comparison between the opening still frame of *Picnic* and Louis Buvelot's painting *Between Tallarook and Yea* (1880) shows, indeed, striking similarities.
7. Tim Bonyhady in Anne Gray (ed.), *Australian Art in the National Gallery of Australia*, London and Port Melbourne, Victoria: Thames and Hudson, 2002, 67.
8. See Scott Murray and Antony I. Ginnane, 'Producing *Picnic*. Pat Lovell', *Cinema Papers*, n. 8, 1976, 299.
9. See ibid.
10. See ibid.; and David Stratton, *The Last New Wave*, 67.
11. See David Stratton, *The Last New Wave*, 68.
12. The AFDC had invested and lost money in *The Cars that Ate Paris*, directed by Weir and produced by the McElroy brothers.
13. See Scott Murray and Antony I. Ginnane, 'Producing *Picnic*. Pat Lovell', 299–300.
14. See David Stratton, *The Last New Wave*, 69. Is it worth pointing out that the generally positive relationship between Weir and the McElroys was under strain because of the difficulties surrounding the distribution of *Cars* and the initially poor performance of the film at the box office.
15. See ibid.
16. The limited budget was a common difficulty that filmmakers had to overcome in the early period of the Australian Revival. Recalling his experience Russell Boyd points out that the scarce resource available meant that filmmakers had to be more inventive. 'On the early Australian films' says the cinematographer 'because of their much smaller budgets and the fact that a lot of the specialised equipment wasn't even in the country, we had to be very resourceful often creating a piece of equipment for a particular shot with the Key Grip welding up a few bits of metal for a rig shot or fabricating a piecemeal something or other to effect a shot'. Russell Boyd, personal communication, 12 January 2006.
17. There are two versions of who actually approached the SAFC: according to Lovell she approached it, according to David Stratton the McElroys did.
18. See ibid., 301; and David Stratton, *The Last New Wave*, 70.
19. James McElroy breaks down the film finance as follows: 'AFDC, SAFC and GU [Greater Union] at about $150,000 each, with a later additional investment of $20,000 each, as overages'.

The producer is keen to stress that the film was effectively completed under the auspices of the AFDC, which he describe as the 'least intrusive of the any of the government agencies'. James McElroy, personal communication, 30 November, 2010.

20. On St Valentine's Day 1900, a group of schoolgirls goes on a trip to the titular location. After lunch, Miranda and four others ask permission to explore the rocks and wander around in amazement. They disappear without a trace. A group of locals help the police in their search and a young Englishman Michael, who has fallen in love with Miranda, finds one of the girls, Irma, who has no recollection of the events. The police investigation fails to find out what really happened at Hanging Rock.
21. Michael Dempsey, 'Inexplicable Feelings: An Interview with Peter Weir', *Film Quarterly*, 8, http://www.jstor.org/stable/1211985?&Search=yes&term=interview&term=peter&term=inexplicable&term=weir&term=feelings (last accessed 4 July, 2008).
22. *Picnic* was, indeed, the collaboration of several creative minds. To make one example, the original ending of the film (Mrs Appleyard returns to the rock and is found dead) was changed following Max Lemon's suggestion to step print the *Picnic* sequence. See David Stratton, *The Last New Wave*, 70.
23. Wendy Stites married Weir in 1966, and is credited in Weir's films with either last name.
24. The Australian Film commission (recently renamed Australian Film Authority), has always been keen in promoting the representation of Australia for overseas audiences. Images from Baz Luhrmann's *Australia* (2008), to make a recent example, have inspired a recent tourist campaign featuring landmark locations of the film to lure tourists and cinemagoers to visit the region.
25. Sue Mathews, *35mm Dreams*, 94.
26. Russell Boyd, 'Cinematographers Speak'. Russell Boyd. '*Picnic at Hanging Rock*', *American Cinematographer*, vol. 57, no. 9, 1976, 1038.
27. Sue Mathews, *35mm Dreams*, 112. With *Picnic*, Weir started a long-lasting relationship with Russell Boyd. 'The first time I met Peter', Boyd recalls in my interview, 'was on the drive to the airport to do a location survey of Hanging Rock in Victoria. [Our collaboration] really only started while we were climbing over the Rock and looking for locations for specific scenes in the script'. Personal communication, 12 January, 2006.
28. Here, I purposely only mention such interpretations of the films, not intending to repeat an analysis that has already been done. See, for example, Rayner, Jonathan, *The Films of Peter Weir*. 2nd Edition, New York and London: Continuum, 2003, 74–78.
29. Edith's reluctance to speak openly about Mrs McCraw's missing skirt reflects, undoubtedly, the spirit of the time, which was quite censorial regarding such matters.
30. The overtly homosexual nature of Sarah's love for Miranda has been analysed by critics, including, for instance, Rayner, Jonathan, *The Films of Peter Weir*, 74–78. Here, I do not aim to repeat or to question such interpretations of the film, but only to draw attention to them.
31. Peter Weir's *Gallipoli* (1981), for example, contrasts the stiffness and formality of the British officers with the more relaxed attitude of the Australian soldiers during the titular battle; Beresford's *Breaker Morant* (1979), portray a similar contraposition in the Boer war. In *Picnic*, such contrast is further emphasized by the contrast between the simplicity of Australian policemen, whose house is cluttered and overcrowded, and the sophistication of the schoolmistress and of the school's interiors.
32. Personal communication, 12 March, 2006.

33. *Picnic at Hanging Rock*, dialogue transcript. See also Edgar Allan Poe, *The Works of Edgar Allan Poe: The Cameo Edition*, New York: Funk and Wagnall, 1904, 102.
34. See Michael Dempsey, 'Inexplicable Feelings'.
35. See ibid.
36. See, for instance, Jenny Craven, '*Picnic at Hanging Rock*', *Film and Filming*, vol. 23, n. 3, December 1976, 31–32 , and Michael Ventura, 'The Angels of Peter Weir', *Los Angeles Weekly*, vol. 1, n. 35, 34–35.
37. See Anon, 'Peter Weir. Dialogue on Film', *American Film*, March 1986, vol. 11, n. 5, 13.
38. See David Stratton, *The Last New Wave*, 73. According to Dermody and Jacka, the film grosses AUD 1,776,000. See Susan Dermody and Elisabeth Jacka, *The Screening of Australia. Anatomy of a Film Industry. Volume I*, Sydney: Currency Press, 1987, 222.
39. Weir was known to the American public since he made *The Last Wave*, which was distributed in the United States by United International Pictures. Indeed, the extent to which Weir was known to the American public depends upon the scale of his films' distribution in American theatres. As Peter Weir was a promising director of the emerging Australian revival, distributors were keen to release his films in America starting in a small range of theatres to taste the reaction of the public before eventually opening them to the bigger market. The distribution of Peter Weir's films also depended upon their success in international festivals (*Cars*, for instance, won the grand prix at the Tehran film festival and was critically acclaimed at Cannes. It was then distributed in the United States, by New Line Cinema, with different editing and the title, *The Cars that Ate People*).
40. I have not defined the presence of such stars as a transnational characteristic of the film because the aforementioned actresses cannot be called transnational: they were cast by Weir and the producers for this film only, and were otherwise permanently based in England.
41. In 1976 (when *Picnic* was premiered in the United States) and 1979, when *Picnic* was widely released in the United States, America saw the release of several national films, in particularly French, Italian and German and. To make few examples, films released in 1976 are the French Robin Davis' *Ce Cher Victor* (1975) with Alida Valli; Yves Robert *Salut l'artiste* (1973) with Marcello Mastroianni and the German *Der amerikanische Soldat* (1970) and *Der Richter und seine Henker* (1975), by Rainer Werner Fassbinder and Maximilian Schell. 1979 saw, for instance, the release of the Italian Franco Zeffirelli's *The Champ* (1979) with Faye Dunaway and Visconti's *L'Innocente* (1976), with Jennifer O'Neill and Massimo Girotti; and of the West-German/Austrian co-production *The Fifth Musketeer* (1979) with Olivia de Havilland and Ursula Andress.
42. Metro Goldwyn Mayer, *The Year of Living Dangerously*, Press Kit, December 27, 1982.
43. See Alan Markefield, 'Dangerously was too True for Crew', *Calendar*, June 6, 1982, 23.
44 Metro Goldwyn Mayer, *The Year of Living Dangerously*, Press Release, December 28, 1981. See also Anon, 'First Aussie Film Backed by US Major', *Screen International*, n. 380, February 1983, 6.
45. For more details on Linda Hunt's casting, see Ken Ferguson, 'Why Weir Decided on a Piece of "Weir-d' Casting', *Photoplay*, vol. 34, n. 9, 1983, 4 and Emmanuel Decaux and Bruno Villien, 'Entretien avec Peter Weir', 26.
46. See Pamela G. Hollie, 'Theatres to "*Living Dangerously*" Come too Close for Comfort', *New York Times*, April 13, 1982, 20.
47. Metro Goldwyn Mayer, *The Year of Living Dangerously*, Preliminary Production Notes, 1982.
48. Ibid., 23.

49. See Ibid., 24 and Don Groves, '*The Year of Living Dangerously*', *Daily Variety*, December 16, 1982.
50. See Metro Goldwin Mayer, 'Peter Weir and Mel Gibson to U.S. and Canada for *The Year of Living Dangerously*', Press Release, January 13, 1983.
51. For examples of unenthusiastic reviews, see Andrew Sarris, 'Journalistic Ethics in Java', *Village Voice*, February 1983, vol. XXVIII, n. 5, and Kalb Berndard, 'Cinematic Art versus Reality in Indonesia', *New York Times*, December 23, 1983. Interestingly, *Variety* speculates on the film's chances in America, affirming that Peter Weir's fame was not only limited to Australia ('few events are as eagerly awaited in Australian Cinema as a new film by Peter Weir') but it was also extended to overseas audiences: '[the film]', says the journal 'opens in the U.S. next month, where the director's reputation and word-of-mouth should enhance its prospects of finding a niche'. Don Groves, '*The Year of Living Dangerously*', *Daily Variety*, December 16, 1982.
52. Michael Ventura praised the film's authenticity whereas Ira Sohn, in a letter published on *Los Angeles Weekly*, dismissed the film's portrayal of Indonesian culture. See Michael Ventura, 'Hollywood Shoots the Third World', *Los Angeles Weekly*, March 25–31, 1983, and Ira Sohn, 'An Opinion: The Politics of Poverty in *Living Dangerously*'s Indonesia', April 15–21.
53. See http://www.imdb.com/title/tt0086617/awards (last accessed 24 May, 2008).
54. http://www.imdb.com/title/tt0086617/business (last accessed April 2, 2009).
55. It is worth mentioning that Peter Weir and some critics have indeed drawn a parallel between *The Year of Living Dangerously* and *Casablanca*. See Gari Hentzi, 'Peter Weir and the Cinema of New Age Humanism', *Film Quarterly*, vol. 44, n. 2, 1990/91, 9; and Michael Dempsey, 'Inexplicable Feelings: An Interview with Peter Weir', *Film Quarterly*, vol. 33, n. 4, 1980, 10.
56. Personal communication, 12 March, 2006.
57. Metro Goldwyn Mayer Film Co, *The Year of Living Dangerously, Screenplay by David Williamson, from the book by C.J. Koch, using additional material from Screenplays by Alan Sharpe, Peter Weir and C. J. Koch*, Second draft, August 1981.
58. Metro Goldwyn Mayer, *The Year of Living Dangerously* (1982), dialogue transcript.
59. John of Salisbury, *Metalogicon*, vol. 3, translation in Henry Osborn Taylor, '*The Mediaeval Mind*', vol. 2, 1919, 159, http://en.wikiquote.org/wiki/John_of_Salisbury (accessed 3 July, 2008).
60. The package includes Weir as director, William Anderson as screenwriter, the McElroys as producers and Gibson and Weaver as stars.
61. See Claudia Springer, 'Comprehension and Crisis: Reporter Films and the Third World', in Lester D. Friedman (ed.), *Unspeakable Images: Ethnicity and the American Cinema*, Urbana and Chicago: University of Illinois Press, 167–189.
62. The 'more serious attention' that Hollywood was paying to the third world is underlined also by Vincent Canby in his review of *The Year of Living Dangerously*. See Vincent Canby, 'Hollywood Shoots the Third World', *Los Angeles Weekly*, March 25–31, 1983, 24.
63. In 1982, Twentieth Century Fox partially financed Ken Annakin's *The Pirate Movie*.
64. Susan Dermody and Elisabeth Jacka, *The Screening of Australia. Volume 1*, 115.
65. In the last film directed to date, *The Way Back* (2010), Peter Weir does return to representing issues of displacement. Arguably, *The Way Back* is the only other film by the director that does respond to the characteristics of a transnational film, for its subject matter: the story of a group of World War II prisoners who escape from a Siberian camp, walking 4000 miles to freedom, in India.

66. Greg Elmer and Mike Gasher (eds), *Contracting out Hollywood. Runaway Productions and Foreign Location Shooting*, Lanham, MD: Rowan & Littlefield, 2005.
67. See Elizabeth Ezra and Terry Rowden (eds), *Transnational Cinema. The Film Reader*, London and New York: Routledge, 2006.
68. Michael Ciment, 'Entretien avec Peter Weir', *Positif*, n. 314, 1987, 23.
69. Ibid.
70. Ibid.
71. See The Saul Zaentz Company, '*Mosquito Coast*. Production Information', 1986, 4, and Michael Ciment, 'Entretien avec Peter Weir', 23. See also Digby Diehl, 'The Road to Belize'.
72. Peter Weir, 'Dialogue on Films', *American Film*, vol. 11, n. 5, March 1986, 15. See also The Saul Zaentz Company, 'Mosquito Coast. Production Information', 1986.
73. Ibid., 14.
74. See John Powers, 'No Buzz, No Bite', *Los Angeles Weekly*, December 5–11, 1986, 51 and Virginia Campbell, 'Love, Fear and Peter Weir', *Movieline Magazine*, September 1993, http://www.peterweircave.com/articles/articleb.html (last accessed July 5, 2008).
75 See Digby Diehl, 'The Road to Belize', 23; John Powers, 'No Buzz, No Bite', 51, and See Virginia Campbell, 'Love, Fear and Peter Weir'.
76. Ibid., 24. For Hellman's narrations of the search for a new producer, see The Saul Zaentz Company, '*Mosquito Coast*. Production Information', 1986, 5. In my interview, Peter Weir says that the producer 'failed to raise the money' for *Mosquito Coast*. Personal communication, 12 March, 2006.
77. See Robert Hill, 'Moments to *Witness*', *Paramount Picture Corporation News*, January–February 1985. Pamela Wallace was credited for *Witness*' story only after a prolonged correspondence with the Writers Guild of America. See 'Notice of tentative writing credits', Paramount correspondence to the Writers Guild of America, 23 August, 1984; 'Notice of tentative writing credits. Revised', Paramount correspondence to the Writers Guild of America, 29 October, 1984; Paramount Picture Corporation, West Coast Legal Department, 'Note For Files', 16 November, 1984.
78. Ibid.
79. Pat Broeske, 'Keeping up with the Indiana Joneses', *Cinema Papers*, n. 51, May 1985, 34.
80. See 'Paramount Picture Corporation. Files', 23 March, 1983.
81. See 'Paramount Picture Corporation, Files', 11 November, 1983.
82. Ibid.
83. According to Paramount Production Notes, it was Feldman who sent Weir the script in Australia when hearing that a project [*Mosquito Coast*] he was involved in had come to a halt. Weir received the *Called Home* script through his agent when *Mosquito Coast* came to a standstill. See Paramount Pictures Corporation, '*Witness*'. An Edward S. Feldman Production, Press Kit, July 1, 1985, and Peter Weir, personal communication, 12 March, 2006.
84. Personal communication, 12 January, 2006.
85. Roderick Mann, 'Peter Weir pays *Witness* to the Amish', *The Los Angeles Times*, January 27, 1985, 17.
86. Personal communication, 12 March, 2006.
87. Ibid.
88. Ford's performance, indeed, was a departure from his other less dramatic roles in the *Indiana Jones* and *Star Wars* sagas, and the actor was also nominated for the Best Actor Academy Award.

89. Personal communication, 12 March 2006.
90. For an account of Ford's reputation, see, for instance Pat Broeske, 'Keeping up with the Indiana Joneses', *Cinema Papers*, n. 51, May 1985, 31.
91. Personal communication, 12 March 2006.
92. See Peter Weir, 'The Director's voice 2. Peter Weir', in Raffaele Caputo and Geoff Brown (eds), *The Third Take. Australian Filmmakers Talk*, St Leonard (NSW): Allen & Unwin, 2002, 61, and personal communication, 12 March, 2006.
93. Seale worked with Weir and director of photography Russell Boyd in *Picnic at Hanging Rock*, *The Last Wave*, *Gallipoli* and *The Year of Living Dangerously*.
94. See http://www.tcm.com/tcmdb/title.jsp?stid=4332&category=Misc%20Notes (last accessed April 19, 2009).
95. Paramount Picture Corporation, 'News Release', 11 May, 1984.
96. Cinematographer John Seale defines the skill of producing good quality filmmaking with a tight schedule and low budgets as the 'Australian style'. In this respect, Seale tells this anecdote about the pre-production shooting of *Witness*: 'We worked fast and compromised easily. Australian films have such low budgets, there's no room to ego-trip into another week's shoot. They're not used to that in America, where it's common for films to go months over schedule and millions over budget. *Witness* was completed one day *under schedule*. An American producer said to us at the time: "You don't realise what that has done for your careers"'. Sue Javes, 'Box-office hit "an Aussie movie"', *The Sun Herald*, June 2, 1985, 18.
97. See Anon, 'Amish Mixed Feelings over Filming of Movie', *The New York Times*, June 7, 1984.
98. See 'Paramount Picture Corporation. Files', 5 August 1983.
99. Frank Cossa, *Lost Girls, Dead Poets, Last Waves: Twenty Years of Living Dangerously in the Films of Peter Weir*, http://www.finearts.uwaterloo.ca/juhde/cossa982.htm (accessed November 6, 2005).
100. Peter Weir, in Mike Bygrave, 'Down Under in L.A.' *Still*, May 1985, n. 19, p. 47.
101. Robert S. Birchard, 'John Seale, ACS', in *American Cinematographer*, April 1986, vol. 67, n. 4, p. 78.
102. Nick Roddick, 'Among the Amish', in *Sight and Sound*, Summer 1985, vol. 54, n. 3, p. 222.
103. See Peter Weir, 'Dialogue on Film', *American Film*, vol. 11, n. 5, March 1986, 14, and Alex McGregor, 'Seale Settles down after three solid years', *Encore*, November 20–December 10, 1983.
104. Ibid.
105. Bob Haak, *The Golden Age. Dutch Painters of the Seventeenth Century*, Zwolle: Wandeers Publishers, 2003, 447 (image 981).
106. The *ordnung* is the unwritten Amish Behavioural Code that commands humility, family, community, and separation from the world. See http://www.britannica.com/EBchecked/topic/20820/Amish/233461/Beliefs-and-way-of-life#ref=ref794840 (accessed May 25, 2009).
107. See 'Paramount Picture Corporation, Files', November 11, 1983.
108. Janet Maslin, 'Cooper and Inspiration for *Witness*', *New York Times*, February 8, 1985, 20.
109. See Paramount Picture Corporation, 'Press Release', 11 February 1985.
110. Recouping the $12 million of the cost and making $50 million profits. See Imdb.com.
111. See, for instance Ellis, Kirk, '"*Witness*" Offering Moviegoers Glimpse of Ford's Acting Talent', *Hollywood Reporter*, January 25, 1985, 3, 34; Michael Ventura, 'Witnessing *Witness*', *Los Angeles Weekly*, February 8, 1985; Jack Kroll, 'A City Cop in Amish Country', *Newsweek*, February 11, 1985; for a positive review with reservations about the script, see Sheila Benson, '*Witness*:

A Gorgeous Look, but the Script Falls Short', *Los Angeles Times*, February 2, 1985, 1, 16; for more negative review see Vincent Canby, '*Witness*. A Tough Guy among the Amish', *The New York Times*, February 8, 1985, http://movies.nytimes.com/movie/review?_r=1&res=9903E6DD1739F93BA35751C0A963948260&scp=2&sq=*WITNESS*+CANBY+WEIR&st=nyt&oref=slogin (last accessed 7 June, 2008).

112. See James Park, '"*Witness*" Kicks off Cannes Fest', *Variety*, May 5, 1985, p. N/A.
113. Personal communication, 12 March, 2006.
114. See Mike Bygrave, 'Down Under in L.A.', *Still*, n. 19, May 1985, 47.
115. Personal communication, 12 January 2006.
116. See Christian Moerk, John Evan Frook, Kathleen O'Steen and Michael Fleming, 'Rudin Picks up spec script', *Weekly Variety*, October 25, 1993.
117. Niccol directed his first feature film, *Gattaca*, after having being turned down as *The Truman Show*'s director.
118. See Michael Fleming, in *Variety*, October 8, 1993, 31
119. Personal communication, 23 December, 2005.
120. See Anita M. Busch and Beth Laski, 'Carrey Caught in $mil "Liar"',*Daily Variety*, August 21, 1995, 40.
121. Ibid.
122. Ibid.
123. Ibid.
124. Personal communication, 23 December, 2005.
125. See Bernard Weinraub, 'Director Tries a Fantasy as He Questions Reality', 6.
126. On hearing about Carrey, Weir commented 'My God, what an interesting idea!' Rob Blackwelder, '"Truman" director tells tales about making Jim Carrey's first serious film', Peter Weir talking at the Ritz Hotel in San Francisco, April 20, 1998, http://www.contactmusic.com/new/home.nsf/interviewee/weir (last accessed April 24, 2009).
127. Judy Brennan, '"Cable Guy" Gets $20.5-Million Reception', *The Los Angeles Times*, March 3, 1996, 29, http://articles.latimes.com/1996-06-17/entertainment/ca-15803_1_cable-guy (last accessed April 24, 2009).
128. Ibid.
129. See ibid.; see also Christine Spines, 'Peter Weir', *Premiere*, July 1998, 40, Nancy Kapitanoff, 'The Peter Weir Show', *Pulse!*, July 1998, 89 and Anita M. Busch, 'Carrey, Weir Talk "Truman"', 22.
130. Personal communication, 23 December, 2005.
131. Ibid.
132. See Paramount Pictures Corporation, '*The Truman Show*. Production Information', 1998.
133. Personal communication, 23 December, 2005.
134. Personal communication, 12 January, 2006.
135. See Anita M. Busch, 'New "Truman" villain: Harris', *Variety*, April 7, 1997. On the Hopper case for *The Truman Show*, see also Edward Feldman and Peter Weir interviewed in 'How is it going to End? The Making of *The Truman Show*', DVD Extra, Paramount Pictures Corporation, 2005. In this context, it is important to stress neither author attributes Hopper's departure from the film to a sour relationship between the actor and Peter Weir.
136. See Edward Harris in 'How Is it Going to End?', 2005.
137. Ibid.

138. See http://everything2.com/index.pl?node=The%20Truman%20Show, accessed 25 July, 2007.
139. Jonathan Rayner, *The Films of Peter Weir*, 245.
140. See Noah Emmerich, 'How is it Going to End? The Making of *The Truman Show*', Special Collector's edition, 2005.
141. Paramount Pictures Corporation, '*The Truman Show*'. Production Information, 1998, 9.
142. Ibid.
143. Ibid.
144. According to Paramont the production notes, 'over 5000 continually running hidden cameras are stationed to capture the action'. Paramount Picture Corporation, '*The Truman Show*'. Production information, 1998, 5.
145. The film follows a classic linear narrative, with an establishment (Truman's routine is followed for a few days as he gets the first signals of something unusual), a disruption (when Truman's father walks onto the set and the full extent of the show is revealed), and a resolution (Truman attempts to break free, hits the skyline with the boats, confronts Christof and walks out the door).
146. Peter Weir and Andrew Niccol, *The Truman Show. The Shooting Script*, New York: Newmarket Press, 1998, xv.
147. See Françoise Truffaut, *Alfred Hitchcock. A Definitive Study of Alfred Hitchcock*, New York: Simon & Schuster, 1985.
148. It is worth noticing, that when Truman attempts to drive away, he exits the range of Christof's bird-eye-view camera, and the only available shots of him (for the audience within the audience that are the spectators of the show) is from the built in radio camera in the car's dashboard.
149. Personal communication, 23 December, 2006.
150. In Niccol's original draft, the film was set in a bleak Manhattan and the overall tone was very dark. See Bernard Weinraub, 'Director Tries a Fantasy as He Questions Reality', *New York Times*, May 21, 1998, 6. Producer Edward Feldman underlines that Florida's Seaside where the film was shot, looked like a set when he first saw it. See 'How is it Going to End? The Making of *The Truman Show*', Special Collector's edition, 2005.
151. Paramount Picture Corporation, '*The Truman Show*'. Production information, 1998, 7. The original New York setting, according to Noah Emmerich, had 'a very different film, a very different tone'. Referring to the original script, Weir says that it was the first time that he wanted to change something that he admired. See Paramount Picture Corporation, 'How is it Going to End?', 2005.
152. Personal communication, 23 December, 2005.
153. See Eric Rudolph, 'This is Your Life', 76.
154. Andrew Niccol and Peter Weir, *The Truman Show. The Shooting Script*, New York: Newmarket Press, 1998, 78.
155. Weir researched pre- and post-war clothes on *Saturday Evening Post* magazines and visual consultant Wendy Stites, together with costume designer Marilyn Matthews, 'took their inspiration from a variety of sources, including Norman Rockweel paintings, Cocteau a book containing "Everyday Fashion of the 1940s" and photos of Cocteau and of Jimmy Stewart'. See Paramount Picture Corporation, '*The Truman Show*'. Production information, 1998, 8.
156. Andrew Niccol and Peter Weir, *The Truman Show. The Shooting Script*, New York: Newmarket Press, 1998, 162.
157. Lunar studio is the script's name for Christof's headquarters. See Ibid.

158. Peter Weir, 'Introduction', in Andrew Niccol and Peter Weir (eds), *The Truman Show. The Shooting Script*, 67.
159. Ibid., 68.
160. It is interesting to notice that, although *The Truman Show* is produced by Paramount, Peter Weir was able to film the sequence within another Hollywood studio (incidentally, the tank that was used was the same employed by James Cameron in *Titanic*). This contributes to demonstrate Peter's Weir status and reputation in Hollywood, to the extent that Universal, which was not involved in the production of *The Truman Show*, was happy to put its facilities at the disposal of the director and his crew.
161. Personal communication, 12 March, 2006.
162. Personal communication, 23 December, 2005. When I asked Weir the same question, the director refers to 'Zubaran,... who goes back to the 60s or 70s, I think he was an Eastern European primitive who did a lot of skies with very uniform cloud patterns'. Although Weir's description matches *The Truman Show*'s style, it is possible that Weir had in mind a different artist, because Francisco Zubaran is a Spanish artist of the seventeenth century with a very different style. Personal communication, 12 March, 2006.
163. See, for instance, Todd McCarthy, '*The Truman Show*', *Variety*, April 27, 1998, www.variety.come/review/VE1117477427?categoryid=31&cs=1 (accessed May 12, 2005); Roger Ebert, '*The Truman Show*', *Chicago Sunday Times*, June 5, 1998, http://rogerebert.suntimes.com/apps/pbcs.dll/article?AID=/19980605/REVIEWS/806050302/1023 (accessed 18 June, 2008), Jason Caro, '*The Truman Show*', *Film Review*, July 1998, 12.
164. See Bernard Weinraub, 'Director Tries a Fantasy as He Questions Reality', 1. *The Truman Show*'s pre-production and production were not immune to difficulties, so it came to no surprise when, in June 1998, Mark Dunne, a New York playwright, accused Paramount Pictures of largely basing his 1992 off-off-Broadway play for Truman's screenplay, and filed a multi-million dollar suit against producer Scott Rudin and Andrew Niccol. Dunne's legal action, however, was not successful. See Reuters, '"Truman" suit filed. Playwright files suit against Par', *Variety*, June 17, 1998, http://www.variety.com/article/VR1117471916.html?categoryid=13&cs=1&query=the+truman+show (accessed 18 June, 2008). See also Tom Rhodes, 'Writer to sue for $200m over "copycat" Carrey film', *The Sunday Times*, September 27, 1998, 22.
165. See Erika Milvy, 'Paramount Shows Creative Use of the Web with Site to Free Truman', *Los Angeles Times*, June 25, 1998 (The site is not longer available at this address).
166. Ibid.
167. *Witness* and *The Truman Show* are not the only Hollywood films that Weir joined when they were already in pre-production. In fact, he was attached to direct the majority of his American films when the project had already started: this was the case of *Dead Poets Society*, *Fearless* and *Master and Commander*. For more details on Weir's involvement in *Dead Poets*, see See Touchstone Picture, '*Dead Poets Society*. A Peter Weir Film', Production Information, 1989, 8. According to Nancy Griffin, Weir received the script directly from Jeff Katzenberg in 1988. See Nancy Griffith, 'Poetry Man', *Premiere Magazine*, July 1989, http://www.industrycentral.net/director_interviews/PW01.HTM (accessed 9 June, 2008); for *Fearless* see Martha Southgate, '"Fearless" Flying', *Premiere*, October 1993, 50; finally, for Weir's involvement in *Master and Commander* see Paul F. Duke, 'Weir Likely to "Master" Helm for Fox Voyage', *Variety*, August 10, 2000, http://www.variety.com/article/VR1117784874.html?categoryid=13&cs=1&query=paul+duke+weir+master (last accessed June 4, 2009).

168. Personal communication, 12 January 2006.
169. The schoolgirls in *Picnic* seem to suffer rather than absorb the Victorian education; Harrison Ford understands that he will never be able to fit within an Amish context and renounces his love; Truman realized that he has been framed in an artificial life and struggles to break free. As mentioned, the only really displaced character is Guy Hamilton in *Year.* For an extensive analysis of Weir's body of work, see, among others, Jonathan Rayner, *The Films of Peter Weir. 2nd Edition*, London: Continuum, 2003.
170. Personal communication, 12 March 2006.
171. Ibid.
172. Personal communication, 12 March 2006.
173. See Ibid.
174. Ibid.
175. See Appendix 1.
176. Weir's wife is credited, in the films, as both Wendy Stites and as Wendy Weir.
177. Personal communication, 12 January 2006.
178. Personal communication 12 January 2006.
179. Weir highlights that maritime paintings (such as John Chancellor's *The Perfect Hurricane*) inspired not only the visual look of the film but also the special effect crew. See Universal, Twentieth Century Fox and Miramax, '*Master and Commander*. Peter Weir on directing in the wake of O'Brien', *Master and Commander. The Far Side of the World*, DVD Special Features, 2003.
180. I am aware that such affirmation comes close to adopting the auteur theory to Peter Weir. However, it is important to bear in mind that Weir has not originated all the projects of the films that he has directed, is not the author of all the screenplays, and as I have shown, in particular in Hollywood, he has agreed to direct films whose subject was chosen by others.

Conclusions

When I started investigating Peter Weir's productions in relations to transnational cinema, I was expecting to come across studies on the application of transnational cinema theories to the case study of specific filmmakers. In particular, I was expecting an answer to the issue concerning the case of filmmakers who migrate within two different production contexts: do they change or do they maintain their way of working and their approach to filmmaking? Based on my research on national and transnational cinema theories, I assumed that scholars analyzing the differences between national cinema productions and the productions of foreign filmmakers in Hollywood would conclude that filmmakers who change context tend to change style. My preliminary research, in fact, showed that the studies on national cinemas and national filmmakers tend to emphasize the differences between national cinemas – and the productions of national filmmakers within these cinemas – and Hollywood.

During the course of my research, however, I have come to realize that some scholars not only highlight the differences, but also draw attention to on the similarities between some national cinemas and Hollywood, as Tom O'Regan does in his work on Australian cinema.[1] O'Regan, in fact, highlights that national cinemas compete with Hollywood in two ways. On the one hand, they seek to differentiate their production from Hollywood, whereas on the other hand, on parallel lines, they seek to compete with Hollywood by imitating Hollywood productions.

As consequence, I sought to apply these general theories on national and transnational filmmakers to specific case studies of migrant filmmakers, and I aimed to compare and contrast these studies with the case of Peter Weir, who migrated from Australia to Hollywood in the 1980s, to understand in more depth the dynamics that intervene when a filmmaker changes context.

I intended to investigate to what extent two different production contexts, the one of origin and the other of destination, as it were, influenced Peter Weir's filmmaking and how they affected his way of working, his creative choices and the choices of his collaborators. I was expecting to compare my conclusions on the specific case study of Weir, with studies on contemporary filmmakers who migrated to Hollywood, and I was expecting that the contribution of this book would be the study of Peter Weir from the point of view of his migration to Hollywood, an aspect that had not been investigated by scholars, who consider him as an auteur within the context of Australian cinema.

In the light of existing theories on national cinemas and their comparison with Hollywood cinema, I was also expecting to find more differences than similarities between Weir's American and Australian productions. Instead, as the last chapter of this book has shown, I have found more similarities than differences, because, as the book has demonstrated, Weir's Australian work already exhibited some of the characteristics of Hollywood production.

As I continued my research, moreover, I realized that not only there was a lack of studies on Peter Weir as a transnational filmmaker, but there was also a more general lack of studies on the migration of contemporary filmmakers to Hollywood. In other words, I realized that I could not compare and contrast my findings on transnational filmmakers with other case studies because I encountered a lack in the application of theories on transnational cinema to the specific case study of a contemporary filmmaker.

Therefore, I have appreciated that the contribution of this book to the field is not only, as I originally thought, the fact that this is the first study on Peter Weir within the context of transnational cinema, but also that this is, with all its limitations, the first – attempted – application of theories on transnational cinema to a contemporary filmmaker. As I have highlighted in the first chapter, I am aware that studies on filmmaker's migrations have already been done, but these were not in the context of the most recent theories on transnational cinema. What is striking is the lack – or at least the very limited presence – of the application of such theories to case studies on contemporary filmmakers who voluntarily moved to Hollywood.

Furthermore, I have also identified an absence of a proper definition of transnational cinema. I have encountered what I have called a general theory on transnational cinema on which scholars generally agree, that considers transnational cinema mainly on two levels. On the one hand, the level of representation, transnational films depict the lives of Diaspora individuals, whereas on the other hand, transnational cinema is made by filmmakers who have directly experienced transnationalism. The studies do not, however, state if these two criteria are both necessary to be able to define cinema as transnational, and this, as my final chapter has pointed out, has complicated my application of transnational cinema theories to the case study of Peter Weir.

Another trait of transnational cinema on which scholars agree, is that it has to both presuppose and transcend national cinema. The latter is in itself a complicated concept, and scholars, as my research has revealed, more recently have agreed to consider any national cinema as being in constant development, and have acknowledged the necessity of studying national cinemas, as I have aforementioned, in relation to Hollywood. Different national cinemas relate to Hollywood in different ways, and it is possible to find, within the same national context, a variety of answers to the challenges that the dominance of Hollywood cinema poses. Australian cinema has reacted to Hollywood by both trying to imitate it and to differentiate its products from Hollywood – with the production of what O'Regan has called cinemas of the festivals. Ultimately, national cinemas also tend to differentiate their characteristics not only from Hollywood but also from other national cinemas.

My chapter on transnational cinema has also identified a recent trend to, as it were, join forces with Hollywood, with the proliferation of what scholars have called alternatively, runaway productions (seen from the point of view of Hollywood) or foreign productions (seen from the point of view of the host countries); that is, films produced by Hollywood using the facilities and sites of local national cinemas (shooting locations, but also studios and local cast and crew). These productions have brought benefits not only to Hollywood in terms of reduced film costs, but also to local industries, that have seen an injection of Hollywood money and have taken advantage of the publicity that such productions have generated. From a tourist point of view, these productions in fact generate the interest of worldwide audiences in visiting 'remote' locations (such as the New Zealand of *The Lord of the Rings*).

Australian producers and filmmakers quickly understood the need to accept Hollywood money to boost the local industry and also to increase the level of distribution of Australian films in America. In the early 1980s, Australian producers realized the importance of having foreign production in Australia: Peter Weir's *The Year of Living Dangerously* is a good example of this new trend within the Australian national cinema. Hollywood had indeed been following closely the revival of Australian national cinema, to which it had been exposed thanks to the early distribution of Australian films in America and to the presence of Australian revival films in international festivals. Peter Weir's growth as a filmmaker coincides with the revival of the Australian national cinema during the 1970s and 1980s.

In fact, as this book has shown, the 1970s were an ideal period for a young filmmaker to develop; the only important limitation was the limited budgets. However, my interview with Russell Boyd[2] and the discussions between Jim and Hal McElroy with *Cinema Papers*' Scott Murray[3] have shown that the lack of big budgets meant that filmmakers had to be more creative. This situation helped Australian film professionals to reach a level of craftsmanship, as it were, that was appreciated in Hollywood.

In their conversations with *Cinema Papers*, Jim and Hal McElroy have recognized some the merits of the Australian Film Commission (AFC) in breeding Weir's generation of filmmakers, but, have also highlighted the shortcomings and the narrow mindedness of some stances taken by the AFC, such as the endorsement of the Actors Equity Policy in limiting the number of international stars who could feature in Australian productions. Moreover, the McElroys have also highlighted the limitations of the 10B tax scheme that introduced a series of regulations that were very difficult to comply with, and failed to produce a second wave of filmmakers that could replace the first generation of revival directors. Also, the McElroys pointed out the fact that the introduction of tax benefits stimulated the production of too many films, with the result of reducing quality.[4]

Indeed, my research into the development of the Australian film industry in the 1970s and 1980s has highlighted both the positive and the negative aspects of the AFC policies, and has in particular questioned the role of the reviews commissioned by the AFC into the status of the film industry. I have pointed out that such reviews would have been more effective if carried out by independent bodies. Those would have had more power to penalize the industry in cases in which filmmakers did not comply with the recommendations. Despite these shortcomings, my research has highlighted that the

Australian production context during the revival was ultimately favourable to the growth of young professional filmmakers.

It is true that the various Weir, Noyce, Beresford and Schepisi had to comply with some requests, but it is also true that they had the financial backing of the Australian government. The latter promoted the making of films which shared the same 'visual sensibility' and appealed not only to home audiences, as ocker comedies had done, but also to overseas audiences. The AFC genre managed to relaunch the image of Australia that had been damaged by the ocker films.

In Australia, Weir received a good professional formation and was able to work closely with a restricted group of colleagues with whom he shared experiences and labour. This allowed him to acquire the necessary skills to compete in Hollywood both at the production level and at the, as it were, level of working relationships. In other words, Weir in Australia had learned to deal with the demands of Australian producers, the requests of the AFC and also with the personalities of the various international stars that featured in his films, from Richard Chamberlain in *The Last Wave* to Sigourney Weaver in *The Year of Living Dangerously*.

This book has shown that Weir was aware of his weaknesses and also his strengths. Not moving to Hollywood in 1976, when he was first asked, Weir indeed demonstrated that he was able to manage his career with long-sightedness. Weir took a step back and observed his career from a distance, picturing himself in Hollywood in the mid 1970s. At the time, he had only done two feature films and realized that he did not have the necessary skills; by staying in Australia, he gave himself the best possible chance to succeed in the future.

In examining the arrival of Peter Weir in Hollywood, I have considered the type of production context that he found and I have also investigated why he was immediately accepted by Hollywood. I have argued that the reason why Weir was successful in Hollywood was because his Australian films already had some of the traits of Hollywood productions. In the 1980s, Hollywood was experiencing a series of extremely significant changes that resulted in the complete remapping of the structures of all the major studios. The over diversification of products by the studios' parent companies had caused damage to the film production side.

All the studios gradually understood the need to scale down and concentrate on fewer assets, and merged their various activities. In doing so, they obtained a convergence between, as it were, the hardware and the software. The parent companies dismissed activities such as the production of soft drinks and sporting venues to concentrate solely on the production and distribution of the films, triggering a return to a (partial) vertical integration that had characterized the studio system.

In the 1980s, studios also developed home video distribution branches, understanding the need to promote – rather than to impede – technologies such as the VHS[5] that could produce high revenues. This climate also facilitated the emergence of independent cinema productions on one side and enhanced the distribution of those films that, without home video and cable television, would not have been able to reach larger audiences.

It is in this thriving climate that Peter Weir made his Hollywood entrance. Weir's debut on the Hollywood stage was eased, as my research has shown, by the significant presence of Australian filmmakers in Hollywood. The likes of Bruce Beresford but also of Russell Boyd had, in fact, preceded his arrival and had already made themselves known by Hollywood producers. The latter appreciated their ability to work within budget and schedule, and also the type of sensibility that they brought to American subject matters, as Bruce Beresford did in *Tender Mercies* (1983).

As my book as shown, Weir was asked to move to Hollywood for the first time in 1976; however, he decided not to move. I argue that the director has to be given credit for a decision that, at first, might seem risky. Indeed, it would appear that a young and inexperienced Australian director, as Weir was at the time, would be foolish to refuse such an offer by a major Hollywood studio such as Warner Bros. As Weir's agent warned him, he might have run the risk of not being asked again after a refusal. It would appear that a young director who was just starting to know international recognition thanks to the success of *Picnic at Hanging Rock* should have felt honoured to be asked to join Hollywood, and should have accepted such a proposal. I argue however that Weir, by refusing the proposal, demonstrated to be wise and long-sighted.

In fact, Weir was aware that a move to Hollywood then would have been quite risky precisely because he was quite inexperienced. Weir would have had to face the same demands from Hollywood producers and studios that he faced ten years later (such as casting and plot choices), but he would have had to do so with only two feature films in his curriculum, and not enough experience to deal with such demands. Referring to the first proposal to go to Hollywood, in my interview Weir stresses the fact that he did not have the necessary experience and that he did not know enough; he said that he did not feel ready to go to Hollywood. However, he does not specify what the necessary experience would have been, nor he does say what it entailed to be ready to go to Hollywood.

Herein, it is only possible to speculate what the director means by this readiness and what the necessary degree of experience is. He might have referred to filmmaking experience tout court: having only directed *The Cars and Ate Paris* and *Picnic* he felt that he needed more filmmaking experience. It could be that he refers to the fact that he did not have enough experience working with big stars, as he might have been asked to do in Hollywood. It might also be that Weir was referring to experience in terms of dealing with big budgets, that, as I have shown were not available in Australia at the time.

What this statement puts to the fore is that, whatever the type of experience and the degree of readiness he had in mind, Weir, by simply thinking that he was not ready, thought that a certain degree of readiness was necessary to make the move. The fact that Weir thought that he needed 'to be ready to go to Hollywood', suggests that he felt that the Hollywood production context was going to be very different from the Australian one, otherwise he would not have needed more preparation before making the move.

Moreover, the fact that Weir, to this day, continues to refer to Hollywood as 'a foreign' location (as he does in my interview), suggests that Weir still perceives the American production context as different from the Australian one. This book has however shown that there are more similarities than differences between the two contexts, and this suggests that Weir, by not feeling ready, might have over-estimated the task and the challenges that laid ahead of him in America. When he finally moved in 1985, Weir had added three more feature films and one TV movie to his production, and had developed – in his view – the necessary experience to work within the Hollywood production context.

Considering Weir's evaluation that he needed more time and experience before moving to Hollywood, I argue that he has to be given credit for understanding that the Australian production context of the 1970s would have allowed him to obtain the experience that he felt necessary. Weir realized that in Australia he would have the type of backing, from the Australian government, in terms of finance and grants. The Australian production context of the 1970s was, in fact, even considering all its shortcomings, a good working environment to obtain a valid training and level of craft, as Weir puts it, as filmmaker.

Moreover, and equally importantly, Weir, in Australia, had the advantage of working closely with long-sighted producers such as the McElroy brothers, who understood the importance of having Hollywood money in Australia. Jim and Hal McElroy had already produced films with the idea of the package concept (such as *The Last Wave* and *The Year of Living Dangerously*) and welcomed the idea of supporting Hollywood foreign productions (such as *The Year of Living Dangerously*). All these factors meant that when Weir moved to Hollywood he was ready professionally to face the challenges that the Hollywood production context presented.

My research has also highlighted that, to successfully work in Hollywood, Weir had to adapt his way of working to the conditions of Hollywood producers who, if on the one hand were quite similar to the ones posed by Australian producers, whereas on the other hand were different. In particular, Weir as director had to accept what he calls 'studio assignment' projects, such as *Witness*, *The Truman Show*, but also *Dead Poets Society* and *Fearless*, which he was attached to direct after pre-production had already started.[6]

This finding brought me to consider more closely the core question of my book, which was to assess the impact that the different production contexts had on Peter Weir's Australian and Hollywood filmmaking, and to establish, as I mentioned at the beginning of these conclusions, the differences and the similarities between Weir's productions in the two contexts. To establish this impact, I have carried out the textual analysis of four films that, in my opinion, occupy a key position in the director's career: *Picnic at Hanging Rock*, *The Year of Living Dangerously*, *Witness* and *The Truman Show*.

As this research did not aim to be a study only of the films but also of the people behind the films, I have taken into consideration the opinion of some of Weir's collaborators to establish their view on the director's approach to filmmaking, to investigate their contribution to Weir's productions and also, in the case of Russell Boyd, to identify any changes in Weir's way of working from Australia to Hollywood.

My interview with Boyd provides important elements regarding Weir's move to Hollywood, because, having worked with him in both Australia and Hollywood, the cinematographer is in the best position to assess changes in Weir's way of working. Interestingly, Boyd does not mention many differences in Weir's approach to filmmaking, and he only points out that he had found Weir 'more sure footed and confident with his filmmaking and story telling'.[7] What is striking in the cinematographer's account is the depiction of the serious yet humorous attitude that the director has on the set. Importantly, Boyd and Steuer convey the impression of Weir as a director easy to collaborate with, a person respectful of the views of others and open to suggestions coming from filmmakers of all the different creative areas.

Although I did not have the opportunity of interviewing actors or actresses directed by Weir, Philip Steuer's account of Jim Carrey's behaviour on and off the set of Truman Show is indicative of Weir's relationships with actors. Steuer stresses that even Jim Carrey was well behaved on the set, and this suggests that the actor is usually difficult to work with and that Weir found the right way to approach him. Talking about his relationship with Weir, Jim Carrey highlights a significant aspect of Weir: 'Peter would listen to your ideas… he welcomed creativity at every level'.[8]

In the final chapter of this book, I have used interviews with filmmakers as a first hand source to complement my textual analysis of the films, reflecting the methodology that I have used in the chapter on the Australian production context. The difference in the use of this approach in the two chapters is that while in the latter I have used existing material (in particular, the aforementioned interview by Scott Murray with Hal and James McElroy), in final chapter I have used material from my own interviews with Weir, Boyd and Steuer, that gave me the chance to ask questions directly related to the specific research issues of this book.

The analysis of the four selected films has highlighted the extent to which the two production contexts have influenced Weir's filmmaking. In 1970s and 80s, Australia filmmakers worked with the backing of the AFC, but AFC's funding came at the price of having to deal with a degree of control on the productions. This control was not only limited to assuring that the film was completed within budget and within schedule, but also meant, as the case of *Picnic* clearly demonstrates, that the AFC had its say over creative aspects of production. Despite the fact that Weir, in his interviews, wants to come across as a director who was in control, the director was always answerable for his financial but also creative choices.

What changed between Australia and Hollywood was the degree of control that Weir had over his films. In moving to Hollywood Weir did not gain or lose control on his films, what changed is to whom he had to respond in creative and financial terms. In Australia, Weir had to respond to the requirements of the government bodies (the Australian Film Development Corporation first and of the AFC afterwards), and of the producers; in Hollywood Weir ceased to have to respond to the demands of the government, but continued to have to comply with the requests of the studios, the producers, and in addition, he also had to deal with the requests of the actors, as the level of Harrison Ford's involvement in *Witness* has shown.

I do not mean to suggest that Weir neither had control at all over his films, nor does this book suggest that Weir was in constant conflict with studios or that he was not able to take any decisions. On the contrary, the production histories of the films show that there are cases in which the director had his own way. To give two significant examples, Weir completely changed the tone and the setting of Andrew Niccol's script for *The Truman Show*, and he inserts clauses into his contracts that the post-production of his films might take place in Australia. What I intend to point out is that Weir does not have total and unconditional control over all the different aspects of the films that he directs, and that he therefore is not the sole auteur of his films, as the majority of scholars suggest.[9]

Even in this respect, indeed, I have highlighted more similarities than differences between Weir's Australian and Hollywood productions. Despite the fact that the director is keen to come across, in his interviews, as being always in control of the situation, my book has shown that Weir, in addition to having to give account for his choices, also had to change, once moved to Hollywood, his way of working. While in Australia Weir had originated four out of the five movies that he directed, in Hollywood, the director had the original idea only on one film out of seven, *Green Card*, which he also wrote.

While in Australia Peter Weir was always involved in the casting process, in Hollywood, joining a project that was already at the pre-production phase meant that some key decisions, such as the casting of the leading actor, were already made by the studio, as in the cases of *Witness*, *Dead Poets Society* and *The Truman Show*. Weir, however, is keen to represent the compromises that he has had to make in Hollywood as voluntary adaptations on his part. The fact that Weir in Hollywood, had to accept what he has called 'studio assignment', is in my opinion, the biggest change in Weir's way of working across the two contexts.

This is not a small change, but is a change that contributes to explaining the reasons for Weir's success in Hollywood. The case of *Witness* is, in this respect, crucial. With this film, Weir confirmed that he could work under big Hollywood studios and importantly showed that he was capable of working within budget, and within schedule. Indeed, considering that the 1980s had begun with Michael Cimino's *Heaven's Gate* fiasco (the film's burgeoning budget and out of control schedule had bankrupted United Artists), being able to keep within schedule was a quality particularly appreciated in Hollywood. This ability meant that Hollywood studios were keen on proposing Weir direct challenging projects, as in the case of *The Truman Show*, where the presence of Jim Carrey in his first dramatic role required a more experienced director than Andrew Niccol. In this respect, Weir's record with Robin Williams in *Dead Poets Society* proved to be fundamental.

Weir had acquired this capability of working within budget and schedule during his Australian career, and this is another testimony of the fact that the roots of Weir's success in America lie in his Australian years. Another characteristic that Weir gained while working in Australia, which made him appealing for Hollywood, was his ability to work with stars and to bring out of them award-winning performances, as he did with Linda Hunt in *The Year of Living Dangerously*. In fact, and this is another similarity that the Australian and the Hollywood production context share, in Australia Weir had the opportunity of working with actors that, at the time, were well-known international stars such as Richard Chamberlain in *The Cars that Ate Paris*, Rachel Roberts in *Picnic at Hanging Rock*, Mel Gibson in both *Gallipoli* and *The Year of Living Dangerously*, and, in the latter, also Sigourney Weaver.

I have carried out the textual analysis of Weir's films within the broader framework of transnational cinema theories and I have interrogated if, following the assumptions of these theories, Peter Weir's films can be considered transnational. I have pointed out that film scholars agree in considering transnational the cinema that deals with transnational issues, and I have highlighted that the latter concern the displacement of individuals uprooted from their national context and/or diaspora.

The analysis of the films has confirmed that a common thematic element in the films that Weir has directed, is, as scholars have pointed out, the struggle of the individual against the social environment in which he lives and that can be combined with a battle that he has to undertake against the forces of nature, as in the case of *Picnic*. I have argued that the conflicts the protagonists in Weir's films face can also be seen as a form of displacement that takes place within the specific boundaries of one community. All of the characters in the four films analysed experience a form of displacement: the girls in picnic find it difficult to cope with the demands of a Victorian education; *Witness*' John Book understands that he will never be able to fit within the Amish community, and Truman lives a completely made up existence.

I have concluded that the only characters that experience a form of displacement across two different national boundaries are Guy Hamilton in *The Year of Living Dangerously* and the protagonists on *The Way Back*. In other words, *Year* is the only film that treats transnational issues in the sense highlighted by scholars. This has in turn raised the question if, given that his films do not strictly treat transnational issues, Weir can be considered a transnational filmmaker. I have argued that, to answer this question, it is not sufficient to analyse the themes of Weir's films, but it also ought to be taken into consideration if the production context of Weir's films can be considered transnational.

In this respect, I have argued that, once again, the only truly transnational film that Weir has directed is *The Year of Living Dangerously*, which has characteristics of both Hollywood and Australian productions. At first, therefore, it appears that Peter Weir cannot be considered a transnational director. However, I have argued that a transnational director is not only a director that treats transnational issues in his films, but is also a director that has managed to work successfully within two production contexts. In this respect, Weir is a transnational director. Weir is not only a representative of the Australian film revival, as scholars have repeatedly pointed out, but also an established Hollywood filmmaker, as I have argued; in other terms, he is not only a director that has worked successfully within two production contexts, but he is also a director that continues to work successfully across two productions contexts.

In fact, my book has highlighted that, if it is true that Weir is professionally based in Hollywood, it is equally true that he continues not only to live in Australia, but also to work on the post-production of his films from Australia. In this light, Weir ought to be considered a part-time transnational filmmaker.

The fact that I have identified more similarities than differences between Weir's Australian and Hollywood productions, on the one hand goes against the expectations that I had when I started this work, as aforementioned at the beginning of these conclusions, and on the other hand brings to the fore the necessity of continuing to research the issue of migrations of contemporary foreign filmmakers to Hollywood. This book, indeed, constitutes only the beginning in what should be a new area of research in the field of film studies that requires further investigation. I am aware that this is not the only study which investigates the migration of filmmakers to Hollywood, but such studies have on the one hand being limited to past migrations or, as far as migrations of contemporary filmmakers is concerned, have been limited to journal articles or newspaper interviews.

Researching Peter Weir's passage to Hollywood has made me aware that the stream of filmmakers moving to Hollywood, either on a permanent or on a part-time basis, has never been interrupted: it is the academic studies on such migrations that need to be further investigated.

Notes

1. See Tom O'Regan, *Australian National Cinema*, London and New York: Routledge, 1996.
2. Personal communication, January 12, 2006.
3. See Scott Murray, 'Hal and James McElroy. Producers', Cinema Papers, n. 14,1977, 148–150, 183; 'Hal and James McElroy. Producers', Cinema Papers, Cannes Special, n. 16, 1978, 36–39; "Informal Discussion with Jim and Hal McElroy and Peter Weir", Cinema Papers, n. 1, 1974, 20–21; 'Interview with Jim McElroy. Producer', *Cinema Papers*, n. 1, 1974, 21–22; and 'Hal and Jim McElroy', *Cinema Papers*, n. 79, 1990, 13–17, 66–70.
4. Scott Murray, 'Hal and Jim McElroy', *Cinema Papers*, n. 79, May 1990, 14–17, 66–70.
5. Vertical Helical Scan, also know as Video Home System.
6. See Chapter 5, note 159.
7. Personal communication, 12 January 2006.
8. Paramount Pictures, *How is it Going to End? The Making of The Truman Show.* 'Truman Show's Special Collector's Edition', 2005. Interviews with actors and actresses who have worked with Weir over the years all suggest that Weir is capable of establishing very positive relationships, that actors consider it a privilege to work with Weir, and that they would recommend the experience to any actor. See, for instance, interviews with Laura Linney and Ed Harris in ibid.; Mel Gibson, in Marcia Magill, 'Peter Weir', *Film in Review*, vol. 32, n. 8, October 1981, 479. See also Colin Dangaard, 'Sigourney Living Dangerously in the Philippines', *Photoplay*, vol. 34, n. 6, 1983, 17; Gerard Depardieu in Kitty Bowe Hearty, 'French Connection', *Premiere*, vol. 4, n. 6, 1991, 62.

9. Incidentally, one of the arguments used to indicate whether a director is an auteur is to look at who is actually the author of the script and whether this is original. Looking at the fourteen films that Weir has directed which have reached theatrical release, Weir is credited as sole author of the – original – script only in the case of *Green Card*. Moreover, the majority of films directed by Peter Weir both in Australia and in Hollywood are actually adaptations from literary novels.

Bibliography

Books

Bertrand, Ina and William D. Routt (eds), *The Story of the Kelly Gang. The Picture that Will Live Forever*, St Kilda, Victoria: The Moving Image, 2007.

Bliss, Michael, *Dreams within a Dream. The Films of Peter Weir*, Carbondale and Edwardsville, IL: Southern Illinois University Press, 2000.

Bordwell, David and Kristin Thompson, *Film Art. An Introduction*, 7th Edition, New York: McGraw-Hill, 2004.

Caputo, Raffaele and Geoff Burton (eds), *Second Take. Australian Film-makers Talk*, St Leonards, NSW: Allen & Unwin, 1999.

Caputo, Raffaele and Geoff Burton (eds), *Third Take. Australian Filmmakers Talk*, St Leonards, NSW: Allen & Unwin, 2002.

Cavaliero, Roderick, *Italia Romantica: English Romantics and Italian Freedom*, London: I.B. Tauris, 2005, http://site.ebrary.com/lib/uon/Doc?id=10132932&ppg=22.

Cook, David A., *A History of Narrative Film*, New York: Norton & Co., 2003.

Dermody, Susan and Elisabeth Jacka, *The Screening of Australia. Anatomy of a Film Industry. Volume 1*, Sydney: Currency Press, 1987.

Dermody, Susan and Elisabeth Jacka, *The Screening of Australia. Anatomy of a National Cinema. Volume 2*, Sydney: Currency Press, 1988.

Giltaij, Jeroen and de Leeuw, Ronald, *The Dutch Golden Age Book*, Zwolle: Waanders Publishers, 2004.

Gleeson, James, *Colonial Painters 1788–1880*, Dee Why West, NSW: Lansdowne, 1979.

Grainge, Paul, Mark Jancovich and Sharon Monteith, *Film Histories. An Introduction and Reader*, Edinburgh: Edinburgh University Press, 2007.

Gray, Anne (ed.), *Australian Art in the National Gallery of Australia*, Melbourne: National Gallery of Australia, 2002.

Haak, Bob, *The Golden Age. Dutch Painters of the Seventeenth Century*, Zwolle: Wandeers Publishers, 2003.

Haltof, Marek, *Peter Weir. When Cultures Collide*, New York: Twayne Publishers, 1996.

Langman, Larry, *Destination Hollywood. The Influence of Europeans on American Filmmaking*, Jefferson, NC: McFarland & Company, 1999.

Levy, Emanuel, *Cinema of Outsiders: the Rise of American Independent Film*, New York: New York University Press, 1999.

LoBrutto, Vincent, *Sound-on-Film. Interviews with Creators of Film Sound*, Westport, CT, and London: Praeger, 1994.

Lovell, Alan and Gianluca Sergi, *Making Films in Contemporary Hollywood*, London: Hodder Arnold, 2005.

Mathews, Sue, *35mm Dreams*, Ringwood, Victoria: Penguin Books Australia, 1984.

Mayer, Geoff and Keith Beattie, *The Cinema of Australia and New Zealand*, London: Wallflower Press, 2007.

McFarlane, Brian, *Australian Cinema 1970–1985*, London: Secker & Warburg, 1987.

McFarlane, Brian, *Words and Images. Australian Novels into Films*, Richmond, Victoria: Heinemann Publishers Australia in association with Cinema Papers, 1983.

McFarlane, Brian and Geoff Mayer, *New Australian Cinema. Sources and Parallels in American and British Films*, Cambridge: Cambridge University Press, 1992.

Merchant, Ismail, *My Passage from India: A Filmmaker's Journey from Bombay to Hollywood and Beyond*, New York: Viking Studio, 2002.

Miller, Toby, Nitin Govil, John McMurrin, Richard Maxwell and Ting Wang. *Global Hollywood 2*, London: British Film Institute, 2005.

Morrison, James, *Passport to Hollywood. Hollywood Films, European Directors*, New York: State of New York University Press, 1998.

Murray, Scott (ed.), *Australian Cinema. Australian Directors Overseas 1970–1992*, Sydney: Allen & Unwin in association with the Australian Film Commission, 1994, 149–177.

Murray, Scott, Raffaele Caputo and Alissa Tanskaya, *Australian Film 1978–1994. A Survey of Theatrical Features*, Oxford and New York: Oxford University Press and Cinema Papers (Melbourne), 1995.

Nacify, Hamid, *An Accented Cinema. Exilic and Diasporic Filmmaking*, Princeton and Oxford: Princeton University Press, 2001.

O'Regan, Tom, *Australian National Cinema*, London and New York: Routledge, 1996.

Peeters, Theo, *Peter Weir and His Films: a Critical Biography*, Melbourne: Australian Film Institute Research & Information, 1983.

Perkins, Victor F., *Film As Film. Understanding and Judging Movies*, London: Penguin, 1972.

Petrie, Graham, *Before the Wall Came Down: Soviet and East European Filmmakers Working in the West*, London: University Press of America, 1990.

Petrie, Graham, *Hollywood Destinies: European Directors in America, 1922–1931*, Detroit: Wayne State University Press, 2001.

Phillips, Gene D., *Exiles in Hollywood. Major European Film Directors in America.* Bethlehem, PA: Lehigh University Press; London: Associated University Press, 1998.

Prince, Stephen, *A New Pot of Gold: Hollywood Under the Electronic Rainbow, 1980–1989.* London and Los Angeles: University of California Press, 2000.

Rayner, Jonathan, *Contemporary Australian Cinema. An Introduction*, Manchester and New York: Manchester University Press, 2000.

Rayner, Jonathan, *The Films of Peter Weir*, 2nd Edition, New York and London: Continuum, 2003.

Schafer, Dennis and Larry Salvato, *Masters of Light. Conversations with Contemporary Cinematographers*, Berkeley and Los Angeles: University of California Press, 1984.

Sergi, Gianluca, *The Dolby Era. Film Sound in Contemporary Hollywood*, Manchester: Manchester University Press, 2004.

Shiach, Don, *The Films of Peter Weir. Visions of Alternative Realities*, London: Letts, 1993.

Shirley, Graham and Brian Adams, *Australian Cinema. The First Eighty Years*, Sydney: Angus & Robertson and Currency Press, 1983.

Stratton, David, *The Last New Wave: The Australian Film Revival*, London: Angus & Robertson, 1980.

Thompson, Kristin and David Bordwell, *Film History. An Introduction*, 2nd Edition, New York: McGraw Hill, 2002.

Françoise Truffaut, *Alfred Hitchcock. A Definitive Study of Alfred Hitchcock*, New York: Simon & Schuster, 1985.

Turner, Graeme, *National Fictions. Literature, Film and the Construction of Australian Narrative*, St Leonards, NSW: Allen and Unwin, 1993.

Waldman, Harry and Anthony Slide, *Hollywood and the Foreign Touch: A Dictionary of Foreign Filmmakers and their Films from America, 1910–1995*, Metuchen, NJ, and London: Scarecrow Press, 1996.

Wollstein, Hans J., *Strangers in Hollywood: The History of Scandinavian Actors in American Film from 1910 to World War II*, Metuchen, NJ, and London: Scarecrow Press, 1994.

Zollo, Paul, *Hollywood Remembered. An Oral History of its Golden Age*, New York: Cooper Square Press, 2002.

Book chapters

Appadurai, Arjun, 'Disjuncture and Difference in the Global Cultural Economy', in Xavier Jonathan Inda and Rosaldo Renato (eds), *The Anthropology of Globalization. A Reader*, Oxford: Blackwell, 2002, 584–603.

Balio, Tino, 'A Major Presence in All of the World's Important Markets': The Globalization of Hollywood in the 1990s', in Steve Neale and Murray Smith (eds), *Contemporary Hollywood Cinema*, New York: Routledge, 2000, 59–63.

Ezra, Elizabeth and Rowden Terry, 'General Introduction. What is Transnational Cinema?' in Elizabeth Ezra and Terry Rowden (eds), *Transnational Cinema. The Film Reader*, London and New York: Routledge, 2006, 1–12.

Elmer, Greg and Mike Gasher, 'Introduction: Catching Up to Runaway Productions', in Greg Elmer and Mike Gasher (eds), *Contracting out Hollywood. Runaway Productions and Foreign Location Shooting*, Lanham. MD: Rowan & Littlefield, 2005, 1–18.

Higson, Andrew, 'The Limiting Imagination of National Cinema', in Elizabeth Ezra and Terry Rowden (eds), *Transnational Cinema. The Film Reader*, London and New York: Routledge, 2006, 15–25.

O'Regan, Tom, 'Profilo storico e nuove tendenze del Cinema Australiano', in Brunetta Gian Piero (ed.), *Storia Del Cinema Mondiale*, vol. IV, Torino: Einaudi, 2001, 1037–1098.

O'Regan, Tom, 'A National Cinema', in Graeme Turner (ed.), *The Film Cultures Reader*, London: Routledge, 2002, 139–164.

Weir, Peter, 'Gallipoli. Shooting History', in Patty O'Brien and Bruce Vaughn (eds), *Amongst Friends. Australian and New Zealand Voices from America*, Dunedin: University of Otago Press, 2005, 54.

Weir, Peter, 'The Director's Voice 2', in Raffaele Caputo and Geoff Burton (eds), *Third Take. Australian Filmmakers Talk*, Australia: Allen & Unwin, 2002, 56–64.

Winer, Robert, '*Witness*ing and Bearing *Witness*: the Ontogeny of Encounter in the Films of Peter Weir', in Joseph H. Smith and William Kerrigan (eds), *Images in Our Souls: Cavell, Psychoanalysis and Cinema*, London: Johns Hopkins University Press, 1987, 82–96.

Articles

Adept, Michael, 'Under the Influence: Peter Weir's *The Year of Living Dangerously*', http://www.dga.org/news/v27_1/indie_peterweir.php3, February 10, 2005.

Anon, 'Amish Feelings Mixed over Filming of Movie', *The New York Times*, June 7, 1984.

Anon, 'First Aussie Film Backed by US Major', *Screen International*, n. 380, February 5, 1983, 6.

Anon, 'Jim McElroy', *Films and Filming*, vol. 23, n. 6, 1977, 36.

Anon, 'Lovell Slams "Quick Buck" Producers', *Screen International*, n. 312, 1981, 42–43.

Anon, 'Milos Forman: Hollywood est comme une pyramide pour un architecte!', *Ciné-Revue*, vol. 65, n. 22, Cannes Special, May 30, 1985, xiv–xv.

Anon, 'New 'Dangerously' Booking Causes Stir', *Daily Variety*, March 16, 1983, 2.

Anon, 'Weir Tries to Keep That 'Fragile Spark' Intact', *Screen International*, n. 187, 1979, 30.

Anon, 'Weir, Peter', *Current Biography*, August 1984, 41–44.

Anon, '*Witness*. A Dutch Treat', *Los Angeles*, March 1985.

Barber, Susan, 'Neil Rattigan, Images of Australia: 100 Films of the New Australia', *Film Quarterly*, vol. 46, n. 3, Spring 1993, 60–61.

Barber, Susan, 'O'Regan, Tom. Australian National Cinema', *Film Quarterly*, vol. 51, n. 4, 1998, http://www.jstor.org/view/.

Bennet, Ray, 'Finding Direction in Life', *Hollywood Reporter*, March 11, 1991, S-14.

Benson, Sheila, 'Movie Reviews: Unholy Innocents Abroad in the World. '*Witness*': A Gorgeous Look, but the Script Falls Short', *Los Angeles Times*, February 2, 1985, 1, 16.

Birchard, S. Robert, 'John Seale, ACS', *American Cinematographer*, vol. 67, n. 4, 1986, 74–76, 78.

Blackwelder, Rob, '*Truman*'s Director Tells about Making Jim Carrey's First Serious Film', April 20, 1998, http://robio.netwiz.net/features/weir.html.

Boland, Michaela, 'Australia Has Incentive to do Business. New Budget Sets Local Rebates', *Weekly Variety*, May 14, 2007, http://www.variety.com/article/VR1117964789.html?categoryid=1019&cs=1&query=Cate+Blanchett&query=australia+has+incentive+to+do+business.

Boyd, Russell, 'Russell Boyd. *Picnic at Hanging Rock*', *American Cinematographer*, n. 9, September 9, 1976, 1038–1039.

Brennan, Judy, "Cable Guy' Gets $20.5-Million Reception', *The Los Angeles Times*, March 3, 1996, http://articles.latimes.com/1996-06-17/entertainment/ca-15803_1_cable-guy.

Brennan, Richard, 'Peter Weir', *Cinema Papers*, n. 1, 1974, 16–17.

Brillon, Nathalie, "Mexicans with Parkas and Mobile Phones", Transnational Cinema at Hollywood's Edge', *Screening the Past*, 2008, http://www.latrobe.edu.au/screeningthepast/19/mexicans-parkas-mobiles.html.

Broeske, H. Pat, 'Keeping up with the Indiana Joneses', *Cinema Papers* , n. 51, 1985, 31–34.

Busch, Anita M., 'New 'Truman' Villain: Harris', *Variety*, April 7, 1995.

Busch, Anita M. and Beth Lasky, 'Carrey Caught in $20 mil 'Liar', *Daily Variety*, August 7, 1995, 1, 40.

Bygrave, Mike, 'Down Under in L.A.', *Still*, n. 19, 1985, 46–49.

Byrge, Duane, '*Green Card*', *The Hollywood Reporter*, vol. 325, n. 30, 1990, 6, 46.

Campbell, Virginia, 'Love, Fear and Peter Weir', *Movieline*, September 1993, http://www.peterweircave.com/articles/articleb.html.

Campbell, Virginia, 'Poetry in Motion Pictures', *Movieline*, June 9, 1989, 20–22, 56–57.

Canby, Vincent, 'Film: *Last Wave*. Storm of Occultism: Mysticism Down Under', *New York Times*, December 19, 1978, http://movies2.nytimes.com/mem/movies/review.html?_r=1&title1=Last%20Wave%2c%20The%20%28Movie%29&title2=&reviewer=VINCENT%20CANBY&pdate=19781219&v_id=28407&oref=slogin.

Canby, Vincent, 'Chilling Truths about Scaring', *The New York Times*, January 21, 1979, 13, 18.

Canby, Vincent, 'Screen: Australian Hawthorne Romance', *The New York Times*, February 23, 1979, c14.

Canby, Vincent, 'Film. *Witness.* A Tough Guy Among the Amish', *The New York Times*, February 8, 1985, http://movies.nytimes.com/movie/review?_r=1&res=9903E6DD1739F93BA35751C0A963948260&scp=2&sq=*WITNESS*+CANBY+WEIR&st=nyt&oref=slogin.

Canby, Vincent, 'Film: *Mosquito Coast*, with Harrison Ford', *The New York Times*, November 26, 1986.

Canby, Vincent, 'Robin Williams as Hip Mr. Chips', *The New York Times*, June 2, 1989, B1, B9.

Caro, Jason, '*The Truman Show*', *Film Review*, July 1998, 12.

Champlin, Charles, 'Peter Weir: In a Class by Himself', *Los Angeles Times*, June, 4, 1989, 3, 20, 23.

Champlin, Charles, "Poets' Patronage Outclassing Summer Wisdom', *Los Angeles Times*, June 8, 1989, 1, 3

Christon, Lawrence, 'Daviau's Vision Makes Him One for the Ages. ACS Lifetime Achievement Award', *Variety*, February 13, 2007, http://www.variety.com/awardcentral_article/VR1117959421.html?nav=news&categoryid=1985&cs=1&query=allen+daviau.

Chung, Pei-Chi, 'Asian Filmmakers Moving into Hollywood: Genre Regulation and Auteur Aesthetics', *Asian Cinema*, vol. II, n. 1, 2000, 33–50.

Ciment, Michael, 'Entretien avec Peter Weir', *Positif*, n. 314, 1987, 23–28.

Clancy, Jack, 'The Plumber', *Cinema Papers*, n. 23, 1979, 569, 571.

Cossa, Frank, *Lost Girls, Dead Poets, Last Waves: Twenty Years of Living Dangerously in the Films of Peter Weir*, http://www.finearts.uwaterloo.ca/juhde/cossa982.htm.

Combs Richard, '*Picnic at Hanging Rock*', *Monthly Film Bulletin*, vol. 43, n. 512, 1976, 196–197.

Craven, Jenny, '*Picnic at Hanging Rock*', *Film and Filming*, vol. 23, n. 3, 1976, 31–32.

Dalton, Stephen, 'Film Choice. *Fearless*', *The Times*, October 5, 2004.

Dangaard, Colin, 'Sigourney Living Dangerously in the Philippines', *Photoplay*, vol. 34, n. 6, 1983, 16–17.

Daws, '*Dead Poets Society*', *Daily Variety*, May 3, 1989, 2.

Decaux, Emmanuel and Bruno Villien, 'Entretien avec Peter Weir', *Cinematograph*, May 15, 1983, 25–27.

Diehl, Digby, 'The Iceman Cometh', *American Film*, vol. XII, n. 3, December 1986, 20–24, 49–50.

Digby Diehl, 'The Road to Belize', *American Film Bulletin*, vol. XII, n. 3, 1986, 23–24.

Dobson, Patricia, 'Saul Zaentz', *Screen International*, n. 1051, 1996, 36.

Duke, Paul F., 'Weir Likely to 'Master' Helm for Fox Voyage', *Variety*, August 10, 2000, http://www.variety.com/article/VR1117784874.html?categoryid=13&cs=1&query =fearless+peter+weir.

Ebert, Roger, 'Hardcore', *Chicago Sunday Times*, January 1, 1979 http://rogerebert.suntimes.com/apps/pbcs.dll/article?AID=/19790101/REVIEWS/901010314/1023.

Ebert, Roger, '*The Truman Show*', *Chicago Sunday Times*, June 5, 1998, http://rogerebert.suntimes.com/apps/pbcs.dll/article?AID=/19980605/REVIEWS/806050302/1023.

Edelstein, David, 'When Worlds Collide', *Voice*, vol. XXX , n. 7, 1985.

Eyman, Scott, 'The Swat Team', *Moviegoer*, December 1986, 6–7.

Ferguson, Ken, 'Why Weir Decided on a Piece of 'Weir-d' Casting', *Photoplay*, vol. 34, n. 9, 1983, 4.

Fieschi, Jaques (ed.), 'Dossier: L'Europe à Hollywood I: L'Age D'or ', *Cinematograph*, n. 65, 1981, 1–44.

Fieschi, Jaque (ed.), 'Dossier: Europe-USA II', *Cinematograph*, n. 66, 1981, 1–62.

Fleming, Michael, 'Rudin Enters Spec Fray', *Daily Variety*, October 8, 1993, 1, 31.

Fleming, Michael, 'Shantaram Shuffling', *Variety*, July 11, 2006, http://www.variety.com/article/VR1117945086.html?categoryid=13&cs=1&query=weir+shantaram.

Goldman, M.R., 'Russell Boyd. Master and Commander: The Far Side of the World', *Variety*, January 12, 2004.

Gray, Simon, 'Hell or High Water', *American Cinematographer*, vol. 84, n. 11, 2003, 50–63.

Groves, Don, 'The Year of Living Dangerously', *Daily Variety*, December 16, 1982, 3, 31.

Groves, Don, "Hicks' pic is Oz helmers' pick', *Weekly Variety*, May 31, 2004, http://www.variety.com/search/siteall?q=Goldman+M+R+master+and+commander&s=relevance.

Groves, Don, 'Aussie Sound Biz Sets Up in Beijing. Company is Co-Venture with China Film Assist', *Weekly Variety*, October 27, 2003.

Gupta, Akhil, 'The Song of the Nonaligned World: Transnational Identities and the reinscription of Space in Late Capitalism', *Cultural Anthropology*, vol. 7, n. 1, February 1992, 63–79.

Ulf Hannarez, 'Flows, Boundaries and Hybrids: Keywords in Transnational Anthropology', in Ali Rogers (ed.), *Transnational Communities Programme Working Paper Series*, published in Portuguese as 'Fluxos, fronteiras, híbridos: palavras-chave da antropologia transnacional', *Mana*, Rio de Janeiro, vol. 3, n. 1, 1997, 7–39.

Haltof, Marek, 'In Quest of Self-Identity. *Gallipoli*, Mateship, and the Construction of Australian National Identity', *Journal of Popular Film & TV*, vol. 21, n. 1 Spring 1993, 27–36.

Harcourt, Tim, *Hollywood Stars Bring Export Wins Back Home*, March 1, 2004, http://www.austrade.gov.au/corporate/layout/0,,0_S1-1_CORPXID0029-2_-3_PWB110419027-4_-5_-6_-7_,00.html.

Harden, Fred, 'Talking Film Stock', *Cinema Papers*, May 1989, 52–55.

Hentzi, Gary, 'Peter Weir and the Cinema of New Age Humanism', *Film Quarterly*, vol. 44, n. 2, 1980, 2–12.

Hill, Robert, 'Moments to '*Witness*'. Writing Team Tackles Amish Territory', *Paramount Picture Corporation News*, 1985, 9.

Hollie, Pamela G., 'Threats to 'Living Dangerously' Come too Close for Comfort', *New York Times*, April 13, 1982, 20.

Houlton, John, 'Movies LA', *The Pact Magazine*, n. 54, 1996, 6.

Hunter, Allan, 'Harrison Ford', *Films and Filming*, n. 389, 1987, 24–26.

Hutton, Anne B., 'Nationalism in Australian Cinema', *Cinema Papers,* April–May 1976, 97–100, 152.

Jacobs, Diane, 'His Subject. Mysteries of Different Cultures', *New York Times*, January 14, 1979, 17, 26.

Javes, Sue, 'Box-Office Hit 'an Aussie Movie'', *The Sun Herald*, June 2, 1985, 1.

Kael, Pauline, 'The Current Cinema. Doused', *The New Yorker*, January 22, 1979, 102–103.

Kafka, Hans, 'What Our Immigration Did for Hollywood and Vice Versa', *New German Critique. Film and Exile*, n. 89, 2003, 185–189.

Kalb, Bernard, 'Cinematic Art vs. Reality in Indonesia', *New York Times*, January 23, 1983 17, 22.

Kapitanoff, Nancy, 'The Peter Weir Show', *Pulse!*, July 1998, 89.

Kirk, Ellis, '*Witness* Offers Moviegoers Glimpse of Ford's Acting Talent', *Hollywood Reporter*, January 25, 1985, 3, 34.

Klain, Stephen, 'McElroy's Pleasure: Australians Recognize Value of the Producer', *Variety*, January 10, 1979, 4, 64.

Kroll, Jack, 'A City Cop in Amish Country', *Newsweek*, February 11, 1985.

Lee, Nora, 'Mosquito Coast: A Jungle Utopia Gone Awry', *American Cinematographer*, vol. 68, n. 2, 1987, 60–65.

Lee, Nora, '*Dead Poets Society*', *American Cinematographer*, vol. 70, n. 9, 1989. 88.

Magill, Marcia, 'Peter Weir', *Film in Review*, vol. 32, n. 8, October 1981, 474–475, 478–479.

Mann, Roderick, 'Peter Weir Pays *Witness* to the Amish', *Los Angeles Times*, January 27, 1985, 17.

Markfield, Alan. 'Dangerously Was Too True for Crew', *Los Angeles Times*, June 6, 1982, 23–24.

Maslin, Janet, 'Sleeping Dogs', *The New York Times*, February 28, 1982, http://movies.nytimes.com/movie/45162/Sleeping-Dogs/overview.

Maslin, Janet, '*Barbarosa*, Australian-directed Western', *The New York Times*, July 25, 1982, http://movies.nytimes.com/movie/review?res=9B04E7D71038F936A15754C0A964948260.

Maslin, Janet, 'Cooper Film an Inspiration for *Witness*', *New York Times*, February 8, 1985, 20.

McCarthy, Todd, '*The Truman Show*', *Variety*, April 27, 1998, www.variety.com/review/VE1117477427?categoryid=31&cs=1 (last accessed 4 May 2008).

McElroy, James, 'Jim McElroy', *Films and Filming*, vol. 23, n. 6, 1977, 36.

McFarlan, Brian, 'The Films of Peter Weir', *Cinema Papers*, n. 26, 1980, 1–24.

McGilligan, Pat, 'Under Weir ... and Theroux', *Film Comment*, n. 22, 1986, 23–32.

McGrath, Ben, 'Wicked Wind', *The New Yorker*, October 20, 2003, newyorker.com/fact/content/?031020fa_fact1.

McGregor, Alex, 'Seale Settles down after Three Solid Years', *Encore*, November 20–December 10, 1983.

Milliken, Robert, 'Cinematographers' Shot at Stardom. AFI Awards', *The National Times*, September 28–October 4, 1984, 32.

Milne, Tom, '*Picnic at Hanging Rock*', *Sight and Sound*, vol. 45, n. 4, Autumn 1976, 257.

Milvy, Erika, 'Paramount Shows Creative Use of the Web with Site to Free Truman', *Los Angeles Times*, June 25, 1998.

Moerk, Christian, Evan Frook John, O'Steen Kathleen and Michael Fleming, 'Rudin Picks up spec script', *Weekly Variety*, October 25, 1993.

Muellery, Matt, 'The Films of Peter Weir: Visions of Alternative Realities' *Empire*, n. 48, June 1993, 105.

Muńoz, Lorenza and Johnson Reed, 'Mexico's Creative Brain Drain', *Los Angeles Times*, February 24, 2007, http://www.latimes.com/entertainment/news/business/la-fi-mexfilm24feb24,1,4528084.story.

Murray, Scott and Gordon Glenn, 'Production Report. *The Cars That Ate Paris*. Informal Discussion with Jim and Hal McElroy and Peter Weir', *Cinema Papers*, n. 1, 1974, 20–21.

Nichols, Peter, 'In Peter Weir's Whodunit, an Otherworldly Force Did', *The New York Times*, November 1, 1998, 34.

Osswald, Dieter, 'Boat Person. Wolfgang Petersen, Director', *Cinema Papers*, n. 57, 1989, 25.

Park, James, "*Witness*' Kicks Off Cannes Fest', *Variety*, May 5, 1985.

Perez, Christopher, 'Gibson and Weaver Live '*Dangerously*' With Roles', *Daily Trojan* (University of Southern California), February 17, 1983, 8.

Pierce, Nev, 'Master and Commander: The Far Side of the World', November 27, 2003, http://www.bbc.co.uk/films/2003/11/18/master_and_commander_2003_review.shtml.

Pollock, Dale, 'Weir Escalates Aussie Film Invasion', *Los Angeles Times*, August 23, 1981, 31–32.

Powers, John, 'No Buzz, No Bite', *Los Angeles Weekly*, December 5–11, 1986, 51.

Prouty, Howard, 'Peter Weir. Director', *The American Film Institute*, 1985.

Reuters, "Truman' suit filed. Playwright files suit against Par', *Variety*, June 17, 1998, http://www.variety.com/article/VR1117471916.html?categoryid=13&cs=1&query=the+truman+show (accessed 18 June, 2008).

Rhodes, Tom, 'Writer to sue for $200m over 'copycat' Carrey film', *The Sunday Times*, September 27, 1998, 22.

Robbins, Jim, 'Manila Filming of Weir Pic Fees MGM-UA Coin', *Daily Variety*, January 20, 1983, 18.

Roddick, Nick, 'Among the Amish. *Witness*', *Sight and Sound*, vol. 54, n. 3, 1985, 221–222.

Rudolf, Eric, 'This Is Your Life', *American Cinematographer*, vol. 79, n. 6, 1998, 74–85.

Russell, Jamie, 'Paul Bettany and Master and Commander',http://www.bbc.co.uk/films/2003/11/18/paul_bettany_master_commander_interview.shtml.

Ryan, Tom and McFarlane Brian, 'Peter Weir: Towards the Centre', *Cinema Papers*, n. 34, September–October 1981, 323–329.

John of Salisbury, *Metalogicon*, vol. 3, translation in Henry Osborn Taylor, '*The Mediaeval Mind*', vol. 2, 1919, 159, http://en.wikiquote.org/wiki/John_of_Salisbury.

Sampson, Sally and Vidal-Hall Judith, 'Milos Forman. It's Good Out in the Jungle', *Index on Censorship*, vol. 24, n. 6, 1995, 129–135.

Springer, Claudia, 'Comprehension and Crisis: Reporter Films and the Third World', in Lester D. Friedman (ed.), *Unspeakable Images: Ethnicity and the American Cinema*, Urbana and Chicago: University of Illinois Press.

Stanley, Raymond, 'World News. Australia', *Screen International*, n. 312, October 1981.

Schickel, Richard, 'Harrison's Heart of Darkness', *Time Magazine*, December 1, 1986, 167–189.

Schiller, Nina Glick, Linda Basch and Cristina Szanton Blanc, 'From Immigrant to Transmigrant: Theorizing Transnational Migration', *Anthropological Quarterly*, vol. 68, n. 1, 1995, 48–63.

Silverman, Jeff, 'Harrison Ford Takes off his Fedora and Turns Humble', *Los Angeles Herald Examiner*, February 7, 1985, col. 1, b-7.

Sims, Calvin, 'The Media Business. "Synergy": The Unspoken Word', October 5, 1993, http://select.nytimes.com/search/restricted/article?res=F00616FB3A5A0C768CDDA90994DB494D81.

Smith, Margaret, 'Mel Gibson', *Cinema Papers*, n. 42, 1983, 13–17.

Sohn, Ira, 'An Opinion: The Politics of Poverty in *Living Dangerously*'s Indonesia', *Los Angeles Weekly*, April 15–21, 1983, 4, 40, 49, 51.

Southgate, Martha, '*Fearless*' Flying', *Premiere (USA)*, vol. 7, n. 2, 1993, 50–53.

Spines, Christine, 'Peter Weir. The Director of *The Truman Show* Discusses the Very Real Manipulations of Moviemaking', *Premiere*, 1998, 39–41.

Spines, Christine, 'Peter Weir', *Premiere*, July 1998, 40.

Spring, Lory, 'The Other Dream: *The Year of Living Dangerously*', *Cineaction!* n. 3/4, 1986, 58–71.

Steuer, Joseph and Cathy Dunkley, 'Truman Show Elects Hopper', *Hollywood Reporter*, October 4, 1994.

Stratton, David, 'Three to Go', *Variety*, April 1, 1979, 24.

Sutcliff, Phil, 'Maurice Jarre. Composer', *Empire*, n. 38, 1992, 46.

Thomas, Kevin, '"Cars That Eat People" in Long Beach', *Los Angeles Times*, September 21, 1979, 24.

Thomas, Kevin, 'Peter Weir Climbs Hollywood Beanstalk', *Los Angeles Times*, August 30, 1979.

Tulich, Katherine, 'Peter Weir', *Cinema Papers*, vol. 80, 1990, 7–10.

Ventura, Michael, 'Hollywood Shoots the Third World', *Los Angeles Weekly*, March 2–31, 1983, 24, 26–30.

Ventura, Michael, 'The Angels of Peter Weir', *Los Angeles Weekly*, August 3–9, 1979, 34–35.

Ventura, Michael, '*Witnessing Witness*. The Nuts and Bolts of Peter Weir', *Los Angeles Weekly*, February 8–14, 1985, 35–37, 39–40.

Ventura, Michael, 'Writing *The Last Wave*', *Los Angeles Weekly*, June 8–14, 1979, 25.

Vertovec, Steven, 'Conceiving and Researching Transnationalism', *Ethnic and Racial Studies*, vol. 22, n. 2, 1999, 1–25.

Ward, Kyla, 'Weir'd Tales', *Tabula Rasa*, n. 2, 1994, http://www.peterweircave.com/articles/tabularosa.html.

Weinraub, Bernard, 'Director Tries a Fantasy as He Questions Reality', *The New York Times*, May 21, 1998.

Williams, Tony, 'From Hong Kong to Hollywood. John Woo and His Discontents', *Cine Action*, n. 42, 1996, 40–46.

Dissertations

Behlil, Melis, 'Home away from home: global directors of new Hollywood', Unpublished PhD thesis, University of Amsterdam, 2007.

O'Regan, Tom, 'The politics of representation. An analysis of the Australian film revival', Unpublished PhD thesis, Griffith University, 1985.

Press releases and production information

Atlantic Releasing Corporation, '*Picnic at Hanging Rock*', Press Kit, Exclusive Los Angeles Premiere, July 19, 1979.

Atlantic Releasing Corporation, '*Picnic at Hanging Rock*', Press Release, July 19, 1979.

CBS Television Network, '*Witness* to be broadcast on 'CBS Sunday Movie'', Press Release, April 18, 1989.

Metro Goldwin Mayer '*The Year of Living Dangerously*', Press Release, December 28, 1981.

Metro Goldwin Mayer, '*The Year of Living Dangerously*', Press Kit, December 7, 1982.

Metro Goldwin Mayer, '*The Year of Living Dangerously*'. Preliminary Production Notes, 1982.

Metro Goldwin Mayer, 'Peter Weir and Mel Gibson to U.S. and Canada for *The Year of Living Dangerously*', Press Release, January 13, 1983.

Paramount Pictures Corporation, '*Witness*. An Edward S. Feldman Production', Press Kit, July 1, 1985.

Paramount Pictures Corporation, '*Witness*', News Release, May 11, 1984.

Paramount Pictures Corporation, '*The Truman Show*', Production Information, 1998.

Saul Zaent Company, '*The Mosquito Coast*',. Production Information, 1986.

Reports

An Overview of Government Inquiries into the Film and Television Industry 1971–1985, Policy Unit Executive Branch, Australian Film Commission, May 1985.

Interim Report on the Australian Film Industry. A Survey of Industry Activity from October 1980 to October 1981 against the background of industry development from 1969 to 1980, The Australian Film Commission in association with all State Government Film Corporations and the Film and Television Production Association of Australia, January 15, 1982.

Interviews

Anon, 'Dialogue on Film. Peter Weir', *American Film*, vol. 11, n. 5, 1986, 13–15.

Anon, 'Excerpt from an Interview with Peter Weir', *Cinema Papers*, August 1990, http://www.peterweircave.com/articles/articlek.html.

American Society of Cinematographers, Online Chat and Open House, *Transcript of Online Chat With John Seale, ASC*, February 7, 2004, www.theasc.com/magazine.

Bliss, Michael, 'Keeping a Sense of Wonder. Interview', *Film Quarterly*, 1999, http://www.findarticles.com/p/articles/mi_m1070/is_1_53/ai_57798733.

Crowdus, Gary and Udayan Gupta, 'An Aussie in Hollywood: An Interview with Bruce Beresford', *Cinéaste*, vol. 12, n. 4, 1983, 20–25.

Delon, Michael, 'Milos Forman. A Two Part Interview (Part One)', *Film – British Federation of Film Societies*, vol. 2, n. 85, 1980, 6–7.

Delon, Michael, 'Milos Forman. A Two Part Interview (Part Two)', *Film – British Federation of Film Societies* , vol. 2, n. 86, 1980, 6–7.

Dempsey, Michael, 'Inexplicable Feelings: An Interview with Peter Weir', *Film Quarterly*, vol. 33, n. 4, 1980, 10, http://www.jstor.org/stable/1211985?&Search=yes&term=interview&term=peter&term=inexplicable&term=weir&term=feelings.

Farber, Stephen, 'Natural Dangers. A Conversation with Peter Weir', *New West*, 1979, 99–106.

Fonda Bonardi, Claudia and Peter Fonda Bonardi, 'An Interview with Peter Weir', *Cinéaste*, vol. 11, n. 4, 1982, 41–42.

Formica, Serena, 'Interview with Philip Steuer', December 23, 2005.

Formica, Serena, 'Interview with Russell Boyd', January 11, 2006.

Formica, Serena, 'Interview with Peter Weir', London, March 12, 2006.

Griffith, Nancy, 'Poetry Man', *Premiere Magazine*, July 1989, http://www.industrycentral.net/director_interviews/PW01.HTM.

McCarty, John, 'An Interview with Francis O'Brien. Producer of Award Winning Gallipoli', *Classic Images*, n. 81, 1982, 46.

Murray, Scott, 'Hal and James McElroy. Producers', *Cinema Papers*, n. 14, 1977, 148–150, 183.

Murray, Scott, 'Hal and James McElroy. Producers', *Cinema Papers, Cannes Special*, n. 16, 1978, 36–39.

Murray, Scott, 'Informal Discussion with Jim and Hal McElroy and Peter Weir', *Cinema Papers*, n. 1, 1974, 20–21.

Murray, Scott, 'Interview with Jim McElroy. Producer', *Cinema Papers*, n. 1, 1974, 21–22.

Murray, Scott, 'Interview with Ken Hammond', *Cinema Papers*, n. 1, 1974, 25–26.

Murray, Scott, 'Hal and Jim McElroy', *Cinema Papers*, n. 79, 1990, 13–17, 66–70.

Murray, Scott and Antony I. Ginnane, 'Producing Picnic. Pat Lovell', *Cinema Papers*, n. 8, 1976, 298–301, 377.

Murray, Scott and Gordon Glenn, 'Production Report. *The Cars that Ate Paris*. Interview with John McLean and Tony Tegg', *Cinema Papers*, n. 1, 1974, 22–24.

Siebert, T.W., 'Peter Weir. The Well Rounded Interview', http://www.well-rounded.com/movies/reviews/weir_intv.html.

Wiggins, John, 'Feature Film Lighting: Russell Boyd A.C.S. Interviewed by Peter Thompson', doc/57, 1984, http://www.cinematographers.nl/PaginasDoPh/boyd.htm.

Scripts and DVD sources

Anchor Bay Entertainment, *Miracles and Mercies*, 'Tender Mercies Interviews', 2002.

Guerrilla Films, *A Conversation with Barry Humphries*, 'The Adventures of Barry McKenzie', 2006.

Metro Goldwyn Mayer, *The Year of Living Dangerously*, 'Dialogue Transcript', 1982.

Metro-Goldwin-Mayer Film Co, *The Year of Living Dangerously*, Screenplay by David Williamson, from the book by C.J. Koch, using additional material from Screenplays by Alan Sharpe, Peter Weir and C. J. Koch, Second draft, August 1981.

Metro-Goldwin-Mayer Film Co, *The Year of Living Dangerously*, Screenplay by David Williamson, from the book by C.J. Koch, using additional material from Screenplays by Alan Sharpe, Peter Weir and C. J. Koch, Fourth draft, November 1981.

Niccol, Andrew and Weir, Peter, *The Trumans Show. The Shooting Script*, New York: Newmarket Press, 1998.

Paramount Pictures, *How is it Going to End? The Making of The Truman Show*, 'The Truman Show Special Collector's Edition', 2005.

Touchstone Pictures, *Pretty Woman*, 'Dialogue Transcript', 1990.

See Universal, Twentieth Century Fox and Miramax, '*Master and Commander*. Peter Weir on directing in the wake of O'Brien', *Master and Commander. The Far Side of the World*, DVD Special Features, 2003.

Internet sources

http://millimeter.com (online movie magazine).

http://movies.nytimes.com (*The New York Times*).

http://newyorker.com (*The New Yorker*).

http://site.ebrary.com (online electronic library).

http://www.afc.gov.au (Australian Film Commission).

http://www.austrade.gov.au (Australian Trade Commission).

http://www.bbc.co.uk (British Broadcasting Corporation website).

http://www.britannica.com (Encyclopaedia Britannica Online).

http://www.cinematographers.nl (Internet Encyclopedia of Cinematographer).

http://www.findarticles.com (online articles database).

http://www.finearts.uwaterloo.ca (University of Waterloo).

http://www.imdb.com (internet movie database).

http://www.industrycentral.net (provider of links to industry-related websites).

http://www.jstore.org (online journal articles database).

http://www.latimes.com (*Los Angeles Times*).

http://www.nam.gov.za (non-aligned movement).

http://www.nmm.ac.uk (National Maritime Museum, Greenwich, UK).

http://www.peterweircave.com (Collection of articles on Peter Weir).

http://www.screensound.govol.au (National Film and Sound Archive, Australia).

http://www.script-o-rama.com/movie_scripts (scripts transcripts website).

http://www.visitmalta.com/st-johns-cathedral-museum (St John's Cathedral Museum, Malta).

http://www.tcm.com (Turner Classic Movies online database).

http://www.theasc.com/magazine (American Society of Cinematography).

http://www.variety.com (*Variety* online).

Appendix I

Filmography – Main credits

	Picnic at Hanging Rock (1975)	*The Year of Living Dangerously* (1982)	*Witness* (1985)	*The Truman Show* (1998)
Producers	A. John Graves (SAFC) Patricia Lovell Hal McElroy Jim McElroy	Jim McElroy	David Bombyk Edward S. Feldman Wendy Weir (as Wendy Stites)	Edward S. Felman Andrew Niccol Lynn Pleshette Richard Luke Rothschild Scott Rudin Adam Schroeder
Company credits	The Australian Film Commission Picnic Productions Pty Ltd.	McElroy & McElroy Metro Goldwyn Mayer	Paramount Pictures Edward S. Feldman Production	Paramount Pictures Scott Rudin Productions
Main cast	Rachel Roberts Vivean Gray Helen Morse	Mel Gibson Sigourney Weaver Linda Hunt	Harrison Ford Kelly McGillis Danny Glover	Jim Carrey Laura Linney Ed Harris
Screenplay	Joan Lindsay (novel) Cliff Green (screenplay)	C.J. Koch (novel and screenplay) Peter Weir (screenplay) David Williamson (screenplay)	William Kelley (story and screenplay) Pamela Wallace (story) Earl W. Wallace (story and screenplay)	Andrew Niccol (written by)
Cinematography	Russell Boyd (camera operator John Seale, uncredited)	Russell Boyd	John Seale	Peter Biziou

	Picnic at Hanging Rock (1975)	***The Year of Living Dangerously*** (1982)	***Witness*** (1985)	***The Truman Show*** (1998)
Music	Bruce Smeaton Gheorghe Zamfir	Maurice Jarre	Maurice Jarre	Burkhard von Dallwitz
Sound (a) Supervising sound editor (b) Sound re-recording mixers (c) Sound editor (d) Sound recordist	Greg Bell (dubbing editor) (d) Don Connolly	Peter Fenton (dialogue mixer: Australia) Phil Heywood (sound effects mixer Australia)	Cecelia Hall (supervising sound effects editor) (b) Don Digirolamo Humberto Gatica Robert Glass	(b) Phil Heywood (c) Lee Smith
Production design (a) Production designer (b) Art direction	(b) David Copping	(b) Herbert Pinter	(a) Stan Jolley	(a) Dennis Gassner (b) Richard L. Johnson
Editing	Max Lemon	William M. Anderson	Thom Noble	William M. Anderson Lee Smith
Costume design	Judith Dorsman Wendy Weir (associate costume designer)	Terry Ryan	Dallas D. Dornan Shari Feldman (costume supervisors)	Marilyn Matthews

Appendix II

Films made in Hollywood by Australian actors

Director	Title	Year	Genre	DOP**	Main cast
Bruce Beresford	*Tender Mercies*	1983	Drama	Russell Boyd	Robert Duvall
	King David UK/ US co-production	1985	Drama/ Action/ Adventure	Donald McAlpine	Richard Gere
	Crimes of the Hearts	1986	Comedy/ Drama	Dante Spinotti	Diane Keaton Jessica Lange Sissy Spacek
	Her Alibi	1989	Comedy/ Crime/Mystery/ Romance	Freddie Francis	Tom Selleck Paulina Porizkova
	Driving Miss Daisy	1989	Drama/Comedy	Peter James	Jessica Tandy Morgan Freeman Dan Aykroyd
Peter Weir	*Witness*	1985	Drama/Thriller/ Romance	John Seale	Harrison Ford Kelly McGillis
	Mosquito Coast	1986	Adventure/ Drama	John Seale	Harrison Ford Helen Mirren River Phoenix
	Dead Poets Society	1989	Drama	John Seale	Robin Williams Ethan Hawke
Philip Noyce	*Dead Calm* (Aus/ US Co-production)	1989	Horror/Thriller	Dean Semler	Nicole Kidman*** Sam Neill***
	Blind Fury	1989	Action	Don Burgess	Rutger Hauer Mel Gibson***
Roger Donaldson	*The Bounty* (UK/US) Co-production	1984	Adventure/ Drama	Arthur Ibbetson	Anthony Hopkins Daniel Day Lewis Laurence Olivier
	Marie	1985	Drama	Chris Menges	Sissy Spacek Jeff Daniels Morgan Freman

Director	Title	Year	Genre	DOP**	Main cast
Roger Donaldson *(cont.)*	*No Way Out*	1987	Drama/Thriller/ Mystery	John Alcott	Kevin Costner Gene Hackman Sean Young
	Cocktail	1988	Romance/ Drama	Dean Semler	Tom Cruise Bryan Brown***
Fred Schepisi	*Barbarosa*	1982	Western	Ian Baker	Willie Nelson Gary Busey
	Icemen	1984	Drama/Sci-fi	Ian Baker	Danny Glover Timothy Hutton Lindsay Crouse
	Plenty UK/USA co-production	1985	Drama	Ian Baker	Meryl Streep Sting Ian McKellen Sam Neill***
	Roxanne	1987	Comedy/ Drama	Bruce Smeaton	Steve Martin Daryl Hanna
	A Cry in the Dark	1988	Drama	Bruce Smeaton	Meryl Streep Sam Neill***
	The Russia House	1990	Drama	Ian Baker	Sean Connery Michelle Pfeiffer
Gillian Armstrong	*Mrs Soffell*	1984	Drama/ Romance	Russell Boyd	Diane Keaton Mel Gibson***
	*Little Women**	1994	Drama/ Romance	Geoffrey Simpson	Winona Ryder Gabriel Byrne Susan Sarandon
	*Oscar and Lucinda**	1997	Drama/ Romance	Geoffrey Simpson	Ralph Fiennes Cate Blanchett ***

*Even though made in the 1990s, these films are included in this table because of their Australian DOPs.
**Australian directors of photography are underlined.
***Actor/actress either Australian or who had frequently worked in Australia.